THE BLAME GAME

Rethinking Ireland's Sustainable Development and Environmental Performance

BRENDAN FLYNN
NUI Galway

Foreword by
Michael D. Higgins T.D.

D1427635

IRISH ACADEMIC PRESS
DUBLIN • PORTLAND, OR

First published in 2007 by
IRISH ACADEMIC PRESS
44, Northumberland Road, Dublin 4, Ireland

and in the United States of America by
IRISH ACADEMIC PRESS
c/o ISBS, Suite 300, 920 NE 58th Avenue
Portland, Oregon 97213–3644

© 2007 Brendan Flynn

WEBSITE: www.iap.ie

British Library Cataloguing in Publication Data
An entry can be found on request

ISBN 0 7165 2839 8 (cloth)
ISBN 978 0 7165 2839 5
ISBN 0 7165 3351 0 (paper)
ISBN 978 0 7165 3351 1

Library of Congress Cataloging-in-Publication Data
An entry can be found on request

Typeset by Carrigboy Typesetting Services, County Cork
Printed by MPG Books Ltd., Bodmin, Cornwall

For my son Bernardo

Contents

Acknowledgements

Sincere thanks must be offered to several people who helped this book to come about. However, both series editors, Donncha O'Connell and Mike Milotte, deserve particular praise. Without their suggestions, gentle prodding, and initial interest, I simply would never have written it. Their patience was infinite as deadlines slipped. Mike had the stressful task of editing my very rough drafts and bashing some sense out of the more awkward phrases. Obviously, the usual disclaimer applies: all errors are mine and mine alone. Acknowledgement is also due to Brian Dawson, who worked with me as a researcher in the Environmental Change Institute (NUI, Galway). Together, we did some of the research for the section on implementation in Chapter 4. Finally, sincere thanks is offered to all my colleagues, family, and friends, in both Galway and Italy.

Foreword

Dr Brendan Flynn's *The Blame Game* addresses one of the most urgent issues of our times – the need for a new approach to environmental protection. It makes an invaluable critique of the institutional framework in which the debate on environmental issues has taken place in Ireland in recent decades.

Making the case, as it does, for the lodging of the environmental debate in the mainstream, for example as an integral part of future social partnership, the book moves beyond critique and offers an outline of what might be a better, more inclusive and fruitful approach. Such an approach would stress the normalcy of ecological responsibility and would see a seamless connection between the legal system and social policy.

Describing as it does the erosion of trust between the major players in the environmental debate, state, private interests, and environmentalists, the book charts a period of recrimination and litigation which served as a substitute for a period of fruitful discourse.

I served as Minister for Arts, Culture and the Gaeltacht during much of the period under review. Beginning with responsibilities for the Gaeltacht, I had added to my responsibilities duties in relation to, amongst other things, the natural and built heritage. I remain strongly of the view that heritage matters should be represented by a strong and independent Ministry, rather than being subsumed into one where its basic principles are contradicted. I had the privilege of placing the Heritage Council on an independent statutory basis. It still remains. The unit, however, with responsibility for fundamental policy has disappeared into the Department of the Environment, and the Department which I founded has for all practical purposes been demolished. I believe this to be a pity, as heritage issues are best protected within a strong Department of Culture where the Minister has responsibility for both policy and execution. From the chapters of this book, readers may deduce what were the alternatives to litigation, by way of policy discussion and inadequate discourse.

It is also clear from what follows that the general environmental issues which now face us, and which we neglect at our peril, require an entirely different approach to the institutional method which now prevails, and which provokes an ever deeper adversarial context. If we are to follow Dr Flynn's prescriptions we will have a discourse that reduces conflict, builds trust and provides greater certainty. The book is an invaluable contribution in this regard.

The efforts of those concerned environmentalists, however courageous and innovative, will not be sufficient if their marginalisation continues. Again, the abuse of its hegemony by the state through the introduction of such laws as would limit the citizen's right to participate would be little less than a disaster. Unfortunately, both realities seem likely in current conditions. Let us hope this book stimulates such debate as will enable us not just to become aware of the cost of such an outcome, but also to envisage the alternative.

The book discusses the concept of 'ecological modernisation'. This is a debate rich in possibilities, provided of course that some familiar with the term 'modernisation' in previous usages can suspend our reservations. The content of the term as introduced by Dr Flynn offers a model that is both possible and perhaps practical.

It is books such as this that we need now and we are indebted to Dr Flynn for first-class academic work placed in the public realm. It is my hope that such studies as this will lead on to discussion on the jurisprudence we need to provide for inter-generational responsibility. Those of us who have worked on legislative proposals in this regard have accepted as a basic principle that adequate care and protection for heritage and the environment requires such a jurisprudence.

Dr Flynn makes a great case for us choosing to be responsible in relation to environmental matters, towards us having a discourse that is open and tolerant, and towards us moving beyond the misery of being forced to be compliant on matters for which we are responsible not just to present but future generations.

Michael D. Higgins T.D.
September 2006

Chapter One

Blame, Complacency, and Beyond

BLAME, BLAME, BLAME

In late June 2005, the Irish Minister for the Environment, Martin Cullen, stood proudly in front of a gleaming new tram in St Stephen's Green. The occasion was to celebrate both the first anniversary of Dublin's LUAS light rail system and the opening of the final section of the M50 motorway. However, he also took this opportunity to explain to his listeners that he was simply fed up with environmental protestors delaying important infrastructure.[1]

Getting fully into his stride, he went on to argue that persons who sought to use litigation to challenge planning decisions for large government projects could be described as 'robbing money out of the taxpayers of the country by doing this'.[2] He further suggested that their right to a legal appeal of planning decisions should be limited. 'When the proper independent processes have been gone through, that should be the end of it. I want to see an end to the day when people are continually going to the courts simply to stop projects.'[3]

Subsequently a number of persons who had lodged objections to the M50's final section on environmental/heritage grounds issued legal proceedings for defamation. Their claim was that the Minister had inferred that they had 'robbed money from the taxpayer', although he had not named anyone.[4]

Any desire to limit the right of a legal appeal on planning matters sits uneasily with the fact that under Irish constitutional law a clear right exists to legal due process[5] on such matters. This implies that restricting access to courts would be problematic. There is also an important Århus convention on access to information, participation and justice on environmental matters, which Ireland signed in 1998.[6] Under this convention, Irish governments are supposed to facilitate, not restrict, the right of access to justice on environmental planning matters.

This short anecdote provides a good introduction for the reader to modern Irish environmental policy and its problems. We see here much that is wrong with the existing status quo. Irish environmental policy is bedevilled by a climate of mistrust, recrimination, and litigation between environmentalists, economic players, state agencies, and the government. A 'blame game' has emerged, with each side convinced that the other cannot be trusted. Each side disdains the other side's suggestions for solving Ireland's environmental problems. Each side reacts separately to environmental issues as they crop up, rather than co-operate to anticipate environmental problems more proactively.

Nor is the example given an isolated case. In August 2003, the Irish parliament, the Oireachtas, was the setting for what can only be described as an extraordinary anti-environmentalist rant. Representatives of An Taisce, Ireland's largest environmental group, were giving evidence before a joint Oireachtas committee, considering the problems raised by one-off rural housing.

The subject is controversial in Ireland. An Taisce allege such a pattern of housing increases water pollution, leads to pressure on sensitive habitats, or is far too costly for the provision of sufficient waste-water treatment. Such arguments were dismissed out of hand by a majority of the deputies present. One deputy simply refused to accept any evidence from other countries, especially Britain. He argued that Ireland had 'fought to break that link. We have our own culture here, thank God'.[7] Another deputy continued the nationalist theme and likened the An Taisce representatives to 'British landlords', denying Irish people a home to live in.[8]

Incredibly, a serious issue about dispersed rural settlement and rural water quality was ignored. Instead the event provided elected politicians with an opportunity to attack and bizarrely smear An Taisce as somehow unpatriotic or foreign. For daring to suggest there might be serious consequences with such a pattern of housing, the organization was demonized. To those who are familiar with Irish environmental policy and politics it was not a surprise. The blame game was alive and well.

A slightly different variant of the blame game could also be glimpsed in late summer 2005. A new environment Minister, Dick Roche, openly expressed his anger to journalists at the European Commission's decision to initiate legal proceedings against Ireland without having the good manners to inform him first.[9] Such legal measures can be undertaken by the Commission whenever a member state fails to properly implement an EU environmental law. Ireland has failed to implement many.[10] For example, the EU Nitrates Directive (1991) was supposed to be implemented by 1995. Yet regulations to implement the directive were only enacted in late 2005.

However, recourse to litigation by the Commission before the European Court of Justice (ECJ) is usually a fairly drastic measure. Typically, litigation only happens after years of negotiation over individual directives. There is no question here of the European Commission rushing to court, and yet the Minister neglected to point this out. The Irish authorities would have been given plenty of time to sort things out, but had simply not done so, as can be seen in the rather extreme case of the Nitrates Directive.

In fact, Minister Roche's comments were part of a broadside in what has become a tense and fraught relationship between Irish environmental authorities and EU officials. A blame game has also emerged between Dublin and Brussels. The Commission is inundated with hundreds of complaints from Irish environmentalists about pollution incidents, or the failure of Irish authorities to deal with these. Commission officials have increasingly lost patience with Irish governments, as they continue to long-finger environmental laws or refuse to properly resolve issues. Requests for information by the Commission, which could lead to an informal resolution of issues, have sometimes been met with very slow or minimalist replies by Irish authorities. On occasion, Dublin officials have offered the Commission the utterly trite suggestion of contacting Irish local authorities for further information. Faced with such delaying tactics, is it really such a surprise some Commission officials finally lose their cool and press to use their legal powers to the full?

The saga of Ireland's failure to implement the EU Nitrates Directive also reveals much of this blame game logic that I argue is now at the heart of Irish environmental policy. By February 2006, representatives of the Irish Farmers' Association (IFA) and the Irish creamery industry had both decided to leave partnership negotiations with the Irish government, trade unions, and employers. A boycott of Teagasc, the state agricultural science advisory body, was also put in motion. These measures were in protest at the much belated introduction in December 2005 of regulations implementing that directive.

A good example of the nitrates blame game can be seen in the comments made by Padraig Walsh, President of the Irish Farmers' Association on the 2 February, 2006 edition of the RTE Radio 1 currents affairs show 'Morning Ireland'. Commenting on the new nitrate regulations of December 2005, he argued:

> What is being implemented is unworkable at farm level ... there is not a major problem out there (of nitrates) ... I don't see the need for these draconian measures ... and also the implementation is so draconian ... water quality has been improving without these measures and it is continuing to improve ... most of that eutrophication is taking place below towns ... where the sewerage facilities are not up to the mark ... you know there's no point blaming agriculture when agriculture is not the cause ... most of the problems are below towns, that is one of the major causes (of pollution) in our rivers ... I'm saying that farmers are not as much of the problem as is being made out ... I accept that farming has been a contributor in the past but not anywhere near as much.[11]

As I argue in the next chapter, reports by Ireland's Environmental Protection Agency (EPA) confirm that agricultural sources contribute a significant share of water pollution; nitrates pollution is discernible at a level that merits a response. It is not a trivial issue. The bottom line here is that Ireland has a noticeable nitrate water pollution problem. It is not a huge problem, but it is serious enough. Moreover, the sources of such pollution clearly involve a very significant input from agriculture. Denying these realities is a classic form of blame game politics.

The same blame game style can also be seen with regard to controversy over Dublin's traffic problems and how to solve these in a sustainable way. For example, the Irish branch of the Automobile Association (AA) has consistently defended the capital's car drivers by suggesting that the root of the problem in Dublin is not in fact excessive car use but rather the lack of public transport alternatives.[12] Conor Faughnan, the AA's chief spokesman, argued in 1997 that 'Dublin has fewer cars than almost any other European city of comparable size. Our problems are not caused by car use but by inefficient public transport and a lack of resources for traffic management'.[13]

The suggestion here is that thousands of drivers would overnight switch to buses, trams or trains, but only if more of these were available. Apparently, the motorcar and car drivers are not to blame for Dublin's traffic woes: the managers and providers of public transport are.

Of course, the argument is unquestionably valid up to a point. Car drivers cannot reasonably be expected to switch to public transport unless it is available, economically competitive, and of reasonable quality/reliability. Unfortunately, on all these headings Dublin's public transport scores badly, even today.

However, the claim that poor public transport is the root cause of Dublin's transport problems is also a deeply facile argument. It all too conveniently shifts the responsibility away from looking more closely at trends in commuting and the growth or profile of the motor vehicle fleet in Dublin.

A trend towards much bigger, fuel inefficient, and high emissions vehicles is discernable in recent years.[14] Do Dublin car drivers really have to drive diesel-powered large jeep type vehicles in lieu of available buses and trams? Would it not be in the interest of any city government to ensure that the type of vehicles residents are driving would be the most appropriate for city conditions? This insight implies that certain types of cars are very much part of the problem.

PROBLEMS, WHAT PROBLEMS?

Allied with the culture of blame is a widespread complacency about Ireland's environmental problems. Sometimes this manifests itself in the manner of outright denial: the IFA's response to nitrate pollution is a good example of this.

Yet more common and insidious is a view that Ireland's environmental problems are not really that serious. Irish political decision-makers are fond of assuming that Ireland's environmental condition is fundamentally benign. One example of this mindset was provided by a senator from the large nationalist and conservative Fianna Fáil party, who treated newspaper readers to an almost poetic eulogy to Ireland's environmental efforts:

> Ireland is fortunate to have a favourable natural environment, blessed with beauty and fertility and a temperate climate. The weather station at Valentia still provides a base against which air pollution in Western Europe can be measured . . . Air pollution has been successfully tackled, the overall deterioration in water pollution arrested, and a huge effort put into cleaning up amenity waters such as Dublin Bay and the Lakes of Killarney . . . Broadleaf planting has been encouraged. The scourge of the plastic bag has been overcome.[15]

This type of rose-tinted sentiment is not unusual among the Irish political class. The basic view is: 'we have a few little problems, but they are being sorted out, and we are basically a lovely little green Island'. I will argue in this book that such assumptions are nonsense.

Ireland is facing serious environmental problems and is simply not doing enough to solve them. Our environmental record is unimpressive. We are slow to respond to environmental problems. We are unimaginative when we do so, and critically weak in making sure policies get put into practice. Compared with other EU states our environmental performance is too often below par. Yet Ireland has become one of the richest EU states, with one of the strongest performing economies. A more ambitious environmental policy could easily be afforded. Increasingly, greater action on environmental issues will be needed as our new-found economic success reveals a dark underside of costly associated environmental problems.

To return to the senator's gushing praise for Ireland's environmental record, it is also quite easy to show how, at almost every point, his assertions can be challenged. His claim that water pollution has been 'arrested' is just plainly wrong. The town of

Ennis in late 2005 discovered its tap water was undrinkable and the residents were reduced to drinking bottled supplies for several weeks. Other towns have experienced similar water supply crises.[16] This is a new phenomenon unknown in previous decades. Indeed in 2002 it was estimated that as much as 30 per cent of private rural water supplies were contaminated with human and animal excrement.[17]

Official statistics also reveal that there has been a steady reduction in overall freshwater quality. Waters in the pristine 'unpolluted' category declined by roughly 10 per cent between the end of the 1980s and the end of the 1990s. The EPA's water quality report for the period 2001–3 confirms that the stock of unpolluted water continues to slowly decline.[18] The percentage of 'seriously' polluted water, although very small, remained roughly the same for most of the 1990s. It is only now showing signs of real improvement.[19] The number of very seriously polluted lakes, while a small percentage of the total, tripled between 1990 and 2000. They have only been slightly reduced for the period 2001–2003.[20] These trends do not suggest water pollution has been 'arrested', but rather that general water quality shows a slow and insidious decline in quality. Only the very worst pollution cases have been mitigated.

One could also criticize the assertion that air pollution has been successfully tackled. It is true that air pollution is less of a problem in Ireland and most assessments show emission levels are within EU limits. Dublin has moved on from an era of smog caused chiefly by coal burning, thanks to the quite radical action of banning traditional coal use. However, all that means is a Victorian era problem got sorted out in the late 1980s.

The problem today is that much greater vehicle use is pushing up emissions of other types of pollutants, foremost nitrogen oxide (NOx) and particulate matter[21] These types of pollutants are very hard to tackle; one cannot simply ban car use. There are uncertainties about their true safety level. This means they pose much greater challenges and threats to Irish air quality than is often realized. Overall Irish particulate matter emissions have recently reduced, but not as much as many other EU states. A 2005 assessment by the European Environment Agency (EEA) placed Ireland seventh from the bottom out of eighteen European states.[22] Any complacency about Irish air pollution is then unwarranted given growing traffic volumes.

Throwaway comments about the encouraging of broadleaf forestry also need to be put in context. Ireland has one of the lowest rates of afforestation in the EU. Most of the planting that has taken place in recent years has been of coniferous species. These have usually been in dense, high yield, commercial plantations, with typically low nature value. The actual extent of Irish broadleaf species planting remains a subject of controversy.

Environmentalists allege that it remains below the official 1996 target of 20 per cent.[23] In 2000, the Irish government belatedly accepted that 30 per cent of planting should be of broadleaf species.[24] However, the Irish state's own Heritage Council actually argued the case for a 50 per cent target.[25] So Irish government policy on forestry cannot be considered very impressive regarding its green credentials. In any event, major cutbacks in national funding for forestry in the government budget of 2002 have placed the reaching of even the modest goal of 30 per cent further back still.[26]

Ireland's tax on plastic bags, also mentioned by the senator, appears initially to have been successful. Some estimates suggest it has achieved a 90 per cent reduction in littering by plastic shopping bags and it has generated roughly €50m for the Irish government.[27] Nonetheless, there are doubts about whether it has actually reduced the amount of plastic ending up in landfill.

This is because consumers appear to have simply switched to buying plastic bin liners, resulting in about as much plastic being used as before. There is at least anecdotal evidence that sales of bin-liners to consumers have dramatically increased.[28] One source has estimated the increase in sales ranged between 77 and 250 per cent.[29] This problem was openly conceded as a shortcoming with the tax by an Irish civil servant from the Department of Environment, Heritage and Local Government (DEHLG) in testimony before the Scottish Parliament, which was debating a similar tax for Scotland.[30] And even if we accept the Irish plastic bag tax is a success story, it raises the searching question of why the Irish authorities have only recently begun experimenting with such tax instruments? Why were they not being used much more widely and earlier?

It is worth noting that independent professional assessments of Irish environmental performance have also been basically negative. In 2000, the OECD published a formal assessment of

TABLE 1.1 IRISH PUBLIC OPINION ON THE ENVIRONMENT COMPARED WITH EU
AVERAGE RESPONSES AND A PEER GROUP (DENMARK, GREECE, PORTUGAL).

In your opinion should policy makers
consider the environment to be just as
important as economic and social policies?
(Question 7, p.67)
Percentage who answered 'YES'.
EU15 AV: 83 per cent
EU25 AV: 85 per cent
Ireland: 81 per cent
Greece: 95 per cent
Portugal: 85 per cent
Denmark: 84 per cent

Why don't you do more to protect the
environment?
(Question 11, p.75)
*Percentage who replied 'I DON'T BELIEVE THE
ENVIRONMENT IS IN DANGER'.*
EU15 AV: 5 per cent
EU25 AV: 4 per cent
Ireland: 12 per cent
Greece: 0 per cent
Portugal: 8 per cent
Denmark: 6 per cent

Would you say that you personally make
an effort to protect the environment?
(Question 9, p.71)
Percentage who answered 'OFTEN'.
EU15 AV: 45 per cent
EU25 AV: 43 per cent
Ireland: 52 per cent
Greece: 36 per cent
Portugal: 29 per cent
Denmark: 49 per cent

In order to contribute [to] protecting the
environment, which of these would you be
ready to do first?
(Question 16, p.85).
*Percentage who answered 'PAY A LITTLE
MORE IN TAXES TO HELP PROTECT THE
ENVIRONMENT'.*
EU15 AV: 6 per cent
EU25 AV: 5 per cent
Ireland: 8 per cent
Greece: 3 per cent
Portugal: 2 per cent
Denmark: 11 per cent

Commentary: More Irish respondents feel they often do something to protect the environment than the EU average figures. However, there are also more Irish who believe the environment isn't under threat than the EU average or the peer group – a classic symptom of complacency. The number who think environmental questions are as important as social and economic policies, while a clear majority, is also noticeably lower for Ireland. Note: the question on contributions to protect the environment may have produced lower answers for 'pay a little more in taxes' due to the inclusion of 'first' at the end of the sentence. In summary, whereas in the past Irish public opinion used to appear less sympathetic to environmental issues compared with continental and Nordic Europeans, this survey suggests the gap has closed in recent years. For more evidence and debate see Faughnan, P. and McCabe, B. *Irish Citizens and the Environment: A cross-national study of environmental attitudes, perceptions and behaviours. Report for the EPA/Commission of the European Communities* (Dublin: UCD, Social Science Research Centre, 1998); DELG/ Department of the Environment and Local Government and Drury Research, *Attitudes and Actions: A National Survey on the Environment* (Dublin: Government Stationery Office, 2000a); Kelly, M. *Attitudes to the environment in Ireland. How much have we changed between 1993 and 2002?* Paper presented to the Environmental Protection Agency Conference: Pathways to a Sustainable Future, Dublin, 15–16 May 2003.

   Finally, it is important to note that such surveys are rarely reliable guides to voting intentions on the basis of environmental sentiment nor of actual policy changes and outcomes. There is a particular problem with surveys on environmental questions in that they are 'valence issues' (i.e. subjects which attract a wide degree of superficial support). See Stokes, D. E. 'Valence politics', in D. Kavanagh (ed.), *Electoral Politics* (Oxford: Clarendon, 1992), pp.141–64. Thus, surveys tend to overestimate environmental concern or support.

Source: Eurobarometer/Commission of the European Communities. *Special Eurobarometer 217: the attitudes of European citizens towards the environment*, April 2005 (Luxembourg: Eurobarometer, 2005).

Irish environmental policy, which Irish government officials sought to downplay. It is worth quoting their main findings:

> Ireland continues to face many environmental challenges, in particular controlling air emissions from transport and energy production, reducing pollution loading to water from municipal and agricultural sources, and improving waste management and nature protection. These challenges largely reflect insufficient environmental infrastructure, together with changes in consumption patterns associated with recent increases in per capita income.[31]

The EU Commissioner for environmental protection, Dimas, publically stated in 2006 that Irish efforts at dealing with pollution were *not* sufficient.[32] Notwithstanding such advice about the need to improve Ireland's environmental performance from respected international authorities, the mindset of complacency remains in place, both among the governing elite and amidst general Irish public opinion, whose views remain mixed (see Table 1.1).

Some Irish state officials intimately involved in environmental policy, and understandably defensive of their efforts, often like to point to a steady increase in the quantity of Irish environmental laws. They concede privately that Ireland is not an environmental policy 'front runner' comparable to states such as the Netherlands or Denmark. They grudgingly admit that Ireland today has 'a few' serious environmental problems. But they continue to assert that Ireland is more or less holding her own and doing 'not too badly' as regards protecting her environment.

My response here is to suggest that 'not too badly' is no longer good enough. All that has really happened over the last three decades is that under EU tutelage Ireland has played a painstakingly slow and sometimes less than enthusiastic game of 'catch up'. Ireland has 'downloaded' from the EU process all the trappings of a modern environmental policy. Before this era, she had little by way of modern environmental laws or standards. The result is that on paper, Ireland has a modern environmental regulatory apparatus much like any advanced industrial democratic state. Yet the reality in practice can be very different. There are serious institutional problems, which this book aims to uncover. These institutional problems reveal that any modern environmental policy is worth little if it is not implemented in practice.

In any event, just a crude increase in the *quantity* of environmental laws is not in itself evidence of much improvement, unless the *quality* of those laws is itself good. As regards the quality of environmental regulation in Ireland, the legislative efforts by the Irish state over the last three decades have been patchy.

There has also been a notable paucity of new environmental policy instruments (NEPIs), such as green taxes, compared to other EU member states. What one can see instead is a belated introduction of a tax on plastic shopping bags, as discussed before. This was followed by a much more important tax on land-filling of waste in 2002. In contrast, England and Wales have been operating with a landfill tax since 1996. Indeed, Ireland's record on ecological tax reform stands out as among the poorest in western Europe.

Another gaping hole in this smug 'holding our own/doing not too badly' type of argument is that it ignores the reality of non-implementation of laws. The discovery in 2001 of numerous and large-scale illegal waste dumps reveals that enforcement of modern Irish environmental laws has been critically weak.[33]

Ireland appears to be one of the most serious offenders in recent league tables of countries who fail to implement EU laws properly, a topic explored more thoroughly in Chapter Four of this book. Ireland also ranks second last in a league table of EU states' efforts at protecting habitats: the EU average for protected land is 8 per cent of national territory, whereas Ireland has legally protected only 3.2 per cent.[34] So much for 'not doing too badly'.

Any complacent view of Irish environmental policy is certainly no longer tenable in the post 'Celtic Tiger' boom period. Considering that Ireland is today a much wealthier country, it is reasonable that more can and will be expected from her on environmental issues.

THE CELTIC TIGER EFFECT: DECOUPLING GROWTH FROM POLLUTION

Assumptions that Ireland is fundamentally less polluted than other EU states cannot ignore the fact that a decade of 'Celtic

Tiger' economic growth has left its environmental impact on Ireland. Environmental problems have been *magnified* by the surge in economic activity and newly found general prosperity associated with the 'Celtic Tiger' boom.

Economists, at this juncture, are usually quick to counter-argue with the optimistic line that the Irish economy has managed to 'decouple' much greater economic growth from associated pollution. The idea of achieving a decoupling between economic growth and environmental harm implies that pollution emissions and energy use do not increase in proportion to rising measures of production, consumption, and GDP growth. On a first glance, according to OECD data, Ireland would appear to have achieved this.[35]

Between 1990 and 1998 Irish GDP per capita grew by 53.6 per cent and industrial production increased by an incredible 128.2 per cent. By way of contrast, final energy consumption for the same period only grew by 28.8 per cent and CO_2 emissions from energy by only 19 per cent.[36] Chart 1.1 and Table 1.2 both illustrate this data more clearly.

CHART 1.1 HOW MUCH DECOUPLING?
TRENDS COMPARED IN PERCENTAGE (+/−) FOR 7 ECONOMIC AND 7
ENVIRONMENTAL MEASURES IN IRELAND, 1990–98.

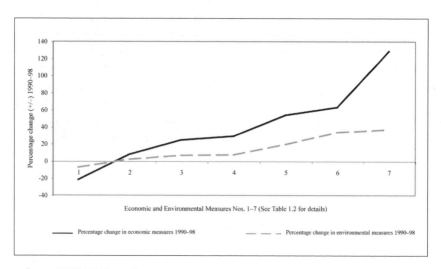

Economic and Environmental Measures Nos. 1–7 (See Table 1.2 for details)

——— Percentage change in economic measures 1990–98   — — — Percentage change in environmental measures 1990–98

Source: OECD (2000), p.100.

TABLE 1.2 PERCENTAGE CHANGE FOR SELECTED ECONOMIC AND ENVIRONMENTAL
MEASURES ILLUSTRATED IN CHART 1.1, FOR THE PERIOD 1990–98

Economic Measures	Description	Percentage change +/_
No.1	Energy intensity (per GDP)	−22.1
No.2	Agricultural Production	+7.4
No.3	Road traffic	+24.2
No.4	Final energy consumption	+28.8
No.5	GDP per capita	+53.6
No.6	GDP	+62.5
No.7	Industrial Production	+128.2

Environmental Measures	Description	Percentage change +/_
No.1	P/Phosphorous fertilizer use	-7.8
No.2	SO_2 (Sulphur Dioxide) emissions	+1.5
No.3	NOx (Nitrogen Oxide) emissions	+6.2
No.4	N/Nitrogen fertilizer use	+6.8
No.5	CO_2 emissions from energy	+19
No.6	Pesticide use	+33.2
No.7	Municipal waste	+36.4

Source: OECD (2000) p.100.

However, what such data really show is greater efficiency in industrial production rather than an absolute decoupling in a stricter sense. The Irish industrial sector can now make greater quantities of products of greater value, but for much less energy and emissions per unit of production. Yet there is still a trend visible here whereby pollution measures follow economic growth indicators. For most of the seven measures compared in Chart 1.1, both trend-lines are pointing upwards. They only differ by order of magnitude as to their rate of increase. This gap between the rate of increase for economic over environmental measures is only then *relative* decoupling. In just a few cases do we find a genuine decoupling, meaning an actual negative trend whereby as economic growth indicators go up pollution measures actually drop down. This happened with phosphorous fertilizer use between 1990 and 1998.

More generally, it is clear that some environmental indicators have risen in pace and scale with soaring economic activity. Municipal waste volumes have jumped an incredible 221.4 per cent between 1980 and 1998, and a more modest 36.4 per cent between 1990 and 1998.[37] Pesticide use also rose by 33.2 per cent. Trends in the transport sector show a relative increase in problem magnitude. The transport sector's share of national CO_2 emissions rose from 17 per cent in 1990 to 26 per cent in 2000.[38]

The decoupling thesis only holds well for the industrial sector of the Irish economy, which has become much more efficient. Yet it remains mostly a relative relationship. In the 1990s Ireland experienced much greater increases in economic activity for relatively smaller associated increases in pollution. This is progress, yet the link between increased economic activity and pollution remains, even if it is not a direct and simple relationship.

As the wealth-generating capacity of the Irish economy continues to grow, ecological harm continues to follow, and not too far behind. Indeed, a 2005 report by the European Environment Agency (EEA) revealed that Ireland had, in 2001, the *second* highest per capita level of resource use for fossil fuels, industrial ores, construction materials and biomass in the *entire* EU.[39] Such evidence casts serious doubt upon arguments about a 'decoupling' of economic activity from environmental harm in Ireland.[40]

PROTEST POLITICS: MISSING THE BIGGER PICTURE?

Complacency of a different sort is also evident within a style of Irish environmental protest politics. The Irish courts are replete with struggles between small environmentalist organizations and the Irish state or commercial developers. This style of politics is complacent because it locks environmental problems into a cycle of confrontation. Many actors within Irish environmental policy neither seek to, nor seem able to, break out of that cycle. They accept it as bizarrely normal.

In a democracy, it would of course be very naïve to expect agreement on environmental policies without some conflict, controversy, or dissent. One cannot assume some type of cosy consensus view will envelop all parties and solve all problems. However, it is equally possible to address environmental problems in a more negotiated and problem-solving style. Such an approach can stress innovation, can build trust, and can treat complex scientific issues in a more pragmatic manner rather than seeing them as moralistic 'black/white' conflicts.

A politics of environmental protest is also complacent because once again the logic of action here is reactive rather than proactive. You protest against something once it has emerged as a problem, meaning environmentalists are left in a reactive mode. It would be more logical to anticipate problems through lobbying in advance, and steering agendas towards better policies or less threatening decisions.

This protest politics is in stark contrast to the way various Irish economic stakeholders, trade unions, and employers' representatives have been integrated within 'social partnership' negotiations. Irish trade unions have moved up a gear in organizational terms by engaging in systematic negotiation with employers and the state since the late 1980s. That partnership experience has shown that it is possible for other problems in Irish society to be addressed in a negotiated way.

Partnership has been one of the success stories of the Irish 'Celtic Tiger' years. It has unquestionably reduced the scope for counterproductive conflict between opposing economic interests groups. It is true that this may now be getting harder to achieve, nor is the approach without its legitimate criticisms. One should have no illusions about what such institutional innovations can achieve.

They do not necessarily bring about a happy consensus or heal antipathy between different social forces. But partnership-style dialogue can avoid open and destructive conflict. It can provide a venue for a fairer negotiation between parties. On balance the argument is very simple: it is better to have imperfect social negotiations rather than extensive social conflict in the guise of strikes. Unfortunately, no comparable type of partnership, negotiation, or consensus has emerged in Ireland to address environmental issues. Instead conflict has reigned, and has actually grown.

At the centre of such an unequal struggle lie Ireland's environmentalists, who remain few in number, and are quite fragmented between several small organizations. It is not an exaggeration to say that they feel isolated and left with few options but to fight, what are for them, desperate environmental rearguard actions. Their self-image is that of an *ad hoc* environmental 'fire brigade' of heroic citizens who must face off a hostile commercial sector or an Irish state whom they assume are both always intent on placing a priority on development over environmental concerns.

Irish environmentalists are very quick then to blame the Irish state, industry, commercial sectors or farmers through a politics of protest which sooner rather than later ends up clogging the Irish and EU legal system. This is the preferred mode of engagement rather than physical 'direct action' protests which remain rarer. As explained before, Irish environmentalists look to the EU to protect Ireland's environment, and a distinctive EU-level 'blame game' circuit has now emerged whereby environmentalists bitterly complain about the Irish state's failings, chiefly to the European Commission in Brussels.

So marked is the antipathy that one interviewee commented on how a visiting EU commissioner for environmental issues in the 1990s advised the Irish government that she had never encountered such hostility towards any EU government as Irish environmentalists displayed towards theirs.

However, her soothing and virtuous Scandinavian advice to calm the conflict down and invite environmentalists into the policy process was largely treated with a mix of incomprehension and indifference by the Irish authorities. By the end of the 1990s, environmental complaints to the Commission would surge as Ireland embarked on an explosion of road-building, infrastructure provision, and a wild housing boom.

Political decision-makers and commercial opinion leaders have been just as quick to blame Irish environmentalists. They are labelled as extremists or as impractical and unprofessional 'nay-sayers'. According to this view, environmentalists are opposed to any form of economic development. Irish governments have become increasingly strident and less interested in engaging with environmentalists. A view has taken hold deep within Irish government circles that no accommodation is really possible with environmentalists. The result is a governing culture which seeks to *impose* environmental policy.

For example, Ireland has implemented controversial waste policy decisions relating to incinerator technology, by national ministerial order and enabling legislation. This has the legal effect of railroading such policies over the heads of local governments, some of whom have expressly voted against such measures. It also simply ignores local environmentalists who oppose the technology of waste incineration due to health fears. In many parts of Ireland, local anti-incineration campaigns have mobilized literally thousands of people, and these campaigns have grown in sophistication and substance. The response of recent governments has been to steamroller over such disquiet and simply force the issue by governmental fiat. Irish governments have very consciously chosen the path of conflict on environmental matters.

The same hostility towards environmentalists can be seen as well in recent changes to Irish planning law, which have made it more expensive for environmentalists to make formal complaints as part of the planning procedure: charges of €250 for individuals and €100 for An Taisce applied since 2003.[41] These charges were challenged by environmentalists at the EU level and the Commission decided to prosecute Ireland in early 2006.[42] There has even been repeated political rhetoric to abolish a legal privilege whereby Ireland's largest and oldest environmentalist organization, An Taisce, can make formal observations as part of the planning process.[43]

On environmental issues Irish political decision-making is steadily moving towards a much more adversarial and aggressive style. Increasingly, Irish governments pay lip service to a formal consultation process. However, once these procedures are gone through with, policies are simply rolled out over any remaining objections.

A continued debate exists deep within the corridors of Irish cabinet government as to whether the entire planning system should not be radically changed. The goal here would be to heavily restrict the right of third party legal appeal and certainly to fast-track large-scale developments, so that objections would be effectively minimized and restricted.

In February 2006 a 'strategic infrastructure' Bill was eventually published by the Irish government.[44] Its stated aim was to speed up the planning process for large infrastructure projects by allowing for the bypassing of the local planning authority. Such cases would instead go straight for consideration by a newly created special panel within An Bord Pleanála, the independent Planning Appeals Board.

Representatives of Irish business lobbies welcomed the Bill. However, Brendan Butler, speaking for the Irish Business and Employers Confederation (IBEC), suggested it could have gone even further. In particular he advocated the need for a special financial bond that third party objectors should pay, once again supposedly to reduce frivolous objections.[45] This ignores the fact that the Planning and Development Act 2000 already included detailed provisions which empower An Bord Pleanála to dismiss appeals where they deem them frivolous or vexatious.

The effect of raising the costs of participation in the planning process for third parties, which now appears to be a punitive government strategy to keep environmentalists in check, will unquestionably mean they will be less able to participate in that process.

Yet, if environmentalists cannot challenge developments in the courts, they may well decide the only option left to them is direct action: protest, occupation, marches, etc. If Irish governments keep imposing very controversial decisions against the will of a small and weak environmental movement, it will likely increase the voices for more extreme and radical action within such groups.

Rather than reduce conflict, build trust, and provide greater certainty, such aggressive measures may then actually increase environmental conflict and make decision-making more heated and unpredictable. Forcing environmental issues and imposing government-led solutions is often a recipe for delay, for excessive litigation, and for the uncertainty this raises. Ultimately it leaves a serious legitimacy deficit as regards the policies which are selected. Working with environmentalists, or at least just negotiating with them fairly, while perhaps neither easy nor swift, may in the long term provide for more stable and workable policy outcomes.

Unfortunately, the failure to develop a forum where environmentalists, economic actors, and the state can negotiate together serves to reinforce the retreat to protest politics. Environmentalists repair to their bunker mentality of activism, mobilization, and litigation. This may be emotionally satisfying for them, but it is not at all clear if it represents a good long-term strategy for engaging with any government, which after all will generally hold tremendous power to get its way. The logic of protest politics can only go so far.

In reality it amounts to little more than countless small tactical skirmishes in the courts. These result in the occasional spectacular victory where some government policy has to be reversed. Yet winning the odd battle does not win a war. Such rearguard 'guerilla actions' through the courts, may in the end do little to really alter the big strategic environmental issues that Ireland faces over energy supply, transport investments, or consumption patterns.

To influence these really strategic environmental policy decisions may well require a very different style of environmental politics than Ireland has seen heretofore. I will argue here that it in fact requires a move towards a politics of systematic negotiation, which in practice should mean bringing environmentalists and environmental questions into partnership negotiations.

A REACTIONARY VIEW OF ENVIRONMENT POLICY?

Allied with the blame game logic and complacency described before, the very conception of environmental policy held by Irish policymakers is deeply problematic. It is what I term a *reactionary* view of environmental policy. It is reactionary precisely because it sees the purpose of environmental policy as akin to that of a fire brigade; to respond only after environmental problems have already emerged as serious. It does not systematically prevent problems before they get worse.

In this guise, environmental policy is reduced to merely fixing the annoying side issues, compared with the core 'bread and butter' policies of public finances or the generation of prosperity and economic growth. Environmental policy becomes somehow a marginal endeavour. In the salience of government policies, environmental concerns quickly become the equivalent of domestic housework: a necessary drudgery.

This type of, usually unspoken, assumption about environmental policy inevitably relegates it to the back burner of government concerns and priorities. This is what has happened in Ireland. Indeed, because so much of the content of Irish environmental policy is effectively imported through our participation in the EU, the political ownership of environmental policy is not strong. It is something 'Brussels wants us to do, and so we better do it'.

However, this sort of reactionary view of environmental policy is not an inevitability. There are alternatives. In other countries a shift has occurred in how environmental issues are prioritized by their governments. Far from being a marginal sector, in a few countries environmental issues have been identified as being of strategic relevance. From being purely problems that must be sorted out at great expense and political cost, environmental issues have been successfully repackaged as national technical, political, and economic challenges, which can produce economic benefits. This shift in viewing environmental issues has occurred also within many large companies, not just governments. If dealt with intelligently and proactively, environmental issues provide opportunities and strategic advantages.

In several states, Japan, the Netherlands and Germany foremost, this type of logic has been well established at the heart of government for decades. Academics have labelled the approach 'ecological modernization'.[46] What that ugly term means is essentially making environmental policy more attractive in a political sense. Instead of seeing environmental regulations as a threat to jobs, competitiveness, or profits, the stress is on searching for ways to apply environmental policies that improve national competitiveness, or that of firms in such countries.

This links environmental policy to advanced technology innovation, whose aim is either to design away pollution, render it inert, or otherwise allow for safe management of waste. More ambitiously, the focus becomes an ongoing engineering challenge to reduce energy or other critical inputs such as water. Seen this way, environmental policy becomes associated with drives for much greater industrial and commercial efficiency.

However, it should be clear that the ecological modernization approach is not some kind of business management fad. It is an inherently political statist strategy, of a distinctly social democratic hue. This may offend those who prefer neo-liberal ideological policies or those who are firm believers in unfettered markets.

As Murphy describes it, arguments for an ecological modernization approach usually involve claims:

> that the state should explicitly intervene in the market in order to achieve economic growth and environmental protection. To do this it should establish demanding environmental standards with the aim of communicating priorities for industrial innovation. It should also pursue macro-economic restructuring in favour of less resource intensive industries . . . governments should make use of a range of more innovative policy measures including, for

instance, environmental taxes, strategic environmental assessment and voluntary agreements. At the same time industry should seek out solutions to production problems through the exploration of cleaner technologies and production techniques. It is argued that if this kind of programme is pursued environmental protection will improve economic competitiveness at the micro and macro-economic levels.[47]

Academics have much studied this 'ecological modernization' approach to environmental policy. They remain divided over whether it should be considered a successful and genuine way of meeting environmental goals. Some have criticized the approach as superficial and ineffective. Others have worried that it amounts to little more than searching for a technical 'quick fix' to environmental problems, or that it is disingenuous in implying no hard decisions might be required within any environmental policy.[48]

Yet on balance the approach represents a useful way to manage and frame environmental problems. It represents one of the best ways of outflanking traditional opposition to ambitious environmental goals and to transcending the usual political opposition from businesses or consumers. Rejecting ecological modernization approaches might well simply return us to a world where any serious environmental demands are met with open hostility by economic interests.

Mindful of potential critics of this approach, it is also possible to ensure that any ecological modernization strategy is pitched in a way that is more substantive and demanding.[49] Crucial to this should be to link ecological modernization approaches with the concept of 'sustainable development', although academics usually see these as discrete debates. I argue here that ecological modernization approaches can actually help make the sometimes woolly concept of sustainable development much more concrete and practical.

The problem in Ireland is that no really serious debate on ecological modernization has occurred. There are pockets of discussion in the third level and research sectors, or a few scattered pioneers in Irish business who seek to harness technology to increase efficiency and improve their environmental profile. The high-tech multinational industrial sector has usually adopted

the most advanced technology to control emissions and reduce exposure to risks. However, these are all isolated cases.

There is no national debate about transforming the paradigm of environmental policy from merely reacting to problems to actually anticipating and avoiding problems. There is no truly significant national green technology fund. The EPA administer an environment technology scheme worth about €32m over the years 2000–6 – less than €5m per annum. Sustainable Energy Ireland spent €5–6 million in 2005 on sustainable energy research. But these amounts are just dribs and drabs of funding in the wider national context of state spending of over €2 billion for the years 2004 and 2005.[50] There is no attempt through industrial policy to promote 'eco-firms' who are front-runners in developing environmental technologies and services. Indeed, in a 1999 assessment, Ireland stood out as exceptionally weak in the field of 'eco-industries', with the second lowest performance by turnover, value added, and direct employment.[51] There seems little comprehension at the political elite level of the possibilities that environmental technologies and investments can yield.

There is however a growing national debate in Ireland on declining competitiveness, due to rising labour and housing costs, inflationary effects for consumers, global competition, and poor infrastructure (energy, transport, broadband). For example, the 2005 annual National Competitiveness Report indicated that landfill of waste in Ireland was among the most expensive in the EU.[52]

Yet, the National Competitiveness Council (NCC) itself has no member who is from an environmental group nor even a recognized independent environmental expert from the third level sector. By way of contrast, IBEC have two representatives, one of whom specializes in environmental issues.[53] The risk has to be that at least part of a growing national competitiveness debate will eventually label environmental policies as too costly and burdensome. Yet another blame game could find a ready audience.

Already, we have seen how Irish governments have uncritically accepted a business led argument that the planning system is too slow. The implication is that the national planning process itself and environmental objectors are to blame for delays and deficiencies in critical national infrastructure, and not the politicians or the civil service. It is this often uncritically accepted

sentiment that informs the proposal to fast-track large infrastructural projects, whose effect may well be to undermine sound planning procedures.

So central is the debate about competitiveness to politics in a small open economy like Ireland that it cannot be simply left as a debate free from any environmental dimension. To step away from engaging with the concept of competitiveness would be a serious mistake. It is true that the concept is problematic. It can be abused politically by those who are ideologically hostile to any form of social regulation, much less environmental protection. And clever ecological modernization approaches may not in every case provide a 'win-win' solution for businesses.

However, there is considerable scope to link competitiveness concerns with environmental objectives. Indeed, Professor Michael Porter, the internationally recognized guru of competitiveness, has consistently argued that environmental objectives do not undermine the competitiveness of most firms. He has even gone further and argued that, if managed well, environmental objectives can provide a spur for innovation and enhanced competitiveness for firms.[54] The most recent Global Competitiveness Report (2005) has also noted that there is a consensus that good environmental standards do not hinder national competitiveness.[55] It is noteworthy that the EU countries that score highest in that study[56] (Finland, Sweden, Denmark, Netherlands) all have ambitious environmental policies and a very high priority placed upon environmental protection by their governments. In many cases they are also leaders in ecological modernization strategies: getting cleaner and more technologically innovative at the same time. Finally, the Network of the Heads of European Environment Protection Agencies has issued an authoritative and well researched statement which argues that ambitious environmental standards and regulation do not undermine competitiveness, and in many cases can improve it.[57] In fact, firms stand to make huge savings if they adopt ambitious waste reduction technologies, explore energy efficiency innovations, or reduce their packaging output.

The need for a greening of the hitherto simplistic debate on national competitiveness is one very important argument of this book. That discourse cannot be left to fester in a way which ultimately could threaten to undermine Irish environmental policy efforts made over the last two decades. Competitiveness should be broadened as a concept. It should be made clear that it can be often reconciled with ambitious environmental goals. Yet even where this is not possible, competitiveness should not be allowed to sweep all other values before it.

THE CASE FOR INSTITUTIONAL REFORM

It is abundantly clear, for those who wish to examine official EU and Irish government sources, that Ireland faces very serious environmental problems today. Yet a culture of blame and complacency stands in the way of dealing with these challenges.

One of the main arguments of this book is that Ireland's decision-makers need to break out of that mindset of complacency and their habit of blame politics. To face the environmental challenges that are very real will require a qualitative shift away from a reactive style of environmental policy.

In fact, facing environmental problems in Ireland is no longer simply about what must be done, but as much about *how* responses should be executed. It is not just a question of more laws or money, but the institutional means by which policies can be made more effective. Indeed, we actually have a fairly good idea about what must be done to face environmental problems. There is a wide body of international experience which points to policy solutions that are promising.

What is more in question is the implementation of policy, or even the agreeing of ambitious measures in the first place. Making tough decisions or implementing these is the core of the Irish environmental policy problem. For example, there is extensive evidence about just how effective ecological taxes are in solving some environmental problems, but Ireland has only experimented with a handful of these and has openly refused to adopt a major one to deal with climate change.

Instead Ireland has seen a huge increase in environmental legislation and much higher levels of spending on pollution control. But these measures alone do not necessarily make for a successful environmental policy if the necessary willpower and institutional means to apply laws is absent. On both counts, Ireland is weak.

In summary, the focus of attention in this book is upon the institutional capacity of Irish governments, environmentalists, industry, and other actors to properly respond to our environmental problems. Are they able and willing to take the measures that seem needed?

One stark answer, as things currently stand, is that they are not. Unfortunately, the way in which environmental policy is organized in Ireland is less than ideal. The institutional structures of the state and civil society are both weak. They cannot flesh out clever laws, ambitious environmental targets, or the latest fancy thinking on how to deal with climate change. The institutions of the Irish state and wider society are simply not supportive enough for adopting and implementing the policy innovations which we know exist in other EU countries. We might get around to adopting them, but only after everyone else has led the way and after domestic interest groups have been placated.

Rather than looking outwards for innovations to adopt, Irish environmental policies remain locked in an insular blame game. If it were not for EU membership, which prods the entire system forwards in fits and starts with carrots and sticks, there might be significantly less environmental policy in the first place.

The intellectual tradition which informs this book is then quite a distinct one. It is centred upon an examination of Irish political institutions for environmental policy and an assumption that the institutional dimension is of real importance in politics. This tradition is mainly influenced by ideas drawn from the disciplines of modern public administration studies and political science.

Taking an institutional focus leads rather inevitably to a certain way of looking at things, and no doubt some aspects of Ireland's environmental problems get neglected. An economist would focus on costs, benefits, and distributional issues. A lawyer rather obviously would give pride of place to environmental laws, their content and complexity. Yet neither of these approaches can be divorced from an understanding of the wider societal institutional frameworks that provide the basis for a legal system or a market economy to function. It is timely therefore to examine what is seriously remiss with the institutional foundations upon which Irish environmental policy is built. Are the institutional foundations solid or shaky?

In fact, the metaphors I much prefer to use in explaining my institutional analysis are not those of construction but of information technology: hardware and software. By using hardware as a metaphor here, I mean the established institutional agencies, departments, and other government actors who have responsibility for environmental issues. I also mean how they combine together to set agendas, reach decisions, and enforce policies and laws. The hardware of environmental policy relates to *how* should environmental policy be decided, and then later, *how* it ought to be executed. Or more exactly, *who* should take such critical decisions, *who* should be consulted, and *who* should execute environmental laws.

In practical terms, then, the institutional hardware of Irish environmental policy can easily be identified. It would include the Environmental Protection Agency (EPA), the Department of the Environment, Heritage, and Local Government (DEHLG), the local government system, and numerous other institutional players.

In contrast to this, by using the metaphor of institutional software I mean the body of EU and Irish environmental laws, their policy content or regulatory ideas. I also mean the non-legal policy objectives, the ideas and fashions that inform any environmental policy thinking. This software of environmental policy relates to *what* actions should be taken, *what* measures or laws should be agreed, or *what* standards should be set. It is all about the content of environmental policy.

In practice the software of Irish environmental policy is not really Irish anymore: it is mostly the vast body of EU environmental laws, but also other EU-led initiatives such as ratification of the Kyoto agreement to address global climate change, or a more recent emissions trading scheme.

The reason why I use these metaphors is primarily to illustrate a central argument of this book: Ireland has advanced environmental laws and modern thinking on environmental problems, but she has a very weak institutional structure with which to apply these laws and policies. The core problem is that the environmental policy software does not run well on the Irish institutional hardware. The former is modern and demanding whereas the latter is old-fashioned and brittle.

There is also a systematic mismatch as regards the pace of policy change versus institutional reform. There is a continually fast-paced development of new software in the guise of policy content, led by the EU. Yet Irish environmental institutions only change very slowly to meet this challenge. For example, Ireland only developed a modern environmental protection agency in 1993. Sweden established the first one in 1969 and the USA followed in 1971. Ireland has only had a dedicated environmental enforcement organization, the Office of Environmental Enforcement (OEE) (within the EPA) since 2003. Yet we have known for decades that there are serious problems with enforcing environmental laws.

Under EU leadership, the software of environmental policy content has reached a volume and level of complexity that is truly amazing. At least 200 major EU environmental laws are in force, but that figure underestimates the total load of regulations, standards, and policy documents that Irish officials must address. Moreover, the EU keeps agreeing every year major environmental policy developments that add further demands.

What has happened in Ireland is a serious institutional mismatch between the *inability* of Irish domestic institutions to reform, adapt, or modernize fast enough, and the *ability* of the EU to continually provide ambitious environmental policy leadership, new laws and regulatory ideas.

Ireland has signed up to such laws and legally and formally accepts such policy content. However, in practice the domestic institutional system is unable to digest this vast menu or respond adequately. Hard decisions that might hurt powerful domestic interest groups are fudged, combined with a general Irish 'slowly does it' mentality. Much of the effort is simply expended in turning one set of documents with the EU logo into another set of documents with the harp, the official symbol of the Irish state. This is a minimalist reactive engagement, when what is called for is a major change in Irish institutional responses overall.

The EU of course cannot really force member states to alter their domestic institutional architecture. It just keeps churning out relatively good environmental laws and hopes that some of these will eventually take hold and have an impact. The result is just like what happens when one tries to run a new software package on an old computer. You get a very slow operating speed. Sometimes this leads to overload, and sometimes an entire system crash. It is this mismatch between policy software and institutional hardware which is at the heart of many Irish environmental policy problems.

It follows that the second argument of this book is that significant institutional reforms are urgently required in Ireland if the culture of complacency and the 'blame game' are to be unseated. A more sustainable pattern of development will not simply happen by itself. There is a need for a major rethink and updating of the institutional hardware of the Irish state. How environmental policy decisions are reached, how environmental laws are enforced, and by whom, all need to be re-examined. Unless that happens, Ireland will probably continue on with the counterproductive blame game style of environmental policy and politics already described here.

However, the view that institutional reform on its own will solve problems overnight is not subscribed to here. It cannot be a panacea. Moreover, many academic accounts have stressed how any process of institutional reform is uncertain, often bitterly contested, and certainly difficult to achieve. Institutional reform is more an art than an exact science. Huge sweeping reforms often fail miserably. A smaller set of institutional adaptations might deliver better results. Therefore, the case for institutional reform here is made cautiously, and mostly points to reform within existing structures.

A later chapter in this book provides a more detailed account of the general direction such institutional reforms could take. However, as a possible reform agenda, the extension of the partnership/social negotiation model to address Irish environmental questions is argued for. To enable Ireland's weak environmentalist organizations to participate more effectively in such a framework, there is an urgent need for capacity building. This means in practice that the Irish state should provide higher levels of funding to environmental organizations to develop their expertise and management structures.

Also argued is that there should be much greater experimentation with the so-called 'new environmental policy instruments' (NEPIs), foremost green taxes and charges. With regard to other institutional problems, arguments are made for novel innovations concerning local government, the Environmental Protection Agency, and An Bord Pleanála. In each case the goal would be to ensure regulatory independence. Other reforms advanced here focus on the problem of implementation of laws.

CHANGING MINDSETS ON ENVIRONMENTAL ISSUES

Of course it cannot be all just down to changing institutional features, as if that were simple, easy, or uncontroversial. A deeper and more profound change seems also to be required. What is in question here is a change in mindsets, mentalities, and priorities, especially among the governing elite. However, it is hard to see how such an intangible goal can come about.

In fact, it may well be that there is a systematic link between reforming institutions and challenging governing mentalities. One reform begets the other. Major institutional change can also act as a driver to encourage a shift in social priorities, and in how problems are viewed by the decision-making elite. Changing the institutional architecture can force a debate on values, priorities, and new ways of seeing environmental problems. Of course, there is no guarantee how such debates will unfold, but at least it could unblock the current blame game impasse into something hopefully more positive.

The existing framing of environmental policy in Ireland has not managed to adopt an ecological modernization approach, unlike other countries. This means that for much of the governing elite environmental issues are still seen as marginal side-issues which challenge the economic success Ireland has attained over the last decade. It does not seem to have sunk in that environmental concerns can be reconciled with advanced industrial development. Indeed, they can add to competitiveness.

For real progress to be made, the diffusion and adoption of some kind of ecological modernization strategy at the elite level will be vital. This forms the third part of the argument made here. Considering the ecological pressures unleashed by the recent economic boom, Ireland will have to make a qualitative leap from hovering grudgingly around the average performer position on environmental issues.

Being more specific, any Irish ecological modernization debate needs to engage with two key concepts: sustainable development and competitiveness. Both are vague expressions and are often used in public debate in a clichéd way. However, ecological modernizaton can help to act as the bridge to connect the rhetorical promise of each of these ideals into some kind of pragmatic policy reality that makes a difference.

I have previously explained in this chapter the dangers inherent in allowing any public debate on competitiveness to evolve without an environmental dimension. Considerable scope for integrating environmental goals into competitiveness agendas already exists. Ecological modernization strategies would seem one obvious route to achieve this.

However, the link between sustainable development and ecological modernization requires a little further explanation. Put simply, to make sustainable development a practical reality requires concrete ecological modernization approaches which transform technologies and existing economic models through deeply pragmatic efforts.

This is because sustainable development as a concept is vague and at times simply 'wishy-washy'. The typical definition of the concept is that any form of development should 'meet the needs of the present without compromising the ability of future generations to meet their own needs'.[58] But this raises more questions than it answers. It seems somewhat odd for us to attempt to make hard choices for future generations, whose needs and preferences we cannot possibly know.

A second problem with sustainable development may be its lack of political feasibility as a reform agenda. Advocates of sustainable development have stressed that it necessitates a major shift in values, away from consumption and growth. This implies a voluntary acceptance of much simpler and more austere lives. Many of the conveniences and luxuries we take for granted would likely be heavily regulated, taxed, or even possibly forbidden by environmental law. One might view this as a useful corrective to the overemphasis which some versions of ecological modernization have placed upon greening technologies. However, trying to convince ordinary consumers to give up cars, cheap air travel, and the panoply of electrical appliances now considered as necessities all seems hopelessly naïve and utopian. If this is sustainable development, it seems destined to fail. Allied with the scope for very different visions of what sustainable development means, it is perhaps not surprising that the concept has been viewed by some commentators as inherently ambiguous and contested.[59]

A third problem is that it is rare to see sustainable development worked out in terms of concrete proposals for reform applied to an individual country. Ireland's various sustainable development plans,[60] fail to offer a concrete vision of what the sum of their various aspirations and promises amount to. These plans retain mostly the character of a ritual series of environmental promises; a type of well-meaning checklist of what Ireland ought to be seen to be doing (but in fact is not). Such exercises are not sustainable development but rhetoric about the concept. It is 'talk' about sustainable development rather than action.

For all these reasons, we desperately need to make sustainable development tangible, concrete and deliverable, lest the entire concept ends up becoming discredited. If sustainable development means considering the long-term view, for future generations, then we need a robust means of reaching and enforcing decisions. Especially if those decisions will be tough. Also implied is the need for a debate about discrete technological choices for the future, some of which could impose a long shadow upon future generations.

Recently in Ireland a debate has begun about the merits of nuclear energy, in response to surging oil prices, and general arguments which speak in favour of its low impact on climate change.[61] These arguments conclude that it is a logical avenue for future energy infrastructure. I will argue against such claims here, but it is obvious that, in order to avoid dependence on nuclear sources, massive investment in renewable energy technologies would have to occur. There is no getting away from the need to transform the harmful technological base of society, which is the goal of ecological modernization approaches. Sustainable development cannot turn its back on systematic technological and economic reforms to deliver greener results. Some type of ecological modernization approach seems needed if sustainable development is ever to become a reality.

Ecological modernization can also address the competitiveness agenda. National competitiveness is not just something achieved by a 'race to the bottom' of the lowest level of corporate taxes, trade union rights, relative wages, or environmental regulations. Environmental objectives, if part of a cohesive national or wider EU strategy, can act as a spur to innovation, develop new products and services, and even deliver reductions in costs and wastage. One major answer to the existing blame game then lies with the awkward term 'ecological modernization'.

STRUCTURE OF THE BOOK

Having explained the motivation for this book, and its principal arguments, it is useful to outline the structure of the following four chapters. Considering the extent of complacency over Ireland's environmental problems, the second chapter provides an overview and assessment of trends in Ireland's environment. The question asked is how bad is the state of Ireland's environment? A number of cases are taken to illustrate trends, especially where there has been some controversy over whether the Irish record is good or bad: energy efficiency, nitrates, car dependency, etc. This chapter is also significant because it places Irish environmental trends within a meaningful comparative context. I argue that it is not good enough just to know if Irish water pollution is on the increase, but are we doing better or worse than other comparable EU states?

The third chapter provides a historical overview of the Irish experience of environmental policy and politics. The question asked here is: how did we end up where we are today? This chapter also focuses on providing an account of how the institutional structures of the Irish state have slowly responded to environmental problems over the last thirty years.

The fourth chapter follows on from this, by providing a deeper analysis and critique of the current institutional dimension of Irish environmental policy. The question examined in this chapter is where exactly are the specific institutional problems that are most serious? This chapter is divided into three major sub-themes. The first of these focuses on institutional failures of organization and design. It takes as its cases the failures of Irish local government and wider problems of regulatory independence.

The second theme explored is why and how Irish implementation and enforcement of environmental policy has deteriorated over the last decade. That question has been the subject of some debate, as Ireland faces increasingly high-profile court proceedings before the European Court of Justice over environmental matters.

The third theme examined is the question of what environmental policy instruments have the Irish used and not used. It is argued here that a serious failure lies in not making more use of eco-taxes in particular. This chapter also provides a critical examination of other policy instruments: the new emissions trading approach and the use of voluntary environmental agreements.

The fifth chapter brings together the various strands of argument, but above all it provides a positive and provocative ending. The focus in the final chapter is on making the case for specific institutional reforms, many of which I have already pointed to here. Arguments for an environmental partnership approach are advanced, along with some critical comment on Ireland's environmental movement. Both the sustainable development and ecological modernization approaches are fleshed out in very concrete terms. Examples of the hard choices Ireland faces are taken from the energy and transport policy sectors. Several concrete suggestions for institutional reform are offered, pitched at the local government level, the EPA, and the planning system. The implementation problem is also addressed with specific reform suggestions.

NOTES

1. O'Brien, T. 'M50 plaintiffs sue Cullen over court remarks', *The Irish Times*, 11 August 2005.
2. Ibid.
3. Ibid.
4. Ibid.
5. For an account of the legal rights of third parties to appeal environmental policy decisions of Irish governments, see Ellis, G. 'Third party rights of appeal in planning: Reflecting on the experience of the Republic of Ireland', *The Town Planning Review*, 73, 4 (2002), pp.437–447. Such rights are also legally guaranteed by Article 6 of the European Convention on Human Rights (ECHR). For a wider discussion on the evolution of Irish constitutional law on the right to challenge government decisions with regard to their fairness, see Casey, J. *Constitutional Law in Ireland*, 2nd edition (London: Sweet & Maxwell, 1992), pp.341–5 and pp.286–90.
6. According to the reply given to a Dáil question, Ireland has not formally ratified the convention as of spring 2006. However, the EU has passed two directives, which enact some of the convention's provisions. These are binding on the Irish authorities. These are: Directive 2003/4/EC on Public Access to Information on the Environment, and Directive 2003/35/EC on the Right of Public Participation in Environmental Decisions. See Naughton, D. 'Dáil question 37780/05 with reply by Minister Roche', *Parliamentary Debates*, 611, 4, (2005), p.43 (available at http://www.oireachtas.ie). On the Århus convention see Hartley, N. and Wood, C. 'Public participation in environmental impact assessment:

implementing the Århus Convention', *Environmental Impact Assessment Review*, 25, 4 (2005), pp.319–41; and Morgera, E. 'An Update on the Århus Convention and its Continued Global Relevance', *Review of European Community and International Environmental Law*, 14, 2 (2005), pp.138–47.

7. McDonald, F. 'An Taisce questioned over housing', *The Irish Times*, 24 August 2003.

8. Ibid.

9. See Kelly, O. 'Roche critical over lack of consultation', *The Irish Times*, 12 April 2005 and O'Brien, T. 'Roche angry over action by EC on environment', *The Irish Times*, 14 January 2005.

10. See Pocock, I. 'State loses water pollution case', *The Irish Times*, 13 March 2004.

11. This is an edited transcript of what he said. The original can be found as an audio file at http://www.rte.ie/morningireland/archive

12. See Faughnan, C. 'New Tax would not cut traffic jams', *The Irish Times*, 15 July 2003; Faughnan, C. 'Luas light rail system should not be about trying to curb transport by car in the capital', *The Irish Times*, 21 August 1997; and Dunne, J. 'AA says Dublin is among the least car populated cities in EU', *The Irish Times*, 4 January, 1997.

13. Faughnan, 'Luas light rail system should not be about trying to curb transport by car in the capital', etc.

14. Sales of large engine capacity Sports Utility Vehicles (SUVs) increased in Ireland by 34 per cent in 2004 on the previous year. See McAleer, M. 'SUV sales up 34 per cent last year', *The Irish Times*, 26 January 2005.

15. See Mansergh, M. 'What ordinary people want still counts for something', *The Irish Times*, 13 March 2004.

16. See MacCormaic, R. 'The tidiest town with the dirtiest water', *The Irish Times*, 22 October 2005; Lucey, A. 'Alert issued over contaminated water', *The Irish Times*, 26 November 2004; Siggins, L. 'Public water supply at centre of row in east Galway town', *The Irish Times*, 14 February 2002; Siggins, L. 'Pollutants found in Galway city water', *The Irish Times*, 30 June 2001.

17. See McDonald, F. '30 per cent of group water schemes found to be contaminated', *The Irish Times*, 10 January 2003 and EPA/Environmental Protection Agency (Ireland) Office of Environmental Enforcement/OEE, *The Quality of Drinking Water in Ireland. A Report for the Year 2002 with a review of the period 2000–2002* (Wexford: EPA, 2002b), pp.xi–xiii.

18. EPA/Environmental Protection Agency/Toner, P. (et al.), *Water Quality in Ireland 2001–2003* (Wexford: EPA, 2005).

19. EPA/Environmental Protection Agency and Lehane, M., Le Bolloch, O., and Crawley, P. (eds.), *Environment in Focus 2002: key environmental indicators for Ireland* (Wexford: EPA, 2002a), p.33, and EPA/(et al.), *Water Quality in Ireland 2001–2003*.

20. See EPA/(et al.) *Environment in Focus 2002: key environmental indicators for Ireland*, p.38. The EPA uses the category 'hypertrophic' to indicate a lake suffering from severe eutrophication problems. In 1990 only 1.1 per

cent of Irish lakes were considered to be in this category but by 2000 this had risen to 3.02 per cent: close to a tripling. The percentage of hypertrophic lakes was 2.4 per cent for the period 2001–3. See EPA/(et al.) *Water Quality in Ireland 2001–2003*, p.49.

21. Particulate matter refers to fine particles that hang in the air. They often include ash and soot particles. PM10 is a reference to particles of 10 microns in size (6 times smaller than the diameter of a human hair). PM2.5 and PM1.0 refer to fine and ultra-fine particles respectively, of even smaller size. They are formed usually by gas particles. There is concern that all these particulates lodge in the delicate blood interchange vessels of the lungs (alveoli) and either damage their function or allow toxins to pass into the blood-stream. See http://www.greenfacts.org/glossary/pqrs/PM10-PM2.5-PM0.1.htm

22. Irish particulate emissions (both PM10 and PM2.5) between 1990 and 2002 reduced by 12.4 per cent. This was a better performance than either Greece (+0.2 per cent) or Portugal (+6 per cent), but unimpressive nonetheless considering that the average EU15 reduction was −39 per cent. See EEA/European Environment Agency, *Emissions of primary particles and secondary particulate precursors* (CSI 003) May 2005 Assessment (Copenhagen: EEA, 2005). Available at: http://themes.eea.europa.eu/IMS/IMS/Ispecs/Ispecification20041001123025/Iassessment1116511151442/view_content

23. Friends of the Irish Environment (FIE), relying on data from Irish parliamentary questions and analysis of official records, allege that for the period 1997–2002, circa 15 per cent of plantings have been broadleaf. This is significantly below the 1996 target of 20 per cent. See FIE/Friends of the Irish Environment, *Forestry Network Newsletter/FNN 138: Parliamentary Replies*, May 12, (2004a). Available at: http://www.friendsoftheirish environment.net/fnn/; and FIE/Friends of the Irish Environment, *Forestry Network Newsletter/FNN 136: The Hunt for the Missing Broadleaves*, March 31, (2004b). Available at: http://www.friendsoftheirishenvironment.net/fnn/

24. For a much fuller discussion, see Viney, M. *A living Island: Ireland's responsibility to nature. A Comhar Pamphlet*, (Dublin: Comhar/The National Sustainable Development Partnership, and Ashfield Press, 2003), pp.19–23.

25. Ibid.

26. See Editor/Irish Times, 'Rethink Required (on forestry budget cuts)', *The Irish Times*, Friday, 22 November 2002.

27. See Langendoen, R. 'Irish Tax Cuts Plastic Use Dramatically', (2003). Available at: http://www.futurenet.org/29globalhope/indicatorlangendoen plastic.htm; Reuters, 'Irish tax on shopping bags nets US$3.45 million', 21 August 2002. Available at http://www.enn.com/news/wire-stories/2002/08/08212002/ reu 48207; and Swanson, I. 'Plastic tax did not leave Irish down in the dumps', *Evening News*, 2 November 2005. Available at http://news. scotsman.com.

28. See EA/Environment Australia/Department of Environment and Heritage, *Plastic Shopping Bags – Analysis of Levies and Environmental Impacts Final Report* (Canberra: EA, December 2002). It is worth pointing out that this Australian government consultancy report nonetheless suggested that ultimately the volume of plastics reduced would still likely be greater than any increase in purchases of bin liners. The issue remains uncertain.

29. EA et al., *Plastic Shopping Bags – Analysis of Levies and Environmental Impacts Final Report*, p. 24, and CBC/Carrier Bag Consortium, 'Proposal for Welsh trials of carrier bag alternatives will not help the environment', *Press Information* 03/5888/3, (CBC, 2003a). Available at http://www.carrierbagtax.com/

30. Swanson, 'Plastic tax did not leave Irish down in the dumps'.

31. OECD/ Organisation for Economic Co-operation and Development, *Environmental Performance Reviews – Ireland* (Paris: OECD, 2000), p.19.

32. See O'Brien, T. 'Anti-pollution drive not sufficient', *The Irish Times*, 4 March 2006.

33. See Reid, L. 'Ombudsman criticises lack of enforcement of planning laws', *The Irish Times*, 28 April 2004.

34 King, T. 'EU chides Ireland over wild birds', *The Irish Times*, 30 January 2004.

35. See OECD, *Environmental Performance Reviews – Ireland*, p.100; and also Clinch, P., Convery, F. and Walsh, B. (eds.), *After the Celtic Tiger: Challenges Ahead* (Dublin: The O'Brien Press, 2002), p.139.

36. OECD, *Environmental Performance Reviews – Ireland*, p.100.

37. Ibid.

38. SEI/ Sustainable Energy Ireland, *Energy and CO_2 Efficiency in Transport: Analysis of New Car Registrations in Year 2000* (Dublin: SEI, 2003). Available at http://www.sei.ie/publications

39. EEA/ European Environment Agency, *Sustainable Use and Management of Natural Resources: EEA Report No.9/2005* (EEA: Copenhagen, 2005), p.20.

40. There are other problems with the decoupling thesis. It cannot measure how much environmental pressure a given country can take – the carrying capacity of each state in ecological terms. More seriously, many states have only been able to achieve either relative or absolute decoupling only because they have shifted their more polluting forms of production to developing countries. See OECD/Organisation for Economic Co-operation and Development, *Indicators to measure decoupling of environmental pressure from economic growth* (Paris: OECD, 2002). Summary available at http://www.oecd.org/dataoecd/0/52/1933638.pdf

41. See An Taisce, Press Release: 'Hike in Charges a Tax on democracy and Community', 4 April 2003. Available at http://www.antaisce.org

42. This case was still being litigated as of April 2006. See Smyth, J. 'State accused of impeding participation in planning', *The Irish Times*, 26 April 2006. The case in question is C-216/05. In May 2006 the Advocate General ruled against the argument that the Irish planning fees were illegal as a matter of EU law. The court itself has yet to decide the issue.

43. Deegan, G. 'Clare County Council to debate stripping An Taisce of status', *The Irish Times*, 17 April 2004.
44. Previous versions of 'fast-tracking' had been discussed at cabinet level since 2002, and politically promised since 2003. These were apparently killed off due to internal coalition wrangling over fears incinerators would be 'fast-tracked' for certain electoral constituencies. There may also have been expert legal advice counselling restraint. Fast-tracking could breach basic legal rights to a hearing and appeals over decisions or offend EU norms on public participation on environmental matters. See McDonald, F. 'Bill to fast track incinerators and motorways is withdrawn', *The Irish Times*, 12 December 2004.
45. Brendan Butler, IBEC's environmental policy expert, argued for such a financial bond on the 16 February 2006 edition of 'Morning Ireland', RTE Radio 1. An archived file of the radio programme can be listened to at http://www.rte.ie/morningireland/archive
46. For an introduction to the literature on ecological modernization, see Barry, J. 'Ecological Modernization', in J.S. Dryzek, and D. Schlosberg (eds), *Debating the Earth: the environmental politics reader,* 2nd edition (Oxford: OUP, 2005/2003), pp.303–21; and Murphy, J. 'Editorial – Ecological Modernization', *Geoform,* 31, 1 (2000), pp.4–5. Other sources include: Mol, A.P.J. 'Ecological modernization and the environmental transition of Europe: between national variations and common denominators', *Journal of Environmental Policy and Planning,* 1, 2 (1999), pp.167–181; Neale, A. 'Organising Environmental Self-regulation: Liberal governmentality and the Pursuit of Ecological Modernization in Europe', *Environmental Politics,* 6,4 (1997), pp.1–24; and Weale, A. *The New Politics of Pollution* (Manchester: MUP, 1992).
47. Murphy, 'Editorial – Ecological Modernization', pp.4–5.
48. Barry, 'Ecological Modernization', pp.315–19.
49. For example, recent work by Joseph Murphy makes the case for a much more ambitious agenda of controlling consumption, consumerism and demand in any economy as part of ecological modernization. See Murphy, J. and Cohen. M. (eds.), *Exploring Sustainable Consumption: Environmental Policy and the Social Sciences* (Oxford: Pergamon, 2001), and especially Murphy, J. (2001) *Ecological Modernization: The Environment and the Transformation of Society,* March, OCEES Research Paper No.20 (Oxford: OCEES, 2001).
50. See Forfás, *State Expenditure on Science and Technology,* November (Dublin: Forfás, 2005), p.5, and Forfás, *State Expenditure on Science and Technology Annex* (Dublin: Forfás, 2005), pp.32, 58. See also EPA/ Environmental Protection Agency, Press Release: 'Technological solutions to environmental issues – EPA initiative provides €2 million in funding', Thursday, March 2nd, 2006 (EPA: Wexford, 2006a). Available at: http://www.epa.ie/NewsCentre/PressReleases/MainBody,8890,en.html
51. Eurostat, *Source book of environmentally relevant data on industry: Data 1990–1999* (Luxembourg: Office for Official Publications of the European Communities, 2002a) p.59. This data was for the year 1999 only. The

relevant data can be found in a table which has to be interpreted – no actual rankings are provided. Ireland comes second lowest after Luxembourg for the categories of turnover, value-added, and direct employment. However, for environmental exports Ireland does better. It is in joint sixth place with Denmark.

52. Landfill costs for the year 2004 measured on a euro per tonne basis were 180 €/t in Ireland, 90€/t in Sweden, and €39 €/t in the UK (year 2003 data). More generally, the Forfás annual national competitiveness report (2005) estimated that total costs for waste disposal in Ireland had risen from €35 million in 1995 to €800 million in 2004. In 1999, Ireland was ranked eighth most expensive out of ten countries for landfill of wastes. Source: Figure 68, Forfás (2005), *Annual Competitiveness Report 2005*. October (Dublin: Forfás). Available at: http://www.forfas.ie/ncc/reports/ncc annual 05/ch03 03.html

53. The membership list for the National Competitiveness Council can be found at http://www.forfas.ie/ncc/structure.html. Brendan Butler, one of the IBEC members of the Council, usually comments on environmental affairs for IBEC. There is a civil service advisor from the Department of Environment and Local Government (DELG), Assistant Secretary Mary Moylan.

54. See Porter, M. *The Comparative Advantage of Nations*, 2nd edition, (Basingstoke: Palgrave, 1998), or Porter, M.E. and van der Linde, C. 'Toward a New Conception of the Environment-Competitiveness Relationship', *The Journal of Economic Perspectives: a journal of the American Economic Association*, 9, 4 (1995), pp.97–112. Other sources which explore the concept of eco-competitiveness include: Xepapadeas, A. and de Zeeuw, A. 'Environmental Policy and Competitiveness: The Porter Hypothesis and the Composition of Capital', *Journal of Environmental Economics and Management*, 37, 2, (1999), pp.165–83, and Wagner, M. and Schaltegger, S. 'The Effect of Corporate Environmental Strategy Choice and Environmental Performance on Competitiveness and Economic Performance', *European Management Journal*, 22, 5 (2004), pp.557–73.

55. See Lopez-Claros, A. (ed.), Porter, M,, and Schwab, K./WEF/World Economic Forum, 'Executive summary', in *The Global Competitiveness Report 2005–2006*: Policies underpinning Rising Prosperity (London: Palgrave), p.xxiv. Available at http://www.weforum.org.

56. In the 2005 Global Competitiveness Report, for the macro-economic Growth Competitiveness Index, Ireland was ranked twenty-sixth, which is an improvement from the thirtieth position assigned in 2004. However, the Irish performance is not impressive when placed alongside that of fellow EU states, nine of whom were ranked before Ireland: Finland (1st), Denmark (3rd), Sweden (4th), Netherlands (11th), UK (13th), Germany (15th), Estonia (20th), Portugal (22nd), Luxembourg (25th). For the other micro-economic measure, the Business Competitiveness Index, Ireland is in nineteenth place, but once again there are nine EU states performing better, including the Nordic EU members and other relatively small states like Austria, Belgium and the Netherlands. See Lopez-Claros, A. (ed.), etc.,

'Executive summary', *Global Competitiveness Report* 2005, p.xxiv. Available at http://www.weforum.org.

57. See Network of Heads of European Environment Protection Agencies, *The Contribution of Good Environmental Regulation to Competitiveness*, November 2005. Available at: http://www.umweltbundesamt.de/ius/downloads/prague statement-en.pdf

58. WCED/World Commission on Environment and Development, 'From One Earth to One World: An Overview by the World Commission on Environment and Development', in Dryzek, J.S. and Schlosberg, D. *Debating the earth: the environmental politics reader*. 2nd edition (Oxford: OUP, 2005/1987), p.264.

59. Dobson, A. *Justice and the Environment: Conceptions of Environmental Sustainability and Theories of Distributive Justice* (Oxford: OUP, 1998).

60. See DELG/Department of Environment and Local Government, *Moving Towards Sustainability: A Review of Recent Environmental Policy and Developments* (Dublin: DELG, 1995); DELG/ Department of Environment and Local Government, *Sustainable Development: A strategy for Ireland* (Dublin: Government Stationery Office, 1997); and DEHLG/Department of Environment, Heritage, and Local Government, *Making Ireland's Development Sustainable* (Dublin: Government Stationery Office, 2002).

61. See, for example, Forfás/Hirsch, R.L. *A Baseline Assessment of Ireland's Oil Dependence: Key Policy Considerations*, April 2006. (Dublin: Forfás), pp.23–4, and McWilliams, D. 'Time to discuss our nuclear option, without a meltdown', *The Irish Independent*, Wednesday, 5 April 2006, p.23.

Chapter Two

Ireland's lacklustre environmental performance: a comparative critique

INTRODUCTION

How bad are Ireland's environmental problems? This should be a question that is relatively easy to answer. However, getting an accurate and fair answer to such a question is more difficult than it might appear. Yet it is a necessary question, precisely to challenge the mindset of complacency described in the last chapter. Indeed, there is ongoing controversy over the very seriousness of some Irish environmental problems. On some issues, there is open denial.

For example, farmers' groups claim that Ireland has no serious problem with nitrates in waters and therefore that recent nitrates regulations are unjustified. The Irish Automobile Association (AA) claims that the car is not *the* problem at the heart of Dublin's increasingly unsustainable transport. This is supposedly because Ireland has fewer cars than the EU average. Irish industry spokesmen also claim that industry has done its fair share to address greenhouse gas emissions. They now want burden-sharing from the agriculture and transport sectors. Government sources trumpet much higher levels of recycling activity to claim Ireland is winning the 'race against waste'. Even Ireland's record on energy efficiency has been hailed as a great success. Over the 'Celtic Tiger' years the Irish economy has been able to produce more goods of higher value for relatively less energy.

So what then is the real story here? Might things be not too bad? Is Ireland's environmental record below or above average? Framing the question that way invites a comparative focus on how Ireland's performance measures up with other EU states. In this regard, this chapter provides the reader with a novel systematic comparison of Ireland's environmental record. The first section places Irish environmental trends within an EU comparative perspective. It is argued that it is not good enough merely to examine Irish official statistics on environmental problems in isolation. To get a more critical view we need to compare trends with countries within the EU who are not unlike Ireland. For comparative purposes, two relatively small cohesion states, Portugal and Greece, are chosen. Denmark is also examined as a contrast. These choices are explained below.

There follows a series of case studies, within which reference is made to the 'peer group' of Portugal, Greece and Denmark. For Irish greenhouse gases this approach reveals that the Irish record is truly awful. Ireland is unquestionably among the worst emitters of such gases in the entire EU. This holds true on a per capita basis, but also Ireland has one of the largest percentage rises in volume over time. Moreover, claims by industry that agriculture and transport are more to blame than they are, ignore still rising emissions from the industrial sector.

As regards the problem of the motor car, the crucial insight is that Ireland shows high levels of excessive car use, or car dependency. Anyhow, trends in car ownership are heading fast towards the EU average. On waste, the argument made here is that much improved recycling is being undermined by rising Irish waste volumes. Rather than explore waste prevention as a strategy, Ireland has got itself hung up on a heated debate over the relative merits of recycling versus the risks of incineration. With regard to energy efficiency, the Irish record may not be as impressive as is claimed. Moreover, gains in energy efficiency are being offset by rising dependence on fossil fuels, at a time when oil and natural gas prices have risen. As if to make matters worse, the Irish record on renewable energy is comparatively poor.

Finally, the saga of Ireland's failure to implement the EU Nitrates Directive is discussed. Controversy over whether nitrates are a problem or not should be laid to rest. There is enough evidence to demonstrate both that the problem is genuine and that agricultural sources are implicated as a significant contributor. Once again much of the debate has also ignored the bigger picture. Even low levels of nitrates can cause ecological harm to aquatic biodiversity. Regulations are required on a precautionary rationale to prevent such happening.

IRELAND'S ENVIRONMENTAL PROBLEMS:
A COMPARATIVE ASSESSMENT

Making comparisons is a basic skill which social scientists have always used to help interpret and make sense of complex social phenomena.[1] However, comparing Irish environmental trends with EU average figures can be criticized as of limited significance, because such EU averages reflect quite different countries – some very large and wealthy, others small and quite poor. This can make EU average data misleading.

One technique that can be used to sharpen the analytical focus is to construct a 'peer group' of EU countries as a subset against which to compare Irish environmental trends. I have selected Portugal and Greece on the basis that, like Ireland, they are relatively small 'cohesion' states within the EU. They have also qualified for extensive fiscal support from EU structural and cohesion funds, and their primary social and economic focus over the last two decades has been an attempt to tackle structurally high unemployment and physical remoteness from the main European markets. Both Greece and Portugal have also had predominantly agrarian economies until late, without much of a history of industrialization.

Obviously one must note important differences as well. Both states have at least double the population of Ireland, and have a larger territory. The low latitude of each state and the Mediterranean climate and geography of Greece are, of course, very different. Yet Portugal's Atlantic position means it shares at least some ecological parallels with Ireland. Table 2.1 below outlines some of the main social, economic and environmental trends for the four states.

Regardless of their obvious differences, these states do represent a reasonable peer group for comparison with Ireland, although they have not had anything like the 'Celtic Tiger'. Ireland has achieved a tremendous reversal of her social and economic profile during the 1990s. Levels of economic growth were double the EU average for much of the 1990s. Ireland's 'Celtic Tiger' years have unquestionably transformed her position, and magnified her environmental problems.

In theory this new-found prosperity should have led to an enhancement of her capacity to deal with ecological problems.

TABLE 2.1 COMPARISON OF IRELAND, PORTUGAL, GREECE AND DENMARK ACROSS
SELECTED SOCIAL, ECONOMIC AND ENVIRONMENTAL STATISTICS.[1]

	IRELAND	GREECE	PORTUGAL	DENMARK
Land area	70,000km²	130,800km²	92,000km²	43,000km²
Coastline	7,100km²	13,700km	800km	7,300km
Population (2002)	3.8m	10.6m	10.3m	5.3m
Population density/inhabitants per km² for 2002	55.4	80.7	112.8	124.7
Percentage of population urbanized (in settlements over 10,000)	60%	60%	44%	85%
GDP Growth in the 1990s	+73.3% (1991–99)	+12.4% (1991–98)	+24.9% (1990–99)	+15% (1990–96)
Share of Agricultural sector as part of total GDP (2002)	3.4%	7.3%	3.7%	2.6%
Net EU fiscal transfers as a percentage of GDP (1995–2000)[3]	3.51%	3.88%	2.83%	0.10%
Public Pollution Abatement and Control expenditure, as percentage of GDP[4]	0.4% (1998)	0.5% (1999)	0.5% (2000)	1.4% (2000)
Growth in total final consumption of energy per capita, 1980–2002	+55.9%	+59.9%	+136.7%	–6.6%
Change in greenhouse gases emissions, 1990–2002, measured by CO_2 equivalent	+29%	+26%	+40%	-0.4%
Percentage of population connected to waste water treatment plants	73% (2002)	56.2% (2002)	41.2% (2002)	89% (2002)
Municipal waste, in Kgs/per capita, for 2002	700kgs.	440kgs.	440kgs.	660kgs.
Recycling rate for glass (2002)	49%	27%	35%	76%
Major protected areas, as a percentage of total land area – for 2003	2.4%	5.2%	7.3%	37.2%
Forested land as a percentage of total (2001)	9.4%	22.8%	36.9%	12.7%
Number of mammal species, late 1990s	31	110	96	50
Number of endangered mammal species, (expressed as percentage of total mammal species in brackets)	2 (6.5%)	40 (36.4%)	17 (17.7%)	11 (22%)

[1] Unless otherwise stated, the data here come from the OECD/Organisation for Economic Development and Co-operation, *Environmental Data Compendium 2004* (Paris: OECD, 2004) and the OECD's individual country reports on environmental performance. These include: OECD/Organisation for Economic Co-operation and Development, *Environmental Performance Reviews – Ireland* (Paris: OECD, 2000); OECD/ Organisation for Economic Co-operation and Development, *Environmental Performance Reviews – Denmark* (Paris: OECD, 1999); OECD/Organisation for Economic Co-operation and Development, *Environmental Performance Reviews – Portugal* (Paris: OECD, 2001); OECD/Organisation for Economic Co-operation and Development, *Environmental Performance Reviews – Greece* (Paris: OECD, 2000b).

[2] Note: I have also seen a figure for the Republic of Ireland's coastline estimated as being 5,800km in length. See Government of Ireland, *Ireland National Development Plan 2000–2006: Economic and Social Infrastructure Operational Programme,* (Dublin: Government Stationery Office, 2000), p.53

[3] Source: Mattila, Mikko,'Fiscal Redistribution in the EU and the Enlargement' (Helsinki: Department of Political Science, Helsinki University, 2005). Working paper available at http://www.valt.helsinki.fi/staff/ mmattila/euredist/redist.pdf

[4] Source: OECD/Organisation for Economic Co-operation and Development, Environment Directorate General. *Pollution, Abatement and Control expenditures in OECD countries,* (Paris: OECD, 2003), p.33.

Ireland now has a wealthy enough social and economic base to pay for higher levels of advanced environmental protection. For that reason, I have included where possible data for Denmark, using that country as an example of a relatively small (post-)industrial state which has had for some time the level of wealth which Ireland has attained in recent years. Structural features of climate and latitude are also not very dissimilar. Denmark provides, then, the higher-level case in this peer group sample. It offers an example of a state which is wealthier and has had a longer experience of dealing with environmental problems.

These countries together should not be understood as a literal peer group that Ireland is expected to emulate on every issue. It is important to understand that each country has different environmental pressures and problems. Instead the 'peer group' provides a general background sample against which Irish trends can be interpreted. They can then be used to assess Irish environmental trends, and to spot where Irish deviations are more marked and require explaining or comment.

In the sections below I examine a number of per capita environmental statistics where they are available, comparing Ireland with this peer group, and where possible I try to provide trend data over time.

IRELAND'S CLIMATE CHANGE BLAME GAME

While Ireland's overall contribution to climate change has been assessed as quite small,[2] per capita statistics tell a very different story. They reveal a country which has among the highest per capita greenhouse gas emissions within the EU. The Irish EPA's official assessment of Ireland's climate change performance admits that 'Ireland still has one of the highest per capita greenhouse emission levels in the EU and is rated as being one of the EU countries that is furthest from its national Kyoto Protocol target'.[3] Yet this frank admission is not backed up by a display of the actual comparative statistics which reveal just how terrible Ireland's track record is. Charts 2.1 and 2.2 tell this story.

Not only can Ireland be placed among the top five per capita producers of such gases within the EU, but Irish per capita rates of production of such gases actually rose as well, between 1990 and 2001. Chart 2.1 reveals that by the mid 1990s Denmark was making progress in achieving a net per capita reduction. Even Portugal, who has considerably increased her emissions, has nonetheless still managed to stay below the EU per capita average. Chart 2.2 indicates that Ireland, along with Portugal and Greece, were the states with the greatest increases in CO_2 emissions during the period 1990–2000. This is partly to be expected from fast-growing cohesion economies. Yet Denmark has managed economic prosperity with comparatively less greenhouse gas emissions.

The EEA's 2004 assessment of emissions in greenhouse gases places Ireland as having the second highest level of per capita greenhouse gas emissions for the period 2002 at sixteen tonnes per person.[4] Yet Denmark had a level of thirteen tonnes, Greece twelve tonnes, and Portugal eight tonnes.[5]

Under the Kyoto Agreement (1997), which is the major international approach for dealing with the problem of climate change, Ireland agreed, together with her EU partners, that national emissions of CO_2 should rise by no more than 13 per cent on the country's 1990 level. It is now widely accepted that

CHART 2.1 PER CAPITA GREENHOUSE GAS EMISSIONS 1990–2001,
MEASURED IN TONNES OF CO_2 EQUIVALENT PER PERSON.

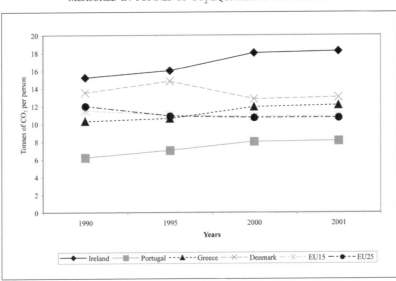

Source: Eurostat (2004b)

CHART 2.2 PERCENTAGE CHANGE (+/−) IN CO$_2$ EMISSIONS
1990–2000 IN SELECTED EUCOUNTRIES.

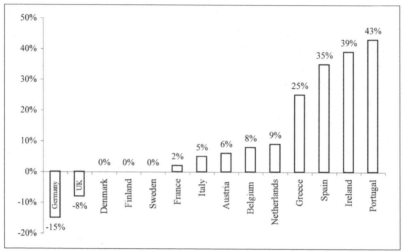

Source: EEA (2002) Annex I.

Ireland had already exceeded that level by 1997.[6] By 2002 Ireland had a level of greenhouse gas emissions which was 29 per cent above the 1990 base year.[7] Given such rises in Irish CO$_2$ emissions to date, it has to be highly questionable whether Ireland can turn the situation around and restore emissions to the Kyoto target by 2010–12.

To be fair, these charts may not capture very recent trends. Irish greenhouse gas emissions for the period 2002–3 did show some signs of reduction, probably due in large part to the closure of both a large fertilizer and steel plant.[8] However, EPA data for 2004 has shown a continued slight rise (+0.15 per cent from 2003) in overall emissions to give Ireland a national output of 68.46 million tonnes of CO$_2$ equivalent.[9] The EPA have estimated that this represents for the year 2004 a 23 per cent increase on Ireland's 1990 base year emissions level.

In plainer language, this is 10 per cent *more* than we have promised to achieve by 2008–12. By those years, the EPA reveal that our annual CO$_2$ equivalent emissions cloud should be no more than 63 million tonnes, yet as of 2004 Ireland was already producing 5 million tonnes more than this limit.

Somehow, Ireland is going to have to find a way to shed several million tonnes of CO$_2$ emissions and very rapidly. Failure to find a way to meet this challenge would not be just a moral defeat. It could cost Ireland a lot of money. For there is scope for financial penalties to be imposed upon member states as part of the Kyoto Protocol legal/diplomatic process. Moreover, our Kyoto targets are binding legal obligations and part of EU law.[10]

This Irish failure to meet Kyoto obligations should, however, be placed in context. The EU as a whole is unlikely to meet its collective goal of an 8 per cent reduction on 1990 emissions by 2010.[11] Even if this is true, Ireland still looks like a poorer performer amid a bad lot. In 2003, for example, Ireland was among the group of worst performers in respect of how far away it was from its Kyoto obligations. While Spain was *the* worst performer in 2003 in terms of deviation from what has been promised under the Kyoto Protocol, Ireland came in as sixth worst.[12] Interestingly, Denmark and Portugal were both serious offenders like Ireland, and actually had greater distances from their Kyoto targets than Ireland.[13]

Such measurements, however, are akin to snapshots at a given moment in time. Perhaps the Irish performance will rally very soon and impressive reductions will be achieved just before the deadline of 2008–12? Unfortunately, European Environment Agency (EEA) assessments of projected *future* greenhouse gas emissions for Ireland are not good either.

They predict Ireland is likely to have a gap between her projected future emissions of greenhouse gases and her 2010 target under the Kyoto Protocol of around 13.6 per cent. Interestingly, Denmark and Portugal once again are predicted to perform worse. Each is likely to have a bigger 'gap' to plug, of 18.7 and 25.1 per cent respectively by 2010. The Greek gap between likely future emissions and their 2010 target is projected to be a more modest 9.7 per cent and for the year 2003 Greece was assessed as actually being on course to meet her Kyoto obligations.[14] Yet the critical point remains that, judged on past performance, one has to say it is very unlikely the Irish will reach their Kyoto obligations on time. To make that possible at such a late stage requires action, and that requires a sense of urgency which can only be fostered once complacency has been unseated.

Unfortunately, complacency abounds. In fact, there is much denial but more especially a 'blame game' logic as various sectoral interest groups jostle to present the facts in a way which suits them. The Irish Business and Employers' Confederation (IBEC) has been consistently sensitive about the climate change record of the Irish industrial sector. When the Irish government announced a planned carbon tax in 2003 (later ditched), Donal Buckley, speaking for IBEC, went out of his way to defend the Irish industrial sector's record on climate change. He argued:

> As regards business, such a tax cannot change the behaviour of the already very clean Irish industry . . . When a company has achieved maximum levels of environmental efficiency and is struggling to compete, the only "behaviour" such a tax will have is to put that enterprise out of business . . . Climate change is a society-wide problem. All sectors emit greenhouse gases, so it logically follows that all must contribute to the solution.[15]

In 2006 Buckley was again repeating the mantra that Irish industry was being unfairly targeted and that other sectors should become the focus of climate change regulation:

> In Ireland, industry emitted 10 per cent of greenhouse gases, transport 17 per cent, agriculture 30 per cent, homes 10 per cent and energy production 25 per cent. A sensible approach would be to spread the burden proportionately. In Ireland the answer seems to be to hit industry . . . A policy that puts this little island out of business is not a sound policy and misses the opportunity to address the issue.[16]

The proposed carbon tax was abandoned as a policy in autumn 2004, after intensive IBEC lobbying among several powerful interest groups who voiced their concerns. These arguments by IBEC are another classic example of the 'blame game' at work. The desire here is to deflect responsibility away from one sector and point to others who should take greater responsibility.

It is worth examining here the claims made by IBEC representatives to get a more balanced picture of responsibility for Ireland's climate change record. Firstly, as regards greenhouse gases, it is completely correct to say that agriculture, forestry and fisheries constitutes the single largest sectoral source: roughly 19 million tonnes between 1994 and 2001. However, what IBEC never admit is that if one pays attention to trends over time in the annual growth of emissions according to sector, the picture for agriculture, fisheries, and forestry appears to be improving (admittedly from a very high base of emissions). Looking at chart 2.3, which describes the percentage rise and fall of Irish sectoral emissions of greenhouse gases between 1994 and 2002, one can see that agricultural sources for greenhouse gases actually reveal signs of a small reduction, in the order of 5 per cent. Emissions from households have also remained very limited between 1994 and 2002: no more than a 2 per cent rise.[17] Neither trend is a great success story, but at least they are not getting much worse.

CHART 2.3 PERCENTAGE CHANGE (+/−) IN ESTIMATED IRISH EMISSIONS, 1994–2002. MEASURED IN 1,000 TONNES CO_2 EQUIVALENT.[18]

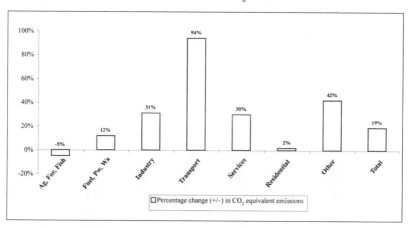

Source: CSO (2003), p.25; CSO (2004), p.25.

By way of contrast, the industrial sector has actually seen its share of emissions grow significantly in the same period: by some 31 per cent. The trend line for transport is the most dramatic of all, with an almost 100 per cent increase.

In summary, while Irish agriculture is certainly the biggest single source of greenhouse gases, it is Irish industry, and especially the Irish transport sector, which are actually getting worse over time.[19] Chart 2.4 also provides a fuller picture of Ireland's greenhouse gas emissions by giving a breakdown of sectoral origins of these gases in 1994 and again in 2002. One can quickly see that while agriculture, fisheries, and forestry still account for the largest share in both charts, that share had fallen well below one-third by 2002. Irish industry has risen from being responsible for *under* one-fifth to accounting for clearly *over* one-fifth of greenhouse gas emissions over the same period. Any simplistic notions that Irish industry is 'relatively clean' or that agriculture should bear more of the blame requires qualification and balance.

Indeed, the one sector where there is the most pressing need of regulatory action is the transport sector, where emissions growth is soaring out of all semblance of control. The transport sector by 2002 was producing almost the same level of emissions as the industrial sector, something that was not at all the case in 1994.

CHART 2.4 CHANGE IN PERCENTAGE SECTORAL SHARE OF ESTIMATED IRISH GREENHOUSE GAS EMISSIONS, 1994–2002.

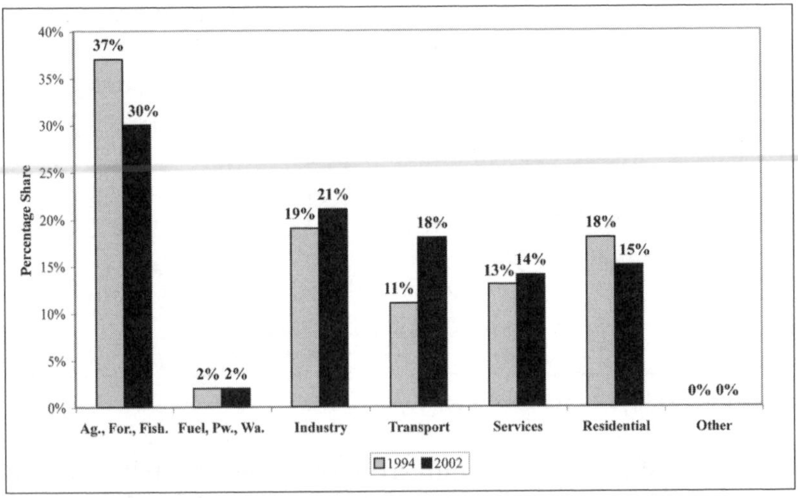

Source: CSO (2003), p.25.

IRELAND'S WASTE CRISIS IN COMPARATIVE PERSPECTIVE

The issue of waste remains one of the most politically contro-versial environmental problems Ireland faces. Since the late 1990s, local disputes have arisen over government waste plans. Irish government thinking on waste has centred on a resolve to move away from landfill. Yet no consensus has been possible about what technical management approach should replace landfill.

The debate has become a highly politicized one. Defenders of incineration face off against advocates of recycling. The result has been numerous small localized 'waste wars'[20] over proposed incinerators. At times the intensity and fervour of this debate has been remarkable. Environmentalists and local community activists are typically the constituency who have passionately opposed any use of incineration/energy recovery. They have argued for very ambitious recycling efforts to replace landfill. Their opposition to incineration has been based on health risks associated with airborne emissions, especially dioxins, the remaining ash, and fine particulate matter.

By way of contrast, business interests and some engineering professionals prefer a mix of both recycling and incineration, motivated chiefly by economic rationales. The profitability of recycling markets can be notoriously unpredictable. Incinerators are, in effect, mini-electricity stations able to sell electricity back into the national grid. This makes their commercial appeal stronger.

At times this debate has resulted in a counterproductive and simplistic 'recycling versus incineration' logic. One casualty has been a failure to pay attention to more subtle issues. For example, it has been widely ignored in the public debate that by far the largest volume of waste originates from the agricultural sector: over 70 per cent of all waste in 2004.[21] This issue is explored in more detail in the discussion on the Nitrates Directive below.

However, also comparatively ignored is the fact that while Irish recycling rates have increased, much of this is exported to other countries to be recycled. As much as 69 per cent of all Irish recycling occurs outside the state, indicating that Ireland is not yet developing a mature domestic recycling infrastructure.[22] In 1992 some 20 per cent of hazardous wastes were exported. By 2004, 70 per cent of hazardous wastes were being exported, the vast bulk to Germany.[23] These trends raise major questions about long-term sustainability.

Opponents of incineration should also note that halting incinerators in Ireland does nothing to prevent the incineration of Irish wastes abroad. Moreover, the Irish EPA already licenses at least ten industrial firms to operate hazardous waste incinerators to deal with their own waste on-site. Obviously, the scale and therefore risk of such activity is fundamentally different from large commercial 'for profit' incinerators.[24] Yet in November 2005, the EPA granted licences for two sites operating no less than three large scale incinerator plants, one of which will be licensed to deal with hazardous wastes.[25] By 2010 Ireland will unquestionably be relying on very controversial 'for profit' and large-scale incineration technology to deal with at least some of its wastes.

Because nearly everyone is, in principle, in favour of recycling, a wider consensus has emerged that much higher levels of recycling are needed in Ireland. Ironically though, the new incinerators may undermine recycling efforts by competing for municipal waste volumes as a fuel-stock. Nonetheless, local governments and the private waste business sector have maximized their efforts on recycling. This has led to some impressive increases. Yet this improvement has come from a very low base of recycling.

For example, for cardboard and paper, Ireland recycled only an estimated 12 per cent in 1992 and this rose to 34 per cent by 2002.[26] However, Denmark saw its recycling of cardboard/paper rise from 36 to 56 per cent over the *same* period. The Greek recycling rate for this material rose by only 32 to 34 per cent during 1992–2002, while Portugal's recycling rate for cardbord/paper grew from 39 to 45 per cent between 1992 and 2002. So Ireland clearly achieved a *faster* increase in the rate of recycling than the two cohesion states. However, the net result was that, by 2002, Ireland reached a level of recycling for cardboard/paper that Greece and Portugal were *already* achieving some ten years earlier in 1992. This is merely catch up mode.[27]

Rather than incineration or recycling, which have received all the attention, the critical issue for Ireland should be waste reduction and waste prevention. It is these two approaches, along with the concept of 're-use', which are the more far-reaching strategies for dealing with waste. Some readers will doubtless be familiar with the concept of the 'waste management hierarchy',[28] endorsed by the EU. This places priority on waste reduction first, secondly minimisation, then re-use, followed by recycling or energy recovery (the politically correct term for incineration). Landfill is usually pitched as a last option. Bizarrely, Irish waste policy has become fixated on strategies which are firmly stuck in the middle of the waste management hierarchy: recycling and/or incineration.

Unfortunately, waste reduction and re-use statistics for Ireland are terrible. For example, the EU average for beer container re-use was 60 per cent in the mid 1990s, whereas Ireland achieved only 17 per cent. Almost 39 per cent of soft drink containers were re-used within the EU in the mid 1990s, whereas in Ireland the rate was less than 10 per cent. Irish rates for re-use of wine and milk containers were both estimated as zero in 1997, whereas the EU average rate was 27 and 9 per cent respectively.[29]

Belatedly, in 2004 the EPA rolled out a four year national waste prevention strategy document as part of a grandiosely titled 'National Waste Prevention Plan'. No firm targets for waste prevention were included. By way of contrast the Dutch policy on waste has a firm target that growth in waste generation should be held at a level of 20 per cent below economic growth.[30] In 2005 a small pilot waste prevention scheme was initiated with funding of €1.7 million. This is a tiny amount in a context where commercial incinerator companies are investing up to €1 billion in individual plants, revealing there can be no doubt about where the focus of Irish waste strategies lie.[31] Waste prevention has been maginalized in the rush for recycling and incinerator 'solutions'.

Above all, the volume of Irish waste shows no sign of stabilizing. Throughout the 'Celtic Tiger' years, waste has increased. One can see this most clearly by using per capita data, which also show that Irish waste levels are significantly higher than our EU peers. Chart 2.5 reveals how Ireland has moved since 1995 from *below* the EU average to soaring well above it. By 2002, Ireland was producing 140 kg more municipal waste per head than the EU15 average, and significantly more waste per capita than any of the 'peer group'. According to the EEA, Ireland had by 2002 the highest per capita level of municipal waste in the *entire* EU.[32]

Such a trend has continued. Between 2002 and 2004 total municipal waste rose from 2.7 million tonnes to over 3 million tonnes: an 11.5 per cent increase.[33] Intriguingly though, the share of household waste as part of total municipal waste[34] loads, has actually *declined*. According to OECD data, in 1995 some 75 per cent of Irish municipal waste loads came from household waste, but by 2002 this share had dropped to 54 per cent. Between 1995 and 2002, household waste generation in Ireland rose only

CHART 2.5 MUNICIPAL WASTE GENERATION PER CAPITA 1980–2002, FOR DENMARK, IRELAND, PORTUGAL AND GREECE. MEASURED IN KGS/PER CAPITA.

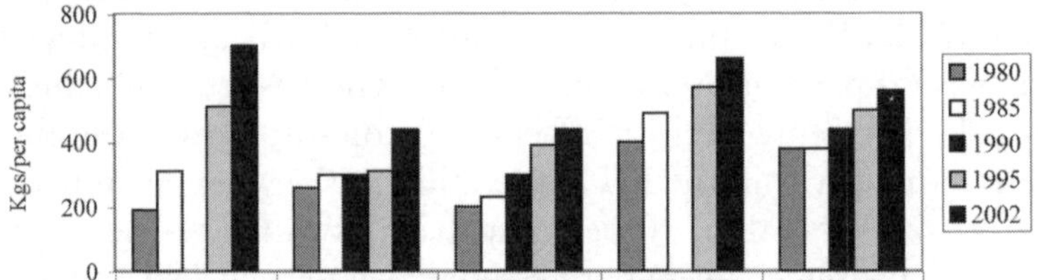

	IRELAND	GREECE	PORTUGAL	DENMARK	EU15 AV.
1980	190	260	200	400	380
1985	310	300	230	490	380
1990		300	300		440
1995	510	310	390	570	500
2002	700	440	440	660	560

Source: OECD (2005), p.174

from 370 kg to 380 kg per capita.[35] EPA data, based on a revised methodology, reveal that household waste per capita was at a significantly higher level in recent years: 428 kg and 430 kg for 2003 and 2004 respectively.[36]

In fairness, there may be an overestimation of Irish municipal waste statistics, because of inclusion of certain types of commercial wastes which other countries do not factor in. The Irish EPA now calculates municipal waste in a narrower way, and the EEA have accepted there may have been overestimation of Irish municipal waste volumes.[37]

However, even using the *revised* Irish EPA data, there is an unmistakable trend: the share of municipal waste coming from households is still declining. Between 2002 and 2004, household waste actually dropped from 61.7 to 57.2 per cent of municipal waste. Yet commercial waste as part of the municipal waste stream rose from 38.5 to 40.4 per cent over the same period.[38] So it is not ordinary Irish consumers who are to blame for pushing up the overall figure for Irish municipal waste way above the EU average. The political ramifications of such statistics are significant, but to date have been ignored.

The situation is not much better with regard to packaging waste, even though there has been a major industry-led voluntary scheme to recycle such waste: the REPAK initiative. Under the EU's Packaging Waste Directive, Ireland has met its targets of 25 per cent recycling by 2001, and 50 per cent recycling by 2005.[39] On first impressions Ireland appears to be making real progress on packaging waste.

In fact, per capita statistics show a poor performance. The problem is that packaging waste volumes are rising. Irish authorities, and especially REPAK, are therefore recycling a growing share of a rising waste mountain. That is not really progress. Moreover, the environmental benefits and cost implications of exporting so much material for recycling are not trivial.

In 1997, around 160 kg equivalent of packaging waste was being produced in Ireland per person. This was actually quite close to the then EU15 average. By 2001 the Irish figure for packaging waste per capita had shot up to an incredible level of 210 kg. The EU average by then was well below 200 kg per person. By 2001 Irish per capita rates of packaging waste were also significantly higher than those for Denmark, Portugal, and Greece. Denmark actually had a higher per capita weight of packaging waste in 1997 compared to Ireland, but by 2001 the Danish rate dropped and was significantly below the 200 kg level.[40] The Irish EPA estimate the per capita level of packaging waste for 2004 had stubbornly remained at 210 kg per person, whereas the EU15 average was 172 kg per capita.[41] In fairness, they also note that comparing packaging waste statistics per capita is tricky because of differing methodologies, noting that the Irish figures are reliable because they are audited, and hinting perhaps that other countries' data may be less reliable.[42] However, even the EPA's own data reveal that packaging waste volumes have been growing from the period 2001–3. It is only in 2004 that a significant reduction in the volume of packaging waste generated is visible.[43]

The bottom line here is clear. Regardless of a growing recycling effort led by REPAK, Irish per capita and absolute volumes of packaging waste have been generally rising. Ireland has gone from hovering around the EU average to being way above that level, and is the worst performer of the 'peer group'.

Comparison also puts into context Ireland's recycling targets for packaging waste. Consider that in the late 1990s the average recycling rate achieved within the EU15 states was over 50 per cent. Ireland only achieved that in 2005, reaching 56 per cent then, and in 2006 REPAK were claiming that packaging recycling was reaching 66 per cent.[44] Yet by the late 1990s, both Portugal and Greece were recycling between 30 and 40 per cent of packaging waste respectively, and Denmark was achieving a rate *above* 55 per cent five years earlier in 2001.[45] Crossing over the target of recycling 50 per cent of packaging waste in 2005 needs to be seriously qualified. It merits applause, but it is a slow pace of catch up compared with what other EU states have been achieving.

Equally, hazardous wastes are something on which Ireland has a distinctly unimpressive record. The types of waste in question here are mainly solvents, contaminated soil, waste oils, medical wastes, etc.[46] Between 1990 and 1998, the production of Irish hazardous wastes rose from 66,000 tonnes to 370,000 tonnes (a 460 per cent increase).[47] Yet both Greece and Portugal saw net *declines* in their production of hazardous wastes during the 1990s (although they started from much higher levels). Danish levels of hazardous waste production have been consistently lower than Irish levels since the late 1990s. Denmark produced 183,000 tonnes in 2000, or just under half the Irish level for 1998. In 2004, Irish hazardous waste production reached 723,931 tonnes. This was an increase of 36 per cent from 2001, or an almost eleven fold increase on the amount for 1990.[48]

Interestingly, the Irish record on hazardous waste fares little better when per capita statistics are used. Although precise data expressed in per capita terms is patchy, Irish per capita hazardous waste generation rose from 28 kg per person in 1992 to 70 kg per capita by 1995. It more than doubled in three years. Portuguese per capita hazardous wastes remained higher, but it was stable over the period 1990–4 at 138 kg per person. Danish hazardous waste levels per capita grew from 21 to 48 kg between 1990 and 1995.[49] From a lower base then, Ireland surged ahead to produce levels of hazardous waste per capita at rates well above those of Denmark. Ireland's record on hazardous wastes, much like its performance for other wastes, is therefore unimpressive.

IRELAND'S CAR DEPENDENCY IN COMPARATIVE PERSPECTIVE

How serious are the environmental problems of the Irish transport sector? More precisely, can we say that the motor car is the core environmental problem for transport, or not? Conor Faughnan, chief spokesman for the Automobile Association

(AA), has agued that Irish rates of car ownership are significantly below those of the EU average.[50] Instead he and others have argued that the failure to develop more sustainable travel within Ireland should be understood as a shortcoming of public transport provision and quality. The car is not to blame.

Unfortunately, such arguments are superficial and breed complacency. They can easily be misrepresented as implying that Irish authorities should not worry too much about seeing even more cars on the roads. The subliminal message could be: 'we can afford to crawl along towards the EU average'.

It is absolutely correct to assert that Ireland has a rate of car ownership that is significantly under the EU average. Chart 2.6, below, shows that for the period 1997–2002, Ireland had an average of 100 fewer vehicles per 1,000 persons compared with the EU average. Ireland's rate of car ownership even appears low for this period when compared with the peer group. Portugal notably stands out as having more cars per head.

However, Ireland has been closing the gap with our EU neighbours in terms of car ownership quite rapidly. In 1990 Ireland had a rate of car ownership that was under 60 per cent of the EU15 average. By 2002, that rate was well over 70 per cent and closer to 80 per cent of the EU average figure.[51] Indeed, there are projections that Ireland could reach the level of 480 vehicles per 1,000 persons by the year 2016.[52]

CHART 2.6 NUMBER OF PASSENGER CARS, PER 1,000 PERSONS,
AVERAGES FOR PERIOD 1997–2002.

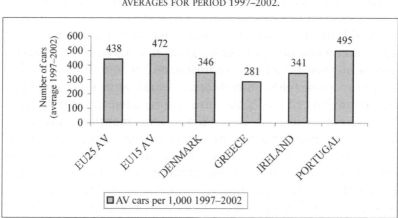

Source: Eurostat (2005), p.90

There has also been a notable increase in large engined vehicles, which have bigger fuel appetites, therefore usually lower fuel economy, and higher relative emissions. Between 1990 and 2004 the number of cars in the 1.7–1.9 litre range grew by 429 per cent and those over 1.9 litres grew by 210 per cent.[53] Sales of so-called Sports Utility Vehicles (SUVs) are also rising very fast. An increase was noted of 34 per cent in the numbers of such cars sold in 2004 from the previous year, and 36 per cent of these were registered mainly in urban Dublin.[54] From an environmental perspective, such vehicles often emit three times as much greenhouse gases as smaller cars and the trend towards larger cars is being blamed for an extra 300,000 tonnes of greenhouse gases in recent years.[55]

However, the big problem with looking at car ownership statistics per capita, or simply counting the total number of cars in each country, is that it tells us comparatively little about their use, especially how often they are driven. Nor do we get from such crude data of car ownership any idea about the actual environmental impacts of widespread car use, especially in Irish cities like Dublin.

One 2001 estimate of the environmental and other costs associated with car commuting in and to Dublin has suggested that these could be substantial: on average, 700 litres of fuel consumed per vehicle; an average of €4,200 running costs for the driver; an estimated average of €5,200 in external costs of pollution and congestion caused.[56]

The EEA has found that Ireland had the *highest* percentage increase of greenhouse gas emissions from the transport sector of any EU state during the period 1990–2003. Irish emissions of such gases showed an incredible 130 per cent increase over that period from the base year of 1990. Portugal by way of contrast had an increase of 95 per cent, Greece 40 per cent, and Denmark, at 25 per cent, was close to the EU15 average of 24 per cent.[57] It is clear that using cars rather than public transport as the primary means of mobility in Ireland has significant environmental consequences.

The Irish Census of 2002 provides findings that allow us to see just how dominant car use has become in Ireland. Chart 2.7, below, describes how, between 1981 and 2002, using the car to get to work has risen from just over one third of respondents to over half. It also reveals that bus and bike usage has fallen, rail travel only slightly increased, and even taking a lift as a car passenger has also declined.

CHART 2.7 CHANGE IN TRANSPORT MODE TAKEN TO WORK BY IRISH PEOPLE
BETWEEN 1981 AND 2002 (MEASURED IN MODAL PERCENTAGE SHARE).

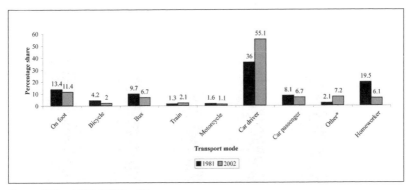

Source: GOI and CSO (2004), p.17

Another possible measure of car (over)use has been to look at distances travelled by various modes (rail, car, bus, etc.). The EEA have produced quite startling findings in this regard, which place Ireland firmly at the top of the league table. Between 1993 and 2002, the kilometres (km) per capita travelled by Irish people on cars, trains, buses and aircraft rose from under 10,000 km to over 17,000 km per person.[58] By 2002 the Irish were doing more travelling per head than any other EU country. The EEA have noted that even when aircraft travel data is removed, 'Ireland still has the highest level of growth and would be at a level comparable to the United Kingdom'.[59]

One other way of examining Irish motor vehicle usage is to look at how much energy cars consume. The OECD has produced a measure of the share of final energy consumption which is taken up by road transport. Of this, private cars make up about 78 per cent of all road vehicles, although road freight has grown substantially.[60] Chart 2.8 describes the situation for Ireland in comparison to EU average and peer group performance.

The share of energy consumption for Irish road transport has gone from being *significantly* below the EU average figure for 1970 (by 10 percentage points), to being *just* below that average by 2002. Interestingly, when per capita statistics are used the situation is not improved for Ireland. Hirsch, writing in a 2006 Forfás[61] report on Ireland's over-dependence on oil, has argued: 'In the early 1990s, Ireland used less oil per capita for

CHART 2.8 PERCENTAGE SHARE OF FINAL ENERGY CONSUMPTION FROM THE ROAD
TRANSPORT SECTOR, 1970–2002 FOR IRELAND, GREECE, PORTUGAL AND DENMARK.

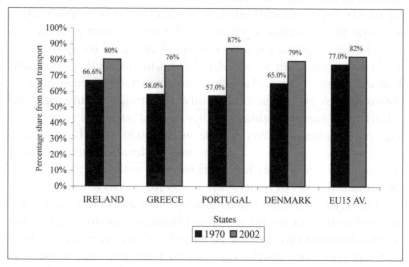

Source: OECD (2005), p.238

transportation than the average of the EU-25 countries. However,
by 2002, Ireland had consumed at least 50 per cent more oil per
capita for transportation purposes.'[62] What such statistics reveal
is that, while Ireland may have significantly less cars and
motorway kilometres per head of population, she is nonetheless
burning as much oil on the roads as the EU average.

Finally, car (over)use can be measured through survey
research. Such studies strongly indicate that the private motor car
is at the centre of Ireland's, and especially Dublin's, transport
problems. The Dublin Transportation Office (DTO) have
estimated the demand for travel in the Dublin area during the
1990s and how this might grow to 2016. According to the DTO:
'Total peak hour trips have grown by 78,000 or 45 per cent
between 1991 and 1997. However, the bulk of that growth has
been accounted for by private car commuting (+71,000) . . . by
2016, total peak hour trips are forecast to be 488,000, a 95
per cent increase on the 1997 level.'[63] A 2003 survey of Dublin
commuting trends, undertaken by Amárach Consulting,
confirmed these DTO findings, discovering that as many as 75
per cent of those surveyed were using cars to travel to work.[64]

Finally, perhaps the most intelligent contribution to our understanding of car use and its associated environmental problems lies in the concept of 'car dependency'. This has been advanced by Wickham and Lohan in their studies on Dublin's traffic problems.[65] By 'car dependency' is meant an excessive or disproportionate need for car use to meet routine mobility needs. The concept also draws attention to how this process happens. It is not just a social trend which is inevitable as countries become richer and buy more cars per head.[66]

Differences in culture, in how public transport is managed and provided for and, above all, variations in planning and spatial development policy together play a huge part in deciding how intensive car use will be. Wickham, writing of the situation in Dublin in the late 1990s, argued: 'Our research showed how the inhabitants of a middle class Dublin suburb used a car in order to carry out virtually every activity: going to work, taking children to school, doing nearly all forms of shopping, visiting friends and relatives, going out for a meal, etc.'[67]

In summary, one cannot fairly say that reliance on the private motor car is much *worse* in Ireland than other EU states. In fact, both Portugal and Greece appear to be more reliant on cars. Nonetheless, it is time to put to rest the mantra of complacency that Ireland has fewer cars than the rest of Europe and therefore not really much of a car problem. Ireland unquestionably *has* a growing problem with the private motor car which needs to be addressed. It does little to simply point to an inadequate public transport sector in an attempt to absolve responsibility for this fact.

Such arguments ignore genuine improvements in public transport provision, especially with regard to Dublin's buses. The number of buses provided by Dublin Bus increased by 32.54 per cent between 1997 and November 2004. The number of bus passengers increased by 49.17 per cent over the same period.[68] Since summer 2004, the entirely new LUAS trams have added the ability to move over 6,000 persons per hour.[69] Yet more buses cannot cope with the parallel greater surge in car use without fairly radical measures to guarantee them road access through special lanes.

The result has been bus 'quality corridors', which although hardly a glamorous or high tech solution, have generally performed well in Dublin, even with the absence of electronic ticketing and proper park and ride facilities. By 2004, Dublin had twelve different quality bus corridors (QBCs) each capable of moving around 4,000 people per hour, or circa 50,000 in total.[70] Yet these QBCs have only become a success by effectively curtailing the rights of road use for ordinary car drivers, who cannot use such lanes at peak times. Progress has come about by actually limiting road access for private cars. In other words, there is a direct relationship between improving public transport and controlling private car over-use, which the AA's argument entirely ignores.

In conclusion, it is far too easy to pan off responsibility for traffic gridlock and the associated environmental problems it causes away from the motor car and onto the woes of Irish public transport. It is equally facile to demonize car drivers and reduce the entire transport and environment debate into an 'anti-car' agenda. The real issues are much more complex than that.

It is not crude ownership rates of cars which matter as much as how often cars are (over)used. It is also not just about controlling the rate at which overall car numbers increase, but in particular the type of cars that drivers buy and drive. Large SUV like diesels becoming an increasing feature of suburban Irish lifestyles is very bad news for Irish air pollution, greenhouse gas emissions, and energy consumption.

IRISH ENERGY EFFICIENCY: SUCCESS STORY OR CHIMERA?

On first impressions, the efficient use of energy in Ireland would appear to be one area where there are signs of real progress from an environmental perspective. According to Sustainable Energy Ireland (SEI): 'In 1990 it required 0.16 kilograms of oil equivalent (kgoe) to produce one euro of GDP (in constant 2003 values) whereas in 2004 only 0.1 kgoe was required. This would suggest that the economy is continuing to become more energy efficient.'[71] Today, the energy used per unit of production has, in real terms, fallen from what it was at the start of the 1990s. Between 1990 and 2002 the value added from industry grew by 224 per cent whereas industrial final energy consumption grew by only 28 per cent over the same period.[72]

To give this discussion a focus for debate, it is worth quoting one industry commentator, Brendan Butler of IBEC, who has argued that this environmental success story has gone unnoticed. According to Butler: 'Ireland has made remarkable steps in reducing energy intensity and now – according to the UN Human Development Report 2002 – is the *second* most energy efficient economy in Europe. Industry in Ireland is efficient and clean, a fact recognized internationally, but unfortunately not here at home.'[73]

However, I argue here that such assertions are not accurate. It is true Ireland has become more energy efficient, but the gains are nowhere near as spectacular as has been claimed by Butler, especially when they are understood in a comparative context. Moreover, more serious issues concerning the sustainability of Irish energy are being ignored by Irish policymakers.

The most worrying of these is a growing reliance on fossil fuels. Ireland is sleepwalking itself into a seriously unsound energy and environmental policy by default. And this is at a time when we appear to be entering a new era of 'peak oil'.[74] The concept of 'peak oil' refers to a period when, due to structural factors in the scarcity of oil and natural gas supply, prices for oil and gas are either set to rise steeply or become more unpredictable. It also implies that risks concerning security of supply are magnified as competition for oil and gas intensifies. At the same time, Ireland has failed to explore renewable energy sources and remains stuck in the 'slow' lane of EU countries who refuse to make a major push towards renewable energy. Regardless of the admitted gains in energy efficiency, the core environmental problem is that Irish energy supply is becoming less sustainable in terms of its source fuels and its security.

Yet what of the argument that Ireland has experienced a revolution in energy efficiency that deserves praise, or that Ireland is ranked European number two in energy efficiency: are these claims accurate? To answer this question requires an understanding of how energy efficiency is usually assessed.

It is typically measured by how many energy units are consumed per unit of economic activity, or whether a country is using more or less energy as its economic activity increases. The standard way to uncover this is to measure the 'energy intensity' of each country. This involves finding a ratio between a measure of energy consumption, usually expressed in units of tonnes of oil equivalent (TOE), against some measure of economic activity, usually expressed in measurements of GDP, set to a standard

CHART 2.9 AVERAGE ANNUAL PERCENTAGE CHANGE IN ENERGY INTENSITY
1995-2002, MEASURED BY TOE (TONNES OF OIL EQUIVALENT) USED PER MILLION OF
GDP EARNED, EXPRESSED IN PURCHASING POWER STANDARDS (PPS).

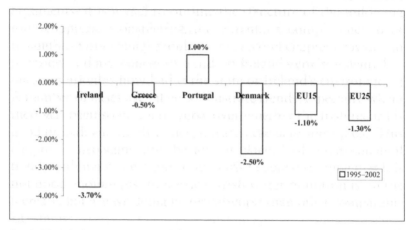

Source: EEA, (2005a), p.336.

pricing index to cope with inflation. Energy intensity is then an
indicator of how much energy is used for a given unit of
economic activity.

So is Ireland less energy intensive in recent years than it was a
decade ago, and how does Ireland compare with our peers or the
EU average performance? According to EEA calculations of each
EU country's energy intensity rate, Ireland stands out as an
excellent performer. An average −3.7 per cent reduction per
annum in her energy intensity rates occurred between 1995 and
2002.[75] The EU15 average for the same period was a −1.1 per cent
reduction per annum. Chart 2.9 describes the Irish performance in
comparison with the peer group used here, and reveals that
Ireland had a greater reduction in its energy intensity rates for the
period 1995–2002 than either Denmark or Greece.

Portugal actually saw an *increase* in her rate of energy
intensity, meaning she became less efficient. However, even this
excellent performance does *not* place Ireland in first or second
place with regard to the best performances overall. According to
the EEA's data, a number of other EU states had either the same
or higher reductions in their energy intensity rates as Ireland:
Estonia (−6.4 per cent), Poland (−5.4 per cent), Latvia and
Lithuania (each −4 per cent), Romania (−3.8 per cent), and

Bulgaria (–3.7 per cent). Ranked this way, Ireland would come in joint sixth place with Bulgaria in terms of reductions of energy intensity rates over the period 1995–2002.

In any event, energy efficiency measured by the concept of intensity, or by per capita consumption, is not necessarily the most important measurement from an environmental perspective. What is often more important is the type of energy supply and its associated pollution characteristics. As the EEA themselves admit: 'Energy intensity is not sufficient to measure the environmental impact of energy use and production . . . the link to environmental pressures has to be made on the basis of the absolute amounts of the different fuels used to produce that energy. Energy intensity should therefore always be put in the broader context of the actual fuel mix used to generate the energy.'[76]

How dependent, then, is Ireland on fossil fuels, or how much progress has she made on alternatives such as renewables? Ireland's reliance on oil and gas has increased over the last fifteen years. Between 1990 and 2004 the share of oil as a proportion of Ireland's total primary energy requirement[77] (a measure of gross energy demand) grew from 45.5 to 55.8 per cent. Coal decreased its share from 23 to 12.9 per cent over the same period, but natural gas surged from 15.4 to 24.3 per cent.[78] By 2004, about 93 per cent of Ireland's energy needs were being met by mostly imported coal, gas, and oil. The share from renewables remained abysmal: from 1.8 to 2.2 per cent of gross energy demand.[79]

Also what is striking is just how fast demand for natural gas has grown during the 1990s and beyond. A 152 per cent increase between 1990 and 2004 is evident for gas, whereas the rate of increase for oil was under 100 per cent. By 2004, natural gas also accounted for 45 per cent of the total fuels used for electricity generation, whereas renewables accounted for just 2.6 per cent.[80] This had been considered a welcome move from an environmental perspective, because natural gas plants are typically highly efficient and produce lower emissions of greenhouse gases and other pollutants. However, on 1 January 2006, Russian gas suppliers disconnected their pipeline to Ukraine for a brief period, and thereby cut supplies to many European states. Ireland was not directly hit, but that single incident has brought into sharp relief the precarious nature of relying on a 'dash for gas' to produce more electricity for lower emissions.

Related to such concerns about energy security, Ireland's dependence on energy imports has grown markedly. The EU15 average for energy imports during most of the 1990s has hovered around 50 per cent of energy needs being imported for most states. Yet Ireland saw between 1990 and 2004 an increase from 69 to 89 per cent of her energy needs being imported.[81]

How does this Irish experience compare with our EU neighbours and the peer group used here? Hirsch, writing in a 2006 report on Ireland's oil dependence for Forfás, argued that the Irish over-reliance on oil was higher than average. He notes:

> Such has been the speed and scale of the increase in Ireland's oil consumption since 1990 that as of 2002 Ireland ranked 3rd among the EU-25 countries in terms of oil consumed per capita . . . while oil consumption per capita has remained constant in the EU as a whole, Ireland's consumption per capita has increased by over 50 per cent between 1990 and 2002. Some of this high dependence on oil is inevitable given the island nature of our economy. However, some is a matter of choice as Ireland has adopted patterns of transportation, spatial development and energy production that are oil intensive.'[82]

The same study revealed that while Ireland could be ranked *third* highest in terms of per capita consumption of oil for 2002, Denmark was ranked 9th and Greece and Portugal 15th and 16th respectively.

However, the comparative weakness of Irish performances with regard to energy is most notable when Ireland's record on renewable energy is subjected to the comparative gaze. Chart 2.10 describes the share of renewables as a percentage of total energy consumption for the period 1990–2002, which is broader than just for electricity generation.

What is completely unambiguous from this chart is how low the Irish share is, and how little it has increased. It is noteworthy that Denmark stands out as the most significant pacesetter in terms of showing what is possible. An effective doubling of the contribution of renewables to Danish energy supply has been achieved within twelve years. A significant portion of this increase has been sourced from wind energy, a sector which the

CHART 2.10 SHARE OF RENEWABLE ENERGY BETWEEN 1990–2002, AS A PERCENTAGE OF TOTAL ENERGY CONSUMPTION, MEASURED IN TOE (TONNES OF OIL EQUIVALENT).

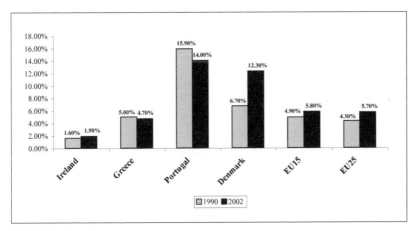

Source: EEA (2005a), p.374.

Danish government have supported and funded since the 1980s and which is now a world leader in wind energy projects. Even Greece had twice as much renewable energy sourcing as Ireland, although some of this reflects older hydro plants.

In fairness, it is worth pointing out that in very recent years the Irish renewable sector has grown fast, and it may yet rise further if proactively supported by government.[83] The Danish experience shows what is possible when there is clear vision, ambition, and willpower to support renewables over fossil fuel dependence.

Yet bizarrely in Ireland, the onset of peak oil has not provoked a resolve to explore greener energy solutions. Instead it has been greeted by some popular commentators as an excuse to make controversial statements about the need to consider nuclear energy. Much of this is merely a fashion to be controversial on the part of commentators. However, the Forfás report already mentioned was perhaps the most authoritative voice in making a more serious case for nuclear electricity imports from the UK,[84] but it is not the only one. The academic and commentator David McWilliams for example, has questioned: 'What are we in Ireland going to do, if the world goes nuclear? Are we going to sit, self-regardingly from the sidelines and 'tut-tut' while we import nuclear powered electricity from the British grid? Are we going to hold our noses while others get on with the dirty business of taking responsibility?'[85]

Well one thing Ireland could simply do is just take a much closer look at what other European states have already achieved with renewable energy. Ireland could seriously try and reach their levels of performance as soon as is possible. Beyond this, the question of nuclear energy is too complex to address here, although I do examine it again in Chapter Five.

THE NITRATES REFUSENIKS

Nitrate pollution of Irish freshwaters and coastal zones has become a live political dispute in Ireland. One of the points of controversy relates to disagreement over whether nitrate pollution in Ireland exists at a serious level, or not. Incredibly, there is still debate in Ireland about whether there is even an environmental problem concerning nitrates.

In fact, what has really made the issue intensely political was that, in March 2004, Ireland was found guilty before the European Court of Justice in Luxembourg for the improper implementation of the EU's 1991 Directive on Nitrates (91/676/EC).[86] This EU law was originally supposed to be fully implemented in 1995.

Since losing that case, there has been huge political and legal pressure on the Irish government to properly implement the Directive. Detailed regulations were introduced in December 2005, but these were partially suspended in February 2006 in the teeth of intense farmer opposition.[87] Incredibly, as of spring 2006 the Irish government was seeking to continue that deferment for a further five years.[88] It remains unclear if Ireland has properly implemented the Nitrates Directive at all. This could leave Ireland facing significant daily fines for non-compliance with a verdict of the European Court of Justice.[89]

Farmers' organizations such as the Irish Farmers' Association (IFA) argue that these latest Irish regulations implementing the directive are draconian, and are anyhow unnecessary. They claim there is not really any serious nitrate pollution problem in Ireland. Or, alternatively, the line taken is that agriculture is not to blame for nitrates in water. Instead the sewage works of towns are pointed to by the IFA as the likely main culprit.

What, then, is the real story on nitrates pollution – are the IFA correct? I argue here that the IFA are inaccurate in their arguments about nitrates. It is true that the scale of Irish nitrates pollution of waters is not extensive. It is also correct to note that levels of nitrates recorded are dropping, meaning the situation appears to be improving. However, there is evidence of *some* pollution arising from nitrates in Ireland. What remains open for dispute is only whether this is significant or not.

The fairest answer is that the levels of nitrates recorded in Irish waters, while generally low, are not trivial. For example, about 23 per cent of groundwater samples taken between 2001 and 2002 had levels which exceeded the EU *guideline* value for nitrates.[90] At the guideline level, such concentrations do not represent a threat to human health. However, they would contribute to eutrophication or excessive nutrient enrichment of waters, reducing aquatic biodiversity.

As regards risks to human health, the EPA's report on water quality for the period 2001–3 reveals that, for groundwaters, there were at least a few cases where the actual safety *limit* value has been breeched. The number of monitoring stations whose average recorded concentrations went over the safety level of 50 milligrams per litre (mg/l) actually increased from 1.5 per cent in 1998–2000 to 1.7 per cent in 2001–3.[91]

The situation is broadly similar when nitrate pollution of rivers is examined. Ireland's EPA cautiously revealed that 'levels in the larger rivers remain within the limit set for drinking waters. However, the guideline concentration has been exceeded on occasion in several of these rivers, and in some smaller rivers and streams in the south-east there have been exceedances of the limit itself.'[92]

For drinking water supplies there can be no grounds for complacency either. The EPA's 2004 report on drinking water reveals that, for that year, about 1.5 per cent of Irish drinking water was actually *exceeding* the safety *limit* value of 50mg/l. That level is not a mere guideline, but a mandatory public health standard. Commenting on similar levels of compliance in previous years and 2003,[93] the EPA admitted that:

> Some of the supplies reporting breaches were abandoned as sources and the improving results (or indeed the high rates

of compliance) should not be interpreted as suggesting that nitrate levels in Irish waters are low as many of the elevated supplies are simply abandoned rather than remediated . . . there appears to be a reduction in the number of moderate and serious exceedances (for nitrates measured in drinking water) and a concurrent increase in the number of very serious and gross exceedances. This indicates that those supplies that are exceeding are actually deteriorating and that levels of nitrates are rising in these supplies.[94]

In cases where the EU limit value is exceeded there could be a remote risk of a very rare[95] blood condition in babies, methaemoglobinaemia. However, a much more likely scenario by which human health can be damaged is that eutrophication caused by nitrates will also increase the scope for a multiplication of water-based pathogens such as faecal coliforms, for example the infamous Escherichia (E.) coli.[96]

One other reason why any complacency about nitrates should never be accepted is because nitrate pollution can take a long time to show up – as long as decades. The EEA have noted this feature, which makes nitrate pollution particularly tricky to regulate and manage: 'Substantial time lags can occur before changes in agricultural practices are reflected in groundwater quality.'[97]

In this regard it is important to realize that the Nitrates Directive requests designation of Nitrate Vulnerable Zones (NVZs) not just where limit values are already being exceeded but where they are likely to be in future. The critical concept within the directive is then the precautionary principle, which is recognized as a principle of EU law.[98] This requires regulatory action to be anticipatory, especially when faced with scenarios where there is a possibility of serious future ecological harm, but not yet certainty as to its probability or extent.

Of course, when faced with evidence of a problem with nitrates, it is sometimes argued by Irish farmers' representatives that Irish levels of nitrates are well below the EU average, and therefore that the directive should not apply to Ireland. However, trying to claim that the Irish experience of nitrates is somehow structurally different is simply not credible.

The OECD have provided data comparing recorded average nitrate levels in selected European rivers for the period

1999–2001. In the absence of better comparative statistics, this provides something of a general indicator of whether the Irish experience is really that different. Chart 2.11 describe this data for the reader.

CHART 2.11 RECORDED AVERAGE NITRATE LEVELS FOR 1999–2001, FROM SELECTED DANISH, IRISH, GREEK AND PORTUGESE RIVERS.

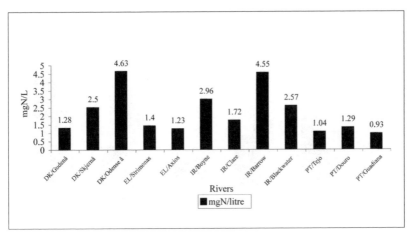

Source: OECS (2005), pp.85–6.

This chart reveals that Greece and Portugal had systematically lower levels of nitrates recorded. Denmark and Ireland had a more mixed record. Both Denmark and Ireland had at least one river where recorded levels were high. Thereafter, the Irish river measurements are, on average, actually higher than Danish ones, even though historically nitrates have been a bigger environmental priority in Denmark. On the basis of an admittedly very limited sample, it is dangerous to reach too many conclusions, but there does not appear to be strong evidence that Ireland has much lower levels of nitrates than other EU states.

Another important way of looking at the Irish problem with nitrates is to ask what level of nitrogen inputs does Ireland have, compared with other states? Two measurements are vital here: the consumption of artificial fertilizers, which typically have a high nitrogen loading, and the size of Ireland's grazing animal herd, which produces nitrogen-rich manures.

Chart 2.12 specifically provides details on nitrogen (N) fertilizers, based on OECD data, and shows a clear trend. Ireland stands out as having had a major increase in the total consumption of such fertilizers over the years 1980–2001, whereas trends for the peer group used here and the EU15 average both revealed steady reductions.

CHART 2.12 CONSUMPTION OF NITROGEN (N) FERTILIZERS 1980–2001, MEASURED IN 1,000 TONNES.

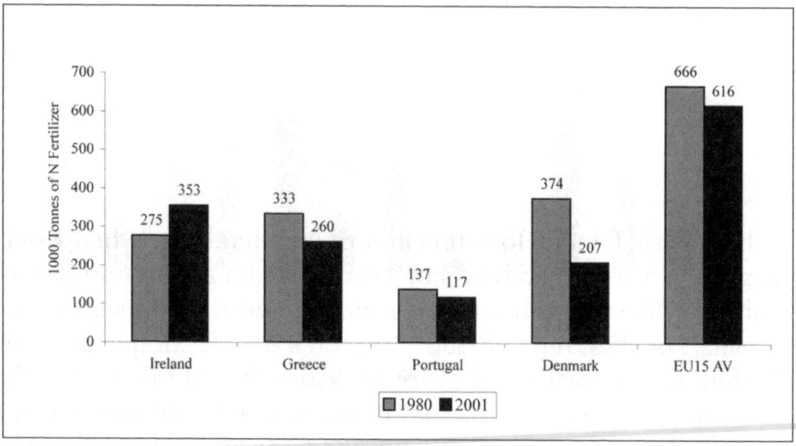

Source: OECD (2005), pp.263–6.

In percentage terms, Irish N fertilizer usage grew by 28 per cent between 1980 and 2001. By way of contrast Danish rates of N fertilizer use dropped by −45 per cent, and the EU average was a more modest −7 per cent reduction between 1980 and 2001.[99] Even when one examines the trend for all fertilizers, for example including phosphorous (P) or potash (K) mixes, only a very low Irish reduction is evident: in the order of just −5 per cent. By way of contrast, the EU average reduction was −26 per cent. For the years 1980–2001, Denmark actually managed a −49 per cent reduction in total fertilizer use, and Greece and Portugal reductions of −20 and −12 per cent respectively.

In fairness, one must note that Irish rates of use of all fertilizers have dropped since the late 1990s,[100] but there is no getting away from what this data shows: Ireland has experienced a sustained and large scale nutrient increase, especially from Nitrogen fertilizers. Moreover, scientific studies have found that many Irish farmers are overusing fertilizers, wasting money, and potentially damaging the environment, in some cases exceeding the required level by a factor of four.[101]

OECD data also reveal that Irish livestock numbers have risen significantly, which has implications for the wastes these animals produce. Between 1980 and 2002, the numbers of Irish cattle in absolute terms grew by 6 per cent, sheep by 16 per cent, and pigs by 74 per cent.[102] In each case the trend for the EU15 average figure was either a reduction, or only a modest increase. By way of comparison, Danish cattle numbers dropped heavily over the same period (–39 per cent), while their pig numbers grew by 28 per cent.

Finally, what of claims by the IFA that nitrate pollution does not come from farmers, but from town sewage works or other sources? The Irish EPA, after a careful study undertaken in 2000, estimated that four out of every five tonnes (83 per cent) of nitrogen entering Irish waters came from agriculture, with the balance coming mainly from domestic industrial wastewater and background sources. Earlier scientific studies have also shown a clear link between intensive agricultural land-use practices in Ireland's south-east and higher nitrate levels in waters there.[103]

However, this estimate by the EPA has been challenged in the Irish parliament during committee hearings.[104] Senator Bradford (Fianna Fáil) argued the figure of 83 per cent was five years old, implying it was no longer accurate. John Dillon, then president of the IFA, went further, dismissing the 83 per cent EPA figure as only 'based on a desk-top assessment and has nothing to do with actual science or fact'.[105]

Yet the 83 per cent figure was based on a scientific published study by the EPA. Suggesting it has been arrived at unscientifically is simply inaccurate, and it is unlikely to have reduced much since it was calculated. Moreover, the EPA have pointed to the link between higher nitrate levels in the south-east and certain agricultural practices there: 'The higher nitrate levels in the rivers of the south-east reflect the differences in respect of land use, particularly the extent of tillage in the two areas.'[106]

Unfortunately, for the nitrates refuseniks of the IFA such evidence is simply not accepted. Denial reigns and a blame game thrives. All of this allows the row over implementing the Nitrates Directive to drag on and on.

CONCLUSIONS

This chapter has not claimed that Irish environmental problems are worse than those of other EU states. Indeed, when one asks how Ireland performs within its 'peer group', some of the evidence presented here actually shows Ireland to be a *better* performer than its peers. For example, the performance of both Portugal and Greece on energy efficiency is worse than Ireland. Portugal would also appear to have a higher level of hazardous waste generation per capita, and a greater dependence on motor cars. However, there should be no grounds for complacency. If there is one strong message from this chapter it is that a comparative perspective allows us to see that Ireland is in general not doing so well on environmental issues.

The 'Celtic Tiger' has spawned simply unsustainable trends in consumption. This can be seen in the Irish transport sector, where car numbers and use are increasing. Even worse, greenhouse gas emissions from the Irish transport sector are surging out of control. With regard to waste generation, there are yearly rises in waste volumes, which undermine the logic of increased recycling. Ireland has failed to seriously explore waste prevention.

What is also revealing is that a comparison with a peer group of EU states suggests that Ireland could and should do so much better. For example, Ireland is now significantly wealthier than either Greece and Portugal, but it is worth asking has her ability to clean up her environmental problems become relatively better than those states?

This chapter suggests not. When the rest of our EU peers were reducing their use of nitrogen fertilizers in the 1990s, Ireland was actually increasing it compared to them. In 1992, Greece and Portugal had already achieved levels of cardboard and paper recycling which Ireland only managed in 2002.

The strongest example of how Ireland could do better lies in looking at how Denmark has improved its environmental perform- ance. Leaving aside the controversy over incineration, which Denmark is heavily reliant on, its record on renewable energy and waste re-use offers Ireland valuable examples about what is possible. While Ireland gorged itself on oil and natural gas over the last decade, Denmark quietly doubled the contribution of renewable energies to its total energy demand. In doing this it has also managed to build up a global leadership in wind energy technologies – a classic ecological modernization strategy.

Finally, a strong theme of this chapter has been that awareness and perception of the seriousness of many environmental problems has been wanting. A lack of basic awareness that there is even a problem lies at the heart of the issues on nitrates, energy policy, and car dependency. Instead the line has been trotted out that Ireland is among the most energy efficient, has fewer cars, or lower levels of nitrates.

Only very recently are these issues beginning to be debated. Unfortunately, that debate has often been skewed by interest groups. IBEC claim industry is now doing *too much* on greenhouse gases and that agriculture or transport should do more. This neatly ignores a still rising level of greenhouse gas emissions from industry. The IFA deny there is any serious nitrate pollution problem at all. That evasion ignores the precautionary logic of the Nitrates Directive and clear evidence from the EPA that there is a problem.

Hopefully this chapter has allowed the reader to better judge such controversies. It is time both policy-makers and the general public became aware of a more critical understanding of Irish environmental problems. Ireland is unquestionably among the very worst European performers on greenhouse gases. Our waste production on a per capita basis is also among the highest within the EU. Irish dependence on fossil fuels or encouragement for renewables is very poor in comparative terms. Against this backdrop, it is time to rethink fundamentally the style and substance of Irish environmental policy. However, before we can do that, we need to know something of its history, which the next chapter uncovers.

NOTES

1. Landman, D. *Issues and Methods in Comparative Politics* (London: Sage, 2000), and Mackie, T. and Marsh, D. 'The comparative method', in D. Marsh, and G. Stoker (eds.), *Theory and Methods in Political Science* (Basingstoke: Macmillian/Palgrave, 1995), pp.173–88.
2. One source estimates Ireland's contribution to global CO_2 production at circa 0.2 per cent for 1998. See World Resources Institute, *Earth Trends:*

the Environmental Information Portal, (2004). Available at: http:// http://earthtrends.wri.org/text/climate-atmosphere/country-profiles.html

3. EPA/Environmental Protection Agency, *Ireland's Environment 2004* (Wexford: EPA, 2004), p.245–6.

4. EEA/European Environment Agency, *Greenhouse gas emission trends and projections in Europe 2004. EEA Report No. 5/2004*, (EEA: Copenhagen, 2004a), p.9. Available at http://reports.eea.eu.int/eea report 2004 5/en

5. Ibid.

6. According to the Irish state's own Central Statistics Office (CSO): 'Based on the EPA's official estimates, national greenhouse gas emissions exceeded the Kyoto target in 1997 and were 31 per cent above the 1990 baseline level in 2001'. See CSO/Central Statistics Office and ESRI/Economic and Social Research Institute, *Environmental Accounts for Ireland, 1994–2001* (Cork: CSO, 2003), p.14. Available at http://www.cso.ie/publications/enviracc.pdf, p.14).

7. EPA, *Ireland's Environment 2004*, pp.245, 241.

8. EPA, *Ireland's Environment 2004*, p.145.

9. EPA/Environmental Protection Agency, 'Press Release: 'Ireland's greenhouse gas emissions increased slightly in 2004 – final figures released', Wednesday 29 March 2006, (Wexford: EPA, 2006). Available at: http://www.epa.ie/NewsCentre/PressReleases/MainBody,9033,en.html

10. Hempel, L.C. 'Climate Policy on the Installment Plan', in Vig, N.J. and Kraft, M.E. *Environmental Policy: New Directions for the Twenty-First Century*, Sixth edition (Washington: CQ press, 2006), pp.294–5; and Council of Ministers of the European Communities, 'Council Decision 2002/358/EC of 25th April 2002 concerning the approval on behalf of the European Community, of the Kyoto Protocol to the United Nations Framework Convention on Climate Change and the joint fulfilment of commitment thereunder', *Official Journal of the European Communities*, L 130, 45, 15 May 2002, pp.1–20.

11. A 2005 comprehensive overview of environmental performance by the EEA has commented: 'After more than half the time period between 1990 and the first commitment period (2008–2012) under the Kyoto Protocol, the reduction by 2003 was less than a quarter of that needed to reach the EU15 target.' EEA/European Environment Agency, *The European Environment: State and Outlook 2005* (Copenhagen: EEA, 2005a), p.415.

12. In 2002 Ireland was the *third* furthest away from its target (after first Spain, then Portugal second, with Denmark and Greece coming sixth and seventh respectively). EEA, *Greenhouse gas emission trends and projections in Europe 2004, etc.*, p.14.

13. The EEA uses a 'snapshot' statistic called 'distance to target'. This calculates the percentage deviation from an estimated line of emissions required to meet each state's Kyoto reductions by 2010. The exact 'distances' from the line of reductions in percentage terms were: Ireland (12.3 per cent), Denmark (15.8 per cent), Portugal (19.1 per cent). Greece was nearer its liner path being only 7 per cent above the level of emissions it should have by 2003. EEA, *The European Environment: State and Outlook 2005*, Figure 2, p.294.

14. EEA, *The European Environment: State and Outlook 2005*, Figure 1, p.297, and also EEA, *Greenhouse Gas Emissions trends and projections in Europe 2005*, etc., p.14.
15. Buckley, D. 'A crude way to address a very complex problem', *The Irish Times*, 5 September 2003.
16. Buckley, D. 'Putting Ireland out of business is no answer to climate change', *The Irish Times*, 2 February 2006.
17. CSO/Central Statistics Office and ESRI/Economic and Social Research Institute, *Environmental Accounts for Ireland, 1995–2002* (Cork: CSO, 2004), p.25 and CSO and ESRI, *Environmental Accounts for Ireland, 1994–2001*, etc., p15. Both Available at http://www.cso.ie/publications/enviracc.pdf
18. The abbreviations 'Ag, For, Fish', stand for agriculture, forestry, and fisheries. 'Fuel, Pw, Wa', stand for Fuel, Power and Waste.
19. EEA, *Greenhouse gas emission trends and projections in Europe 2004*, etc.,p.14. Available at http://reports.eea.eu.int/eea_report_2004_5/en
20. The expression 'waste wars' is from Davies, A. 'Waste wars – public attitudes and the politics of place in waste management strategies', *Irish Geography*, 36, 1, (2003), pp.77–92.
21. EPA/Environmental Protection Agency and Collins, C., Le Bolloch, O., and Meaney, B. *National Waste Report 2004* (Wexford: EPA, 2005h), p.3.
22. EPA/Environmental Protection Agency, *National Waste Database 2003. Interim Report* (Wexford: EPA, 2004b), p.4.
23. EPA (et al.), *National Waste Report, 2004*, p.45. I have calculated this from the raw data provided: 469,501 tonnes out of a total of 673,631 tonnes. Germany took 64.8 per cent of all hazardous waste exports in 2004, and the UK 16 per cent. See Table 23, p.46.
24. According to the EPA's own 2004 National Waste Report, the existing capacity of industrial incinerators was 39,692 tonnes, which is significantly less than the planned 350,000 capacity that will come on stream when (or if) the two incinerator plants at Ringaskiddy (Cork) and Carranstown (Meath) open. EPA (et al.), *National Waste Report, 2004*, pp.62–3.
25. Ibid.
26. OECD/Organisation for Economic Co-operation and Development, *Environmental Data Compendium, 2004* (Paris: OECD, 2005), p.188.
27. For glass recycling, the story is a little better. Irish recycling of glass rose from 27 per cent of the market in 1992 to 49 per cent in 2002. This was, by then, a higher rate than either Portugal or especially, Greece. However, Denmark had managed to grow its recycling effort from 48 per cent of glass in 1992 to 76 per cent in 2002. The result is that by 2002 Ireland had reached a level of glass recycling just above that which Denmark had already achieved in 1992. See OECD, *Environmental Data Compendium, 2004*, p.189.
28. In the USA the waste management hierarchy is often referred to as the 3R principle: Reduce, Re-use, Recycle. See Imhoff, D. *Paper or Plastic: Searching for Solutions to an Over-packaged World* (San Francisco: Sierra Club Books, 2005), p.28. The EU has recently given added focus to the

concept of waste prevention, which is at the very top of the waste management hierarchy. See CEC/Commission of the European Communities *Towards a Thematic Strategy on the Prevention and Recycling of Waste,* COM(2003)301, 27th May, 2003 (Luxembourg: Office of the Official Publications of the European Communities, 2003a). This document suggests that the EU could in future set minimum targets for waste prevention and mandate waste prevention plans being established in the nation states. See van Calster, G. 'Waste', in Etty, T.F.M. (et al.) *The Yearbook of European Environmental Law,* Volume 5 (Oxford: OUP, 2005), pp.413–16.

29. DEHLG/Department of Environment, Heritage, and Local Government, *Making Ireland's Development Sustainable* (Dublin: Government Stationery Office, 2002), p.26, and AM&R/Abfallberatung Müllvermeidung & Recycling, *Reuse of Primary Packaging, Final Report, Part I–Main Report. Study for Commission of the European Communities* (AM&R, 2000). Available at: http://europa.eu.int/comm/environment/waste/studies/packaging/resue.htm

30. See EPA/Environmental Protection Agency, *National Waste Prevention Programme. Outline Work Plan 2004–2008* (Wexford: EPA, 2004e) and VROM/Dutch Ministry of Housing, Spatial Planning, and the Environment. *Waste Prevention* (VROM: The Hague, 2001). Available at http://www2.vrom.nl/Docs/internationaal/03waste%20prevention.pdf

31. See O'Brien, T. 'Danish firm to invest €1 billion in Poolbeg Incinerator', *The Irish Times,* 20 August 2005; and EPA/Environmental Protection Agency, Press Release: EPA invites local authorities to participate in a waste prevention demonstration grant-in-aid programme', Wednesday 30 November 2005. Available at: http://www.epa.ie/NewsCentre/PressRelease Archive/2005/MainBody,8214,en.html.

32. EPA (et al.), *National Waste Report, 2004,* p.8, and EEA, *The European Environment: State and Outlook 2005,* p.461.

33. See EPA (et al.), *National Waste Report 2004,* Table 2, p.7, and EPA, *Ireland's Environment 2004,* p.7.

34. For the definition of municipal waste, see OECD, *Environmental Data Compendium, 2004,* p.173.

35. OECD, *Environmental Data Compendium, 2004,* Table 2a, p.174. By way of contrast, Danish household waste volumes per capita were significantly higher. A rise of between 500 kg and 580 kg per capita was recorded between 1995 and 2002. But such volumes, as a share of total Danish municipal waste loads, have remained stable, with household waste accounting for 88 per cent of total municipal waste loads between 1995 and 2002. No data is available for Greece, Portugal, or for the EU15 average.

36. EPA (et al.), *National Waste Report 2004,* p.12.

37. EPA (et al.), *National Waste Report, 2004,* p.8, and EEA, *The European Environment: State and Outlook 2005,* pp.319 and 461. Note, however, that the definition used by the OECD is quite broad so it's not clear to me what the Irish were counting as municipal waste that other states do not.

The major issue of confusion appears to be the issue of inclusion of some types of commercial wastes.

38. EPA, *National Waste Report, 2004*, Table 2, p.7. Note: I have calculated the raw data provided in terms of tonnes of waste into percentage shares, keeping rounding to a minimum.

39. See O'Riordan, A. 'The Rise and Rise of Recycling', *Local Authority News*, 25, 6, (2006), p.31. The Irish rate for packaging waste recycling in 2005 was apparently 56 per cent.

40. EEA/European Environment Agency, *EEA Signals 2004 – a European Environment Agency update on selected issues* (EEA: Copenhagen, 2004), p.15.

41. EPA (et al.), *National Waste Report, 2004*, p.27. In Appendix A to that report the EPA provide their calculations of per capita packaging waste statistics in tonnes (1 tonne = 1,000kg) per person for the years 2001–4. These were 0.223 (2001); 0.229 (2002); 0.25 (2003); and 0.21 (2004).

42. EPA (et al.), *National Waste Report, 2004*, p.27.

43. The figures for total packaging waste generated (in tonnes) can be found in Appendix A of the National Waste Report 2004. They were respectively; 872,917(2001); 899,125 (2002); 1,006,287(2003); 850, 911 (2004). EPA (et al.), *National Waste Report*, p.71.

44. O'Brien, T. 'Ireland now recycling 66 per cent of used packaging', *The Irish Times*, 22 May 2006.

45. EEA, *EEA Signals 2004*, p.15.

46. EPA (et al.), *National Waste Report, 2004*, p.45. For the year 2004, contaminated soils and solvents represented by far the two biggest shares of the total hazardous waste volumes, at 46 and 24 per cent of the total respectively.

47. OECD, *Environmental Data Compendium, 2004*, pp.183–5.

48. EPA (et al.), *National Waste Report, 2004*, p.43. Note that much of the recent increase is due to contaminated soils now being considered as hazardous wastes.

49. EEA/European Environment Agency, *Hazardous waste generation in EEA member countries: Comparability of classification systems and quantities. Topic Report No.14/2001* (Copenhagen: EEA, 2001), p.7. Available at: http://reports.eea.eu.int/topic_report_2001_14/en/Hazwaste_web.pdf. The only data entry for Greece for the period 1990–5 gives a figure of 44 kg per capita for 1992. No average EU figure is offered here, but it would appear to be roughly 100 kg per capita for much of this period.

50. See Faughnan, C. 'New Tax would not cut traffic jams', *The Irish Times*, 15 July 2003; Faughnan, C. 'Luas light rail system should not be about trying to curb transport by car in the capital', *The Irish Times*, 21 August 1997; and Dunne, J. 'AA says Dublin is among the least car populated cities in EU', *The Irish Times*, 4 January 1997.

51. Forfás/Hirsch, R.L. *A Baseline Assessment of Ireland's Oil Dependence. Key Policy Considerations*, April 2006 (Dublin: Forfás), p.16. Note that if the EU25 average is used post enlargement, this would bring Ireland's rate of car ownership much closer to a new lower EU average – to within 80

per cent. The reason why the EU25 average is lower is because most of the new entrants have historic low rates of car ownership.

52. DTO/Dublin Transportation Office, *A Platform for Change: Strategy 2000–2016* (Dublin: DTO, 2001), p.5.
53. SEI/Sustainable Energy Ireland and Howley, M., O'Leary F., and Ó Gallachóir, B. *Energy in Ireland 1990–2004: Trends, issues, forecasts and indicators* (Dublin: SEI, 2006), p.54.
54. McAleer, M. 'SUV sales up 34 per cent last year', *The Irish Times*, 26 January 2005.
55. See Reid, L. 'SUVs blamed for increasing greenhouse gas emissions', *The Irish Times*, 3 April 2006.
56. SEI/Sustainable Energy Ireland, *The Route to Sustainable Commuting: an employer's guide to Mobility Management Plans* (Dublin: SEI, 2001), p.24. Note that as no date is given for the Euro valuations in this survey, I assume they are Euro valuations at 2001 prices.
57. EEA/European Environment Agency, *Transport and Environment: facing a dilemma. TERM 2005: Indicators tracking transport and environment in Europe. EEA Report No.3, 2006* (Copenhagen: EEA, 2006), p.17. It should be noted that these EEA figures were generated in a way which did *not* consider international aviation or marine transport. In other words, much of the bulk of this huge increase must be due to road traffic and private vehicle use.
58. EEA, *Transport and Environment: facing a dilemma*, p.15.
59. Ibid.
60. SEI (et al.), *Energy in Ireland 1990–2004: Trends, issues, forecasts and indicators*, p.54, and Eurostat. *Energy, Environment and Transport Indicators: Data 1992–2002* (Luxembourg: Eurostat, 2005), p.110.
61. Forfás is the Irish national advisory board for enterprise, trade, science, technology and innovation. See http://www.forfas.ie/.
62. Forfás/Hirsch, R.L. *A Baseline Assessment of Ireland's Oil Dependence. Key Policy Considerations*, p.15.
63. DTO, *A Platform for Change: Strategy 2000–2016*, p.6.
64. Amárach Consulting, *Teleworking – the Shortest Route to Work. Report commissioned by Telework Ireland, Telecom Éireann and Dublin Transportation Office* (Dublin: Amárach, 2004). Available at: http://www.amarach.com/study_rep_downloads/telew.htm
65. See Wickham, J. *Contextualising Car Dependency*, Paper prepared for the ECMT/OECD workshop on managing car use for sustainable urban travel, Dublin, December 1–2, 1999 (Dublin: Employment Research Centre, Dept. Sociology, TCD, 1999). Available at www.cemt.org/UrbTrav/Workshops/Carscities/Dubldoc.htm/. Also see Wickham, J. and Lohan, M. *The Transport Rich and the Transport Poor: car dependency and social class in four European cities*. Paper for conference, 'Urbanism and Suburbanism at the End of the Century', Friday, November 26th and Saturday, November 27th, 1999, National University of Ireland, Maynooth (Dublin: Employment Research Centre, Dept. Sociology, Trinity College Dublin, 1999), p.5. Available at: www.tcd.ie/ERC/pastprojectcars.php/

66. See Wickham, J. and Lohan, M. *The Transport Rich and the Transport Poor*, p.5. Available at: www.tcd.ie/ERC/pastprojectcars.php/.
67. See Wickham, J. *Contextualising Car Dependency*, and Wickham, J. and Lohan, M. *The Transport Rich and the Transport Poor.*
68. DTO/Dublin Transportation Office, *Quality Bus Corridor Monitoring Report* (November, 2004). Available at http://www.dto.ie/.
69. For example, the two LUAS lines together can move about 6,220 persons per hour, which is entirely new capacity. See Nix, J. 'Sick of jams? Take the bus', *The Irish Times*, 2 February 2004.
70. By 2004, Dublin had twelve different quality bus corridors (QBCs). According to Nix, these QBCs have a typical people moving capacity of 4,410 persons per hour, which implies the QBC system can move just under 52,920 Dubliners per hour, although actual numbers carried may vary widely.
71. SEI (et al.), *Energy in Ireland 1990–2004: Trends, issues, forecasts and indicators*, p.16.
72. SEI/Sustainable Energy Ireland and O'Leary, F. *Energy Efficiency in Ireland 1990–2002: An analysis based on the ODYSSEE database of energy efficiency indicators* (Dublin: SEI, 2004), p.15
73. Butler, B. 'Industry has risen to challenge of Kyoto', *The Irish Times*, 1 December 2004). I could find no direct reference to Ireland being ranked a second best performer for energy efficiency in the UN Human Development Report for 2002. However, there is a table (No.19) which provides data on GDP per unit of energy used which could be taken as a measure of energy intensity. The report for 2002 includes actual data for 1980 and 1999. However, as I read the table, and based on the 1999 data entries, Ireland would not be ranked second, but rather fourth. Italy, Switzerland, and Austria all had higher GDP units earned per 1 kg of oil equivalent in 1999. The 2005 UN Human Development Report, using the same measure, does however, place Ireland first (in Europe) with the highest GDP units earned per 1 kg of oil equivalent. See UNDP/ United National Development Programme and Fukuda-Parr, S. (et al.), *Human Development Report 2002: Deepening Democracy in a fragmented world* (New York: Oxford University Press, 2002), Table 19, pp.212–13 and UNDP/United National Development Programme and Watkins, K. (et al.), *Human Development Report 2005: International cooperation at a crossroads: Aid, trade and security in an unequal world* (New York: UNDP, 2005), Table 22, pp.289–90.
74. Forfás/Hirsch, R.L. *A Baseline Assessment of Ireland's Oil Dependence. Key Policy Considerations.* p.3.
75. The SEI have estimated energy intensity reductions of 3 per cent per annum between 1990 and2003. Howley, M. and Ó Gallachóir, B./SEI/Sustainable Energy Ireland, *Energy in Ireland, 1990–2003: Trends, issues and indicators* (Cork: Energy Policy Statistical Support Unit, 2005), p.17.
76. EEA, *The European Environment: State and Outlook 2005*, p.367.
77. The SEI use two different measures of energy demand or consumption, one a gross figure and the other a net measurement. Primary energy demand is the

overall amount of energy accounted for in a country. Total Final Consumption of Energy is the net energy supplies taken up by end users, either for electricity or other uses, less the energy lost in conversion to energy uptake.

78. SEI (et al.), *Energy in Ireland 1990–2004: Trends, issues, forecasts and indicators*, p.10.
79. Ibid.
80. SEI (et al.), *Energy in Ireland 1990–2004: Trends, issues, forecasts and indicators*, p.20.
81. SEI (et al.), *Energy in Ireland 1990–2004: Trends, issues, forecasts and indicators*, p.37.
82. Forfás/Hirsch, R.L. *A Baseline Assessment of Ireland's Oil Dependence. Key Policy Considerations*, p.12.
83. SEI/Sustainable Energy Ireland, *Renewable Energy in Ireland: Update 2005* (Dublin: SEI, 2006), p.2. The contribution of renewables to the total primary energy demand rose from 1.9 to 2.2 per cent between 2003 and 2004. This was an impressive 18 per cent annual increase. Most of the sources were either biomass or wind. Installed wind turbine capacity increased by 46 per cent in the year 2003–4.
84. Forfás/Hirsch, R.L. *A Baseline Assessment of Ireland's Oil Dependence. Key Policy Considerations*, pp.23–4.
85. McWilliams, D. 'Time to discuss our nuclear option, without a meltdown', *The Irish Independent*, Wednesday, 5 April 2006, p.23.
86. See Case C-396/01, *European Commission v. Ireland*, judgement delivered March 11, 2004.
87. Legally, the only part of the regulations which were suspended pending a scientific review were those measures that relate to phosphorous rates and applications. A ruling of the European Court of Justice (Case C-258/00, *Commission* v. *France*) decided that when applying the Nitrates Directives, member states must also have regard to phosphorous levels as well. This is because these can just as easily cause the type of pollution which the aims of the Directive seeks to mitigate or prevent. This ECJ ruling has widened the scope of the original Nitrates Directive, which is literally now no longer just about nitrates. This could mean that suspending any regulations on phosphorous might undermine the Irish position yet again. For a discussion of the phosphorous issue, see also Raftery, M. 'Nitrates and vested interests', *The Irish Times*, 23 February 2006.
88. See Editor/Irish Times, 'Diluting the Nitrates Directive', *The Irish Times*, 21 February 2006 and, especially, Reid, L. 'Ireland to delay farm anti-pollution measures', *The Irish Times*, 19 May 2006. These remain proposals only, which the Commission may reject. They reflect in general a reduction in the demands set out by the original regulations made law in December 2005, especially for phosphorous limits. It is clear they are concessions produced by the lobbying power of organized farming interests. See also Kennedy, J. 'Revised Nitrates Action plan sent to Brussels', *The Irish Framers Journal*, 27 May 2006.
89. This power has been written into the Treaty of Amsterdam and the Treaty of Nice, at Article 228(2). In 2000 it was used for the first time in the

environmental field when Greece was taken to the Court for not adhering to a previous verdict. A daily fine of €24,600 was imposed. Ireland could at least expect to face similar fines if not more. See Krämer, L. *Casebook on EU environmental Law* (Oxford: Hart, 2002), pp.390–5.

90. EPA, *Ireland's Environment 2004*, p.39.
91. Note that this was in fact a reduction from the 3 per cent of monitoring stations who recorded levels above the safety limit in 1995–7. EPA/ Environmental Protection Agency/Toner, P. (et al.), *Water Quality in Ireland 2001–2003* (Wexford: EPA, 2005), p.119.
92. EPA, *Ireland's Environment 2004*, p.46.
93. The compliance rates for nitrates in drinking water from public water supplies for the years 2003, 2002 and 2001 were respectively: 99.6 per cent (2003), 99.4 per cent (2002), and 99.3 per cent (2001). EPA/ Environmental Protection Agency, *The Quality of Drinking Water in Ireland: A Report for the Year 2003 with a Review of the Period 2001–2003* (Wexford: EPA, 2004a), pp.24–7 and Table 2, p.xii.
94. Ibid.
95. The last recorded case in the UK was in 1972. Source: DEFRA/ Department of Environment, Farming and Rural Affairs. 'Nitrates – Reducing Water Pollution from Agriculture-Implications' (U.K.: DEFRA, 2006), available at: http://www.defra.gov.uk/environment/water/quality/nitrate/nitrogen.htm. See also WHO/CEC/ World Health Organisation/Commission of the European Communities, *Eutrophication and Health* (Luxembourg: Office for Official Publications of the European Communities, 2002), pp.12–13.
96. EPA/Environmental Protection Agency, *The Quality of Drinking Water in Ireland. A report for 2003 with a review of the period 2001–2003* (Wexford: EPA, 2004a), p.11, p.24–5.
97. EEA, *EEA Signals 2004 – a European Environment Agency update on selected issues*, pp.10–11.
98. The directive explicitly mentions prevention in its Article 1, Article 5, Annex II (which sets out the content for codes of good agricultural practice), and in its Annex V. See Council of Ministers of the European Communities. 'Council Directive of 12 December 1991 concerning the protection of waters against pollution caused by nitrates from agricultural sources (91/676/EEC)', available at: http://www.europa.int/eurolex/. On the Precautionary Principle more generally see De Sadeler, N. *Environmental Principles: From Political Slogans to Legal Rules* (Oxford: OUP, 2002), pp.110–24, and pp.203–5.
99. OECD, *Environmental Data Compendium, 2004*, pp.263–6. Note: I have taken the raw data and calculated the relevant percentage change between 1980 and 2001 or 2002, depending on the table.
100. EPA, *Ireland's Environment 2004*, p.10.
101. MacConnell, S. 'Farmers buy less fertilizer but use more', *The Irish Times*, 2 July 2002.
102. OECD, *Environmental Data Compendium, 2004*, p.274.
103. Neill, M. 'Nitrate concentrations in river waters in the south-east of Ireland and their relationships with agricultural practice', *Water Research*, 23, (1989), pp.1,339–55.

104. JOCELG/Joint Oireachtas Committee on Environment and Local Government, *Parliamentary Debates*, 42, (2005a), February 9th. Available at http://www.oireachtas.ie
105. JOCELG/Joint Oireachtas Committee on Environment and Local Government, *Parliamentary Debates*, 64, (2005b), December 6th. Available at http://www.oireachtas.ie
106. EPA and Toner, P. (et al.). *Water Quality in Ireland 2001–2003*, p.32.

Chapter Three

Muddling through: a brief history of Irish environmental policy

INTRODUCTION

What has been Ireland's historical experience with environmental policy? Such a question is important if one is to get a fuller understanding of Irish environmental performance. This chapter takes a chronological approach to answering this question and provides the reader with a narrative of the main environmental policy developments since the 1970s to beyond the millennium. Obviously not all details can be covered and some readers may quibble about what I choose to highlight.

Nonetheless, this chapter provides an answer to the question above by emphasizing a number of historical themes. Firstly, Irish environmental policy has been considerably modernized through EU membership. That political process emerges in this account as perhaps one of the most critical forces driving positive change. Yet, while this has led to an impressive set of laws and policies on paper (the 'software' of environmental policy), it has not really altered the institutional deficiencies of Ireland's state agencies and bodies (the 'hardware' aspect). It has also not managed to unseat a mentality among the governmental elite which privileges economic development over environmental protection.

Secondly, Irish environmental policy has been consistently marked since the 1970s by its adversarial style. Irish state institutions and Irish environmentalists simply do not trust or respect each other. Finally, Ireland has failed to conceive of environmental policy in strategic terms. There has been little ecological modernization, and much muddling through in a purely reactive way to legislative and policy agendas set by the EU, or by the immediacy of events.

Unlike the large European states, who can trace their first environmental protection activities back to the nineteenth century, Ireland has been unquestionably a newcomer to environmental policy. For the first decades of the independent Irish state's existence, environmental policy in its modern sense was barely conceived of at all. There was heritage legislation to protect national monuments, and above all there was an awareness of public sanitation, for example in the provision of a basic sewerage system for towns and cities. Legislation, such as there was, often followed a British style in its content. For example, late 1950s Irish laws on river fisheries simply carried over a Victorian era provision for relatively small-scale strict liability fines to be imposed in cases of fish stocks being harmed by pollution.[1] This provision was useful because it did not require authorities to establish proof of actual wrongdoing before a lower court. It was still being used by Irish authorities in the late 1990s to tackle much more serious pollution arising from intensive agriculture.

The 1940s and 1950s saw the first but tentative rumblings of a modern environmental awareness. In the late 1940s the famous naturalist, Robert Lloyd Praeger, established An Taisce and this organisation, usually described in English as the Irish National Trust, slowly began to emerge as an important conservationist body. By the 1970s An Taisce had become the largest mainstream environmental group, which it remains today. Also founded in the late 1950s was the Irish Georgian Society (IGS), whose aim was architectural conservation. This goal took it into the domain of challenging the demolition of Dublin's old Georgian squares in the 1960s, and thereby conflicting with officialdom.

Important legislation to govern planning was made law in the early 1960s. Yet again this copied extensively from relevant British legislation. However, one modification proved crucial. Provision was made whereby local political representatives sitting within the county council, Ireland's primary unit of local administration then and now, could vote to rezone land use designations. This allowed them to ignore the advice of the council's own planners, or local environmentalists. Eventually, this provision would be associated with the systematic planning corruption that was uncovered around Dublin in the 1990s.

The social milieu from which many of these early Irish conservation activists came was typically the Dublin-based upper middle class. Quite a few were of the distinctive Anglo-Irish protestant community. English sounding accents were not unknown. However, such trivial facts allowed for an entirely facile but still pervasive stereotype to be associated with those in Ireland who campaigned for conservation and environmental issues; namely that they were (or are) 'tweedy types'.

Somehow, the image grew of a small group of supposedly posh Dublin-based intellectuals lobbying against needed 'national development', motivated by allegedly snobbish ideas about conservation. This view sometimes remains today, although it is no more accurate than it was in the period before the 1970s. In fact, membership of organizations such as An Taisce was always more widely representative.

THE SEVENTIES: THE ARRIVAL OF MODERN ENVIRONMENT PROTEST AND POLICY

What existed of an Irish environmental policy before the 1970s was essentially then a thin corpus of British style laws, and in some cases actual Victorian-era legislation.[2] The paradigm of a wider environmental policy was mostly absent. Environmental questions were really understood as being small-scale public sanitation matters of limited importance. It was to take a long time to broaden that conception.

By the start of the 1970s, Ireland had actually missed out on the international rise in environmental awareness which can be traced back to the 1960s. A comprehensive environmental critique of western society had evolved in the USA and other advanced industrial societies. Not only had a radical protest fringe emerged, but official government bureaucracies were fast responding to environmental problems. The US Congress passed significant legislation in the mid 1960s to address water and air pollution, providing much of the template for regulation that was to follow in other countries. In 1969 Sweden established the world's first Environmental Protection Agency, followed by the USA in the early 1970s. The European Economic Community (EEC) only began its first very tentative environmental action programme in 1973. Nonetheless, the 1960s was unquestionably the decade when environmental policy and politics in its modern sense 'arrived'.

In Ireland, however, it would not be until the seventies that a modern environmental protest politics emerged. Nor was it until 1977 that the Department of Local Government was symbolically renamed the Department of the *Environment* and Local Government. Ireland was then a latecomer to mainstream environmental thinking, and one could suggest that the gap was as much as a decade or more in terms of awareness and regulatory responses.

The beginnings of a distinctively *modern* Irish environmental policy date from the early 1970s. A small state agency, An Foras Forbartha (The National Development Agency),[3] was established in the late 1960s to advise on various physical planning and infrastructure development issues. It slowly began to develop an environmental monitoring and management dimension, notably around the issue of water supply. There was also some small-scale legislation[4] to deal with industrial smoke and dust. A start was made on a first survey of river and lake water quality in 1971.

However, the two most important pieces of modern legislation of the seventies were the 1976 Wildlife Act and the 1977 Local Government (Water Pollution) Act. The latter, although substantially revised in 1990, provided the template around which modern water pollution law in Ireland was constructed. It marked an early example of what would later become an important trend – responding to the pace set by the EEC.[5]

It simply became a necessary law because much of the early legislative activity of the then EEC in the mid-1970s was concerned with water quality and pollution. Section 26 of the 1977 Act was notable for introducing a mechanism for the legislative establishment of water quality values in keeping with those outlined in EEC directives, while Section 16 established for the first time a licensing regime for industrial water discharges.

The Wildlife Act, 1976, was also a significant achievement for its time. It provided statutory protection for certain species and brought hunting under greater control. However, it is significant that certain of its provisions were seldom used. For example, its Section 18 allowed for land use management agreements with private landowners, which could be used to protect flora and fauna. This anticipated legal protection for ecosystems, which Ireland would be obliged to protect under EU law in the 1990s.

More colourful and certainly more noticeable by the later seventies was the arrival in Ireland of an entirely novel environmental protest politics. According to Allen,[6] one of the earliest examples of an environmental protest was where local residents led (successful) opposition against a planned asbestos factory in Cork in 1970. However, the most dramatic and large-scale environmental protest was centred around Irish nuclear energy ambitions of the late 1970s.

Following the oil shocks in 1973 and 1979, a body of opinion within government and the state electricity monopoly (ESB) began to advance the idea of building a nuclear electricity plant. Plans reached an advanced stage and a prospective site was nominated at Carnsore, County Wexford, along the extreme southeasterly coast. In 1979,[7] local residents who had been campaigning against the plant received an unexpected boost. The 'Three Mile Island' nuclear accident in the USA highlighted the risks of nuclear energy in a tangible way. Also, a protest festival at Carnsore attracted folksingers and counter-culture environmentalists in tow: the sixties had arrived, but in 1979! On television, for the first time, Irish people could see a large-scale and colourful modern environmental protest.

In fact, internal government decisions were taken by 1980 not to build Ireland's first nuclear reactor. This was not necessarily because of the impact of Ireland's new anti-nuclear environmental groups. According to Baker,[8] what was more decisive were classic old fashioned lobbying by local residents within Ireland's clientelist party political system. The politicians simply feared a loss of votes in a key constituency during an era of very close elections. Another decisive blow to these nuclear energy ambitions became obvious by 1980. Ireland was facing serious problems with her public finances, inflation was soaring, unemployment rising, and the economy in recession. The grim eighties had arrived.

THE GRIM EIGHTIES: CUTBACKS, SMOG, AND SELLAFIELD

The economic recession of the early 1980s was inauspicious for the growth of a more ambitious environmental policy and politics. Yet there were small steps forwards, even if first came setbacks.

One casualty was the intermittent freezing of public sector employment throughout the 1980s. Only limited environmental policy expertise could then be built up in fits and starts. Nationally, An Foras Forbartha quickly found itself the target of cutbacks and staffing curbs. After a serious row over government attempts to relocate the bulk of its staff outside Dublin, the agency was marginalised.

The result was the running down of an agency of considerable promise and potential. It could have become a fully-fledged national environmental protection agency. Indeed, An Foras Forbartha was starting to move in that direction. For example, in 1985 it produced Ireland's first 'state of the environment' report, although it was largely ignored. Finally in 1988, under a new round of austerity, the entire agency was simply axed.[9] This left only a small and fragmented Environmental Research Unit (ERU) to provide a minimal national monitoring and scientific backup for County Councils.

It was in the 1980s that serious pollution incidents began to receive attention from the national media. There were two principal events. The first related to the pollution of lake waters with animal wastes in the north-east of the country near the border with Northern Ireland, most notably at Lough Sheelin. The source of this pollution could be traced to local intensive piggeries. This was a turning point because it revealed the serious environmental consequences arising from changing agricultural practices. Even in the mid-1980s, Ireland was a country where agriculture remained economically salient and where farmers were politically powerful. Previously, Irish decision-makers had assumed Irish agriculture was not as intensive as in continental Europe.

Yet some farmers were also on the receiving end. The second turning point was in 1988, when Irish television broadcast harrowing images of dead and dying cattle accompanied by their farmer, John Hanrahan. Openly in tears, he explained to the camera that he attributed blame to a nearby chemicals factory. In any other country the Hanrahan case would be just another individual story of pollution. In Ireland, it was a turning point in public consciousness: industrial pollution *really* existed in Ireland and not just elsewhere. Indirectly, the Hanrahan case underscored the urgent need for a state environmental agency to regulate high technology multinational firms, especially in the chemicals and pharmaceuticals sector.

Of course, such an agency was effectively destroyed by the earlier decision to axe An Foras Forbartha. Yet, it would not be until 1993 that an independent Environmental Protection Agency (EPA) would be established, a critical gap of five years, at a time when Ireland's chemical sector was expanding.

One of the more severe and intense environmental disputes of this period also stands out as a turning point. This was the so-called 'Wood Quay' dispute between 1979 and 1981.[10] On first impressions, this was a conflict over the protection of archaeological heritage and good planning versus the development ambitions of Dublin Corporation, then the city's main local government. It wanted to build for itself administrative office blocks in the heart of old medieval Dublin, beside the river Liffey, and containing significant archaeological heritage. Despite widespread protest, and even site occupation for a time, Dublin Corporation ultimately won and the ugly squat towers went up in 1981. In fact the real issues were always much wider than this.

For the Wood Quay conflict became a touchstone for years of anger over what McDonald has termed the 'destruction of Dublin', through successive appalling planning decisions made for the most part by Dublin's own governing authorities.[11] What was also at stake was a core issue: how could the planning system prevent bad planning if the agent breaching planning laws was the local government itself? How could one expect the planning authority to police its own planning? It had been assumed that local governments did not require planning permission for their own developments, and this was not legally clarified as incorrect until the early 1990s. An Environmental Impact Assessment (EIA) was not made obligatory for their larger schemes until 2000. Of course, their proposed developments could be appealed to a National Planning Board, An Bord Pleanála, founded in 1977. After this level, appeals were possible in certain cases to the higher courts. However, the local council as primary planning authority itself was in a unique 'insider' position.

The wider political significance of the Wood Quay protest was that it was among the first of many examples of a confrontation between the state agencies and environmentalists or conservationists that was to have lasting repercussions for how the Irish state viewed and engaged with environmentalists. After all, weren't they the 'troublemakers' who wanted to block the state from doing obviously sensible things like building ugly office blocks on medieval and Viking heritage? Likewise, Irish environmentalists began to adopt a default position of mistrust towards official government plans and policies.

Finally, it is worth noting that the state's monopoly electricity utility, the Electricity Supply Board (ESB), responded to the rejection of nuclear energy plans by building a large coal-fired generating plant near the Shannon estuary at Moneypoint. This huge plant contributed to a significant increase in Ireland's sulphur dioxide (SO_2) emissions during the mid-1980s. At the same time, the EU was agreeing a directive on so-called Large Combustion Plants (LCP), which was precisely designed to reduce emissions from such facilities with a classic ecological modernization approach: phasing-in of emission control filtration. Ireland sought and got a derogation for Moneypoint from the terms of that directive, pleading basically the need for economic development and insufficient funding to install scrubbers and filters. The significance of this was that Ireland was turning its back on ecological modernization approaches just at the time when other EU states were exploring such strategies.

Yet it was not all bleak. A key legislative achievement was the Air Pollution Act of 1987 which provided the template for a modern air pollution regulatory system, and also gave effect to various EU directives on air pollution. A change of government in 1989 brought new political leadership. Ireland's first Green Party representative was elected to the Dáil and the Chernobyl nuclear accident in 1986 had received widespread publicity in Ireland. The environment finally became a live issue where political reputations could be made or, more cynically, where some votes at the margin could be won.

In this context, Mary Harney, then Minister for the Environment, signed into law regulations that prohibited the burning of bituminous coal in the Dublin urban area from 1990.[12] This was a quite dramatic action that was initially not entirely well received by the Dublin public. In retrospect it was significant because it was one of the first conscious efforts by an Irish politician to make political capital out of an environmental issue needing urgent action.

The Dublin coal ban also offered important lessons for Irish environmental policy, but these have since been largely forgotten. First and foremost it was hugely successful as a measure. Although Clinch and McLoughlin[13] initially suggested the ban merely speeded up an end of reliance upon coal, a careful statistical evaluation of its health related effects has suggested that it 'led to a substantial decrease in concentration of black smoke particulate air pollution . . . there were about 243 fewer cardiovascular deaths and 116 fewer respiratory deaths per year in Dublin after the ban . . . (and) these changes were seen immediately in the winter after the introduction of the ban'.[14]

The obvious lesson here is that relatively simple and bold measures can have dramatic positive results. It remains today a powerful example of the effectiveness of a simple legal prohibition of pollutants. This is a view which is distinctly unfashionable given recent thinking on environmental policy which has tended to view legal instruments and bans as ineffectual.

Finally, the 1980s was the decade when one significant theme in Irish environmental policy clearly emerged: an anti-nuclear stance. Ironically, the same Irish state that had been busy planning nuclear energy electricity generation in the late 1970s had, by the late 1980s, gone 'anti-nuke'. The Irish political class began criticizing the risks of radioactive contamination of the Irish Sea by the operations of Britain's Sellafield nuclear plant in Cumbria. Opposition was to grow throughout the 1990s over plans by British Nuclear Fuels (BNF) to engage in nuclear fuel reprocessing at the site. Ireland has even attempted international litigation to address the issue, although this has been to date unsuccessful.

Much of this anti-nuclear stance reflects the change in consciousness that followed the Chernobyl accident of 1986. However, one might also note how very easy it was for the Irish political class, still much enthralled by nationalist rhetoric, to 'blame the old enemy' of Britain for Ireland's environmental woes. The fixation with Sellafield remains within Irish environmental policy today. Indeed, Irish representatives sometimes join within EU meetings with like-minded 'nuclear phobic' states, such as Austria and Denmark, to raise concerns regarding nuclear energy and radiation pollution.[15]

Undoubtedly, fears about Sellafield, and especially the management of British nuclear wastes, are justified from an Irish perspective, given a woeful record of accidents, negligence, and law-breaking. But Sellafield has also served as a very convenient distraction from facing up to Ireland's own pressing environmental problems and political responsibility for these.

THE ROARING NINETIES: IRISH ENVIRONMENT POLICY IN THE SHADOW OF THE 'CELTIC TIGER'

During the 1990s Irish environmental policy developed fast in terms of its scope and sophistication. The volume of environmental legislation increased as surely as its ambition widened, although much of this was merely implementing EU laws. A distinctive Irish environmental politics took root. The Irish Green Party doubled their parliamentary representation in the election of 1997 and got two members elected as MEPs to the European Parliament in 1994 and 1999. Local environmental protestors grew savvier, pitching their claims around the precise legalities of Irish and EU environmental laws.

Eventually, an Environmental Protection Agency (EPA) was established in 1993 to address the issues raised by the Hanrahan case and persistent complaints from residents and environmentalists in the Cork harbour area, where many chemical firms had clustered. The EPA was also necessary to remedy the failures of Irish local governments. Up until 1993 local governments both granted planning permission to industrial plants and inspected them for pollution. It was not clear whether they had the technical skill to do the first job, nor the political will for the second. Could local Councils be trusted to regulate sophisticated multinational firms that promised local jobs?

From the outset, the EPA concentrated upon one core activity above all others: the granting of so-called Integrated Pollution Control (IPC) licences, now termed Integrated Pollution Prevention Control (IPPC) licences.[16] An IPPC licence covers a comprehensive menu: water, air, wastes, soil, odour, and even noise are all *integrated* into a single licence. In this way it was supposed to prevent any displacement of pollution from, say, water to soil. Firms are given an 'envelope' of acceptable total emissions they must work towards by phasing in agreed technical equipment and techniques, as these evolve over time. It goes without saying that this approach was very detailed and the agency soon became bogged down in the minutiae and paperwork of regulating the larger industrial firms on a plant by plant basis. IPPC licensing is just one typical ecological modernization approach, but crucially its success depends on how exacting and ambitious environmental regulators are in agreeing with firms successive and ongoing improvements in their environmental performance. Environmentalists were unimpressed and probably misunderstood this highly technical and negotiated style of industrial pollution control. They wanted a proactive environmental policing force: they got a technical permitting agency.

The 1990s also marked the modernization of waste legislation, an area which had remained under-regulated over the previous decades. One reason for this was that the bulk of waste management had been historically undertaken by county councils themselves, often to abysmal standards of care. By the end of the 1990s a once small commercial waste management sector had mushroomed, increasingly replacing councils in that role. Waste was one environmental issue where the private sector role would become an almost dominant player – a major change from even a decade before.

The regulatory problem here was the familiar one. County councils had primary responsibility to enforce waste laws. Yet it was often they themselves who were in breach of such laws. Many council landfills were in an appalling state or even illegal because they had no planning permission. The thrust of legislation after 1996 was to hand over waste licensing and supervisory inspection to the EPA. Local governments were again emasculated.

As was explained in the previous chapter, replacing landfills led to governmental support for recycling and, more controversially, incineration. A new institutional player in environmental policy was heavily involved in mapping this change: private consultancy firms. Despite their engineering and commercial savvy, these advisors failed to predict the level of hostility incineration would provoke. Ultimately, many councils rejected incineration plans and their consultants' advice (although national government was waiting in the wings to impose it).

On packaging waste, major developments emerged. An ambitious EU directive had been agreed in 1994, and Germany had introduced a comprehensive commercial 'take back and recycle' syndicate in 1991. Ireland followed these examples in 1997 when REPAK was formed. This was a commercially managed packaging waste syndicate who would manage the packaging waste for fee-paying members. In return, firms who joined REPAK were exempt from the requirements of the 1996 Waste Management Act. However, it soon became clear that not all eligible firms wanted to join. Nor did local governments rush to enforce the Waste Management Acts against firms who were not members. This weakened REPAK's appeal, although somehow they have managed to meet their packaging recycling targets under EU law.

The REPAK story is significant for the wider direction of Irish environmental policy, in that it marked the first major so-called 'voluntary' environmental agreement. The latter had become a fashionable innovation of the 1990s, being widely used in the Netherlands. However, this experiment only happened because the EU provided the initial spur with its 1994 Directive on Packaging Waste.

Intriguingly, no experimentation with ecological taxes was forthcoming in the 1990s. This was no doubt because the EU's role on taxation matters is more restricted. The EU push factor was absent. Instead what emerged was something of an Irish farce concerning environmental charges.

Water charges had been unsuccessfully tried on and off during the 1980s, after fierce political opposition. In 1997 the decision was taken by the then Minister for Environment (etc.), Brendan Howlin, to simply ditch them. This distinctive Irish view on not charging domestic users of water placed Ireland in a difficult position when the ambitious EU Water Framework Directive was being negotiated between 1997 and 2000. This law necessitates the institution of water pricing for end consumers to encourage rational use of water. Ireland was left with no choice but to seek a derogation allowing her to avoid any domestic water charges for conservation purposes.[17]

However, with impressive inconsistency, domestic waste charges have been *imposed*. By the late 1990s Irish citizens were being faced with a regressive annual flat charge that proved very unpopular. Waivers from payment were usually available for those on low incomes. But these were not guaranteed by law and had to be actively requested. There was also significant variation between different councils, in both the scale of annual charges (between €150 and €500 in 2005) and in who qualified for a waiver. The Combat Poverty Agency (CPA) in its research discovered that with the privatization of many councils' waste collection services, waiver schemes were usually abandoned. This was producing significant hardship for some families, against a backdrop of waste charges rising nationally by some 223 per cent between 1997 and 2003.[18] In most rural areas no waiver scheme operated as private waste contractors generally refused to accept such waivers.[19]

Unsurprisingly, a widespread protest movement emerged. At one stage even a member of the Dáil, along with other activists, ended up in prison due to their protests against such charges. When some councils refused to agree charges, that power was transferred to unelected city or county managers in 2003.[20] By 2003 Dublin councils were implementing a draconian policy of non-collection of household waste where charges were not paid. Extensive litigation has emerged which has challenged both the right to levy charges or to refuse collection for non-payment. Some of these cases have been successful. The response of the government was to impose legislative modifications to allow for non-collection of waste.[21]

What was also significant here was that such a scheme of regressive charges was justified by reference to the 'polluter pays' principle.[22] Originally in the 1970s, the 'polluter pays' principle was developed to target industrial firms trying to avoid their responsibility for large-scale pollution. Since then it has been conflated with the much wider idea of taxes or charges on use of natural resources. The goal here was the internalizing of environmental externalities.[23] The reality, of course, was that waste charges were a revenue cash-cow of last resort. Irish local councils were forced to levy them because their fiscal base was so limited. Ireland does not have any system of local property taxes payable to local governments, except for commercial premises.

Citing such a lofty principle was also illogical. Many councils instituted systems that did not distinguish payment according to how much rubbish the householder put out for collection, which was inconsistent with the 'polluter pays' concept.[24] It would not be until late 2004 that councils began introducing complex, opaque, and largely unpopular 'pay by weight' systems. In summary, it was seriously exaggerated to apply the 'polluter pays' principle to domestic householders.

Such labelling involved a dubious conflation of the meaning of waste with pollution. The latter, in the ordinary sense of the word, implies the unnecessary production of an environmental harm due to negligence or malfeasance. Waste is not pollution unless it is dumped or mismanaged. Equally, as was shown in the last chapter, householders' waste did *not* significantly increase within the category of municipal waste during the 1990s.

Moreover, in recent years most citizens have been providing a basic level of waste management themselves, by sorting their waste into different waste categories (recyclable, etc.). This is not polluting activity, and if it were not done, somebody would have to be paid to sort household wastes at huge cost. Yet citizens provide this service free, for it is merely a logical obligation. The fact that at least some of the recycled household waste stream eventually provides a profit for private waste contractors also seems to sit uneasily with the principle. Why should private waste businesses be permitted to make a profit from household waste, which supposed 'polluters' have already paid for?

The wider lesson here is that such principles can be easily abused. They require careful thinking through before they should be applied. In the Irish case, they were just expediently trotted out, to paper over the cracks of a waste policy in perpetual crisis.

The 1990s also marks an era when the self-declared ambitions of the Irish state itself became noticeably 'greener'. In 1990 an *Environmental Action Programme* was published. Other states, notably the Netherlands and Canada, had also published comprehensive green plans.[25] Yet the Irish plan was a very limited document and in no way comparable to the ambitious Dutch National Environmental Policy Plan (NEPP). In 1993 another *ad hoc* advisory environmental group was established to deliver a similar report, calling yet again for more proactive environmental measures. This report, just like the 1990 document, was largely ignored.

The only thing that seemed to get the attention of Irish decision-makers was the urgency of litigation. A notable turning point arrived when Ireland lost an EU Court of Justice case in 1993 over its improper implementation of the vital Environmental Impact Assessment (EIA) Directive of 1985. This was hardly

TABLE 3.1 'SALAMI SLICES?' STATUTORY INSTRUMENTS THAT IMPLEMENTED THE
EU'S ENVIRONMENTAL IMPACT ASSESSMENT DIRECTIVES 1988–2001.

S.I. No. 221 of 1988, European Communities (Environmental Impact Assessment) (Motorways) Regulations, 1988. This was a regulation which required an EIA for large-scale road building projects.

S.I. No. 349 of 1989, European Communities (Environmental Impact Assessment) Regulations, 1989. This was the main general set of regulations that transposed Directive 85/337.

S.I. No. 323 of 1990, Arterial Drainage Acts, 1945 and 1955 (Environmental Impact Assessment) Regulations, 1990. This was a regulation that made an EIA a general requirement of large-scale drainage works.

S.I. No. 220 of 1990, Foreshore (Environmental Impact Assessment) Regulations 1990. This was a regulation that made an EIA a general requirement for foreshore (beach and littoral) developments.

S.I. No. 116 of 1990, Air Navigation And Transport (Environmental Impact Assessment) Regulations, 1990. These regulations made the development or building of airports and aerodromes necessitate an EIA.

S.I. No. 40 of 1990, Fisheries (Environmental Impact Assessment) Regulations, 1990. This was a regulation which made salmon farming an activity that typically required an EIA.

S.I. No. 41/1990, Fisheries (Environmental Impact Assessment) (No. 2) Regulations, 1990. These regulations were related to the previous regulation.

S.I. No. 84 of 1994, European Communities (Environmental Impact Assessment) (Amendment) Regulations, 1994. This regulation integrated the role of the EPA and its IPC licensing process with the EIA Directive's requirements.

S.I. No. 101 of 1996: European Communities (Environmental Impact Assessment) (Amendment) Regulations, 1996. This was a regulation whose purpose was to *reduce* the threshold of forestry developments requiring an EIA from 200Ha to 70Ha.

S.I No. 351 of 1998, European Communities (Environmental Impact Assessment) (Amendment) Regulations, 1998. This was an amending regulation which addressed various details concerning time available for consideration, cross-border effects, and information required.

S.I. No. 93 of 1999. European Communities (Environmental Impact Assessment) (Amendment) Regulations, 1999. This was the main regulation designed to transpose the 2nd EU EIA Directive (97/11/EC).

S.I. No. 450 of 2000, European Communities (Environmental Impact Assessment) (Amendment) Regulations, 2000. This was a regulation that necessitated that local government itself was obliged to undergo an EIA for many of their developments. Previously this had been certified by the national Minister for Environment and Local Government; however, this regulation transferred that certification process to An Bord Pleanála.

S.I. No. 538 of 2001, European Communities (Environmental Impact Assessment) (Amendment) Regulations, 2001. This regulation was introduced expressly to comply with a finding of the European Court of Justice that thresholds adopted by Ireland exceeded the allowed discretion under the EIA Directives of 1985 and 1997.

Source: http://www.statutebook.ie

surprising, as the Irish experience of EIA was shambolic. Rather than introduce a comprehensive legislative act (which Germany did), a series of statutory instruments were made. No less than thirteen were enacted between 1988 and 2001 (See Table 3.1). In some cases these openly amended a previously permissive inter-pretation of the two EU EIA directives.[26] Another deficiency was a failure to make clear what the evaluation process involved under EIA should require. The result was a crude focus on the actual document, the Environmental Impact Statement (EIS), rather than how this should be examined and considered by the parties.[27]

Considerable rhetoric on 'sustainable development' emerged during the 1990s. In 1997 Ireland's first Sustainable Development Plan was published. It was a large and glossy publication, long on generalities but short on specific commitments. It has never become a strategic planning document of real authority, lacking the force of law or dedicated funds associated with it. Of greater significance was the relatively modern framework of environmental laws which were in place by the end of the 1990s.

Nonetheless, there were vital gaps. Transport and energy were two sectors where Ireland had little substantive environmental policy. The only sustainable transport development of real note in the 1990s was the Dublin Transport Initiative (DTI). This promised to balance the hectic new ring-road motorway building around Dublin, with increased investment in priority bus lanes, and a LUAS tramway. Sadly, that plan was nit-picked apart by successive national and local governments of the later 1990s. Dublin got its trams in 2004 and not in 1999 as originally planned! The entire sorry saga of light rail in Dublin was a textbook example of how *not* to make public policy.[28] Yet it was a shambles that had nothing to do with an absence of money or environmental know-how. The problems were rooted in Irish political culture and Ireland's plainly inadequate institutional structure.

As regards sustainable energy policy, the dominant concern of policy-makers in the 1990s was the future of the public electricity monopoly, the ESB. In 1999 the electricity market was dereg-ulated, although the ESB remained the dominant supplier. The promise of renewable energy only managed to find for itself a small niche role.[29] The EU once again remained vital in pushing and prodding the Irish into a more proactive engagement with renewable energy. Unfortunately, the ESB, who retain control of the grid, were sceptical about connecting small wind energy suppliers on the grounds that their output was allegedly too unreliable for sound grid management. Also, renewable energy had to compete for subsidies with the Irish Peat Board (Bord na Móna), who had a declining peat-electricity generation business but strong political connections. EU subsidies in the late 1990s were then directed towards new peat electricity generation projects.

Generous EU funding played a major role in the 1990s in allowing Ireland to develop a modern sewerage infrastructure system for the larger cities and towns. It has been estimated that the level of fiscal transfers involved from the EU were in the order of circa 130 billion ECU between 1993 and 2005.[30] However, there were some serious Brussels–Dublin conflicts as well. For example, in the case of Galway city, the EU Commission challenged that City Corporation's controversial plan to build a sewerage works on a nearby island. After some wrangling, the government took the unprecedented decision to forgo the EU funding but build it anyhow, effectively telling the Commission to 'get lost'.

Other sewage treatment plants were built without as much conflict, and Ireland made steady progress in increasing the proportion of the population which was connected to at least secondary treatment[31] sewage facilities during the 1990s. By 2002, an estimated 73 per cent of the population was connected to public waste-water treatment plants. This compares well with the EU15 average level of 78 per cent. It was less impressive though when compared with the Danish level of 89 per cent.[32]

EU subsidies also unquestionably played the dominant role as regards managing the environmental problems of agriculture. Generous grants were made available for Irish farmers to control farmyard wastes or to farm in an ecologically sensitive manner. The major initiative here was the so-called Rural Environmental Protection Scheme (REPS), which emerged from the mid-1990s onwards in the wake of significant CAP reforms around 1992. These reforms had created dedicated fiscal instruments for environmentally friendly farming, early retirement, and forestry. The Irish Department of Agriculture lost little time in putting together the REPS initiative.

In theory, this meant the Irish agricultural sector was being brought into the fold of modern environmental regulation and by

2002 it was estimated that almost 27 per cent of agricultural land was being farmed under the REPS programme.[33] In practice, the origins and nature of such schemes were as an income support mechanism first and foremost. One independent assessment of the REPS initiative has noted the absence of any coherent monitoring of its environmental effects,[34] and more generally it has been pitched towards smaller farmers, many of whom pose the *least* ecological threat. More politically significant in the agricultural sector was the decision in 1996 to make IPPC licences for large piggeries. Such a level of regulation would have been politically inconceivable a decade before. It effectively recognized that these operations were not small-scale family farms but large commercial operations capable of producing a waste load equivalent to a small town or factory.

The 1990s was also the decade when it became obvious that much of Ireland's countryside was beginning to show signs of environmental harm. One of the more fraught problems was perversely related to EU CAP subsidies. Payments were made to Irish sheep farmers per animal. This quickly encouraged a surge in sheep numbers in the most vulnerable areas, which began to lead to a serious problem of upland soil erosion. Absurdly, by the mid-1990s Irish farmers were being paid per sheep they *removed* from vulnerable hillsides.

Yet the chief source of environmental controversy regarding natural habitats lay with regard to two EU directives: on nature and habitats (from 1991) and on bird protection (1979). Both required an urgent response by the Irish authorities in the 1990s. However, they quickly got bogged down in numerous rows over one key detail that both directives demanded: the legal designation of parcels of land where vulnerable flora and fauna were in existence.

This was politically and legally tricky in Ireland because of a strong cultural sensitivity about property rights. An earlier attempt to compile a list of sites of scientific interest during the early 1980s, and to use these as a basis for designation, had been successfully challenged in the higher courts. But the core of the problem was a more mundane attempt by farmers' groups to get fiscal compensation and limit the number of such designations to the minimum. The various Irish state authorities veered wildly from resisting this to oscillating towards intricate compensation packages with qualifications.[35]

A major weakness here was a failure to revise the 1976 Wildlife Act into a proper biodiversity protection statute. Instead, piecemeal statutory instruments were cobbled together throughout the 1990s to try and give incremental effect to both directives. These have been widely regarded as ineffectual.[36]

In 1995 another new environmental agency was created, although it wasn't necessarily advertised as such. This was the Heritage Council, which has a very broad brief, including everything from archaeological sites to nature conservation. It rapidly moved to produce an impressive quality of reports on rather obviously environmental topics: the state of forestry, the impact of agriculture on the environment, hedgerow conservation, biodiversity, etc. However, its expertise and quality of advice was not matched by strong regulatory powers like the EPA.

The political background to the formation of the Heritage Council is worth recounting, as it was indirectly a by-product of yet another cathartic row in the mould of the Wood Quay saga. In the early 1990s, the Office of Public Works proposed the building of a tourist interpretative centre at Mullaghmore, in the heart of the Burren, County Clare, a unique limestone pavement region. Environmentalists objected that this would undermine the protection of the site, and began a complex number of legal actions that were ultimately successful.

Michael D. Higgins (Labour), who had ministerial responsibility for heritage issues after 1993, decided in the wake of the Mullaghmore controversy to push for the founding of a new Heritage Council in 1995, in part to offer a more sympathetic state response on such questions in future. Yet again, what was interesting here was that this was essentially a conflict between state agencies and environmentalists over contested definitions of development. In this case, the environmentalists won, indicating that the phenomenon of litigation was emerging as a serious factor. Indeed, one key legal victory arising from the Mullaghmore litigation was that state agencies and local governments could no longer simply assume they did not require planning permission for their own developments.

One must conclude by stressing what was arguably the most important development of all during the 1990s. This was the sea-change in background socio-economic conditions which emerged in the latter half of the 1990s. The 'Celtic Tiger' phenomenon should not be underestimated. Ireland by the end of the 1990s had moved from being classifiable as one of the EU's poorer states to being among the wealthiest, at least measured on a GDP per capita basis. In theory, this meant Ireland should have been able to afford a more ambitious and demanding type of environmental policy.

In practice, the roaring forces of economic growth unleashed by the 'Celtic Tiger' left other agendas, such as the environment, very much in the shade. It was not actually until the mid-1990s that Irish unemployment levels began to descend. Irish budgetary policy of the late 1990s was driven by a neo-liberal agenda of delivering cuts in the income tax base. With the new-found prosperity there was an inevitable tendency for conspicuous consumption to take hold. The public mood was not favourable to any sentiments that risked spoiling the good times. In retrospect it was left to beyond the 1990s to face the environmental consequences of rapid growth.

BEYOND THE MILLENNIUM

On 15 November 1999, the Irish government unveiled one of the most important documents for contemporary Ireland with its National Development Plan (NDP) for 2000–6. This was a tremendous opportunity to promote sustainable development in an Ireland that had reached levels of affluence unthinkable in the 1980s. Unfortunately, the NDP was an utterly conventional document. It was little more than a mish-mash of various ministerial wish lists. Sustainable development was not given a central thematic role, despite reference to the concept.

For example, while the NDP did include an environmental infrastructure fund, much of this spending was obligated under EU laws anyway.[37] In theory, the NDP was subjected to a *pilot* 'eco-audit'.[38] Yet this was a banal exercise, being more of a checklist approach rather than a truly comprehensive or critical examination. No proper Strategic Environmental Assessment (SEA) of the NDP was ever done.[39]

Some €51 billion of public spending was committed over the period 2000–6, of which the EU yet again contributed some €3.2 billion.[40] A key part of the NDP was a related national spatial strategy (NSS). This was supposed to identify further urban growth centres besides Dublin, up to 2020, although some reference was also made to the need for rural development for political reasons. However, no substantial policies were offered to address the low-density nature of Irish (sub)urbanization patterns.[41] Future growth would be supposedly concentrated in 'hub and gateway' cities and towns, but of what type? The fear has to be of an American-style sprawl predominating ('doughnut cities')[42] and not compact urban centres. In any event, the NSS was not produced until 2001, *after* the NDP was already up and running. This meant key decisions were made without any prior or coherent spatial development perspective.

The balance within the NDP between roads and public transport, an important indicator of any commitment to sustainability, was also uneven. Some €6.7 billion was promised for the former and about €3.1 billion for the latter, a ratio of roughly 2:1 in favour of roads. In fact, this significantly *underestimates* the actual spending dedicated to roads due to an inflationary spiral which would see road spending eventually budgeted for €16 billion by 2004.[43]

Spending on public transport[44] within the NDP was mostly just paying for replacements or upgrading of obsolescent existing infrastructure, buses, and railcars. Only a small amount was being spent to provide genuinely new capacity. Inclusion of the LUAS trams was disingenuous as it was a project long promised before 2000–6, but much delayed. By way of contrast, the motorway programme was providing a completely new and very costly network. No less than five motorways were to be built by 2006,[45] even though an earlier 1998 'Road Needs Study' by the National Roads Authority (NRA) had indicated investments should be much more selective.

This frenzy of motorway construction did not go unopposed. In the Glen of the Downs (Wicklow), the destruction of native broadleaf forest to make way for an 'improved' N11 was challenged by 'eco-warriors' who camped out in the trees and physically occupied the site. While radical and colourful, they ultimately lost after failing to secure a Supreme Court verdict in their favour, and the aged oaks were culled in the name of road widening.[46] There was opposition to motorways in Kilkenny,[47] Cork, and Galway throughout 2001. Even the state's own

Heritage Council begged the government to rethink its motorway building mania wherever natural heritage was threatened.[48] The authorities replied with cold silence and, later, a new chairperson was appointed to its governing structure. The Heritage Council was later to suffer from controversy over its direction, with at least three high profile resignations from its governing council in 2002 and one from an advisory committee in 2003, after clashes between the chairperson and those members (that chairperson has since been re-nominated as of 2005).

Most of all, by the end of 2004 there was intense concern at proposals for yet another motorway, the M3. This was not originally planned as one of the five promised, and was controversial because it was routed through the valley adjacent to the Hill of Tara. This site was a wide-ranging archaeological zone of international standing. Despite repeated protests for rerouting, and opposition from the National Museum's director, the government decided to proceed. Nothing could be allowed to impede 'critical infrastructure', not even, it seemed, archaeological heritage of world significance.

A serious dispute also broke out over the completion of the crescent shaped M50 around Dublin. This centred on the archaeological remains of Carrickmines Castle. At the heart of this dispute was how the precise routing plan for the motorway was decided. There had been a 1983 assessment by An Foras Forbartha, which noted that the site should be avoided on archaeological grounds. Ultimately, the matter of zoning for sections of this motorway was subject to investigation by the Flood Tribunal into corrupt payments to politicians in return for favourable planning decisions.[49]

In 2000, the entire area of Irish planning law was comprehensively altered by a new Planning and Development Act, which promised to make for an easier and faster planning process. Since the pivotal 1963 Planning Act, there had been nine separate amending laws. The result was a piecemeal and fragmented planning system. Yet this new Act also had a controversial political objective. It contained a systematic attempt to reduce the scope for litigation and planning objections that had been *the* favoured tactic of environmentalists during the 1990s.

The public display period for local government development plans was reduced from three months to five weeks, and a charge was established per objection lodged. For an organization such as An Taisce, the number of submissions in any one year could be several thousand,[50] implying a new cost to this environmental NGO of several thousand euro. It is important to remember here that An Taisce was, since the 1963 Planning Act, listed as a competent body *entitled* to lodge third party objections on public interest grounds. Yet the fee mechanism still applied to them. Unsurprisingly, by 2003 there was a 20 per cent drop in planning objections compared with 2001.[51] As already noted in Chapter One, this charge is facing legal challenge by the European Commission.

In fairness, the new Planning Act of 2000 had positive features. There was supposed to be greater consultation at an earlier stage of planning, and County or City development plans were limited to six years to ensure they were not out of date.[52] That had been a major problem during the last two decades. Another important innovation was the Strategic Planning Guidelines (SPGs).[53] These would be decided by the Minister for the Environment (etc.) in office, but were now given a statutory force of law. This meant they had to be followed by local governments and also, crucially, they had to be considered by An Bord Pleanála when making assessments.

In theory, some discretion remained for the Board in how they chose to apply these guidelines. In practice though, this was a move that reduced the freedom of the Board to decide matters by balancing competing interests more flexibly. For example, in deciding on very controversial waste incinerator cases in 2005, An Bord Pleanála granted planning permission making reference to ministerial strategic planning guidelines which recommended that incineration was a major part of national waste policy.

However, it would be unfair to simply read the entire Planning and Development Act 2000 as only designed to limit planning objections by third parties. One other positive change was to allow An Bord Pleanála to consider environmental issues when making its judgements, and not just narrowly defined planning concerns. Previously, environmental matters were only something that the EPA could decide as part of *their* licensing role. This caused no end of confusion and frustration. Planning and environmental concerns are typically interlinked. Henceforth, environmentalists could raise environmental concerns beyond just planning issues. However, the Planning Board cannot impose environmental related planning conditions, which severely dampens the scope of this reform.

Another controversy which generated considerable media debate between 2000 and 2005 was planning permission for single 'one-off houses' in rural areas. Environmentalists alleged such a settlement pattern risked water supplies, due to their inevitable loading of sewage upon already pressurised rural freshwaters.[54] The other problem was the financial implausibility of ever being able to provide systematic waste-water treatment for such low-density settlements. Yet with soaring house prices, many Irish people were part drawn but also economically pushed to seek better value affordable houses in greenfield sites. This left organizations like An Taisce fighting an unpopular and widely misunderstood cause.

An Taisce's objections were also misrepresented as being a snobby aesthetic abhorrence of so called 'bungalow blitz', or the idealism of a Dublin elite who wanted a pristine rural landscape devoid of people. In fact, the concrete issue was one of commuter lifestyles and rural water pollution. Yet these complex topics were rarely discussed in preference for the familiar portrayal of environmentalists as anti-development 'tweedy types'. In any event the pace of one-off rural housing grew, with perhaps as many as 40 per cent of new homes being of such a type between 2000–5.[55] In April 2005 the Irish government even reversed previously stricter planning conditions for rural one-off housing.[56] The result will certainly be a pattern of fragmented settlement that will have lasting repercussions for the cost of delivering services to dispersed communities, not least environmental protection.

Despite legislative change, disquiet about the planning system actually intensified by 2004–5. Environmentalists alleged that An Bord Pleanála had been emasculated and was being both politically pressurised and legally frog-marched into making decisions favourable to government. County councillors were complaining that local residents could not get permission to build homes.[57] Business representatives argued that the planning system was too slow, unpredictable, and open to third parties making too many objections.[58] IBEC was claiming that, as of 2005, only ten out of forty-six waste projects identified in 2001 had been built. Since the late 1990s it had been a pet project of theirs to have a 'national infrastructure board' established to bypass An Bord Pleanála and 'fast-track' proposals.

When, in 2003, An Bord Pleanála refused permission for a shore-based marine natural gas processing works in Rossport (Mayo), some circles within the governing elite also began to make sounds that the planning system required 'reform'. What they in fact wanted was a guarantee that critical infrastructure could be expedited. In the end, the Corrib Gas pipeline project was resurrected and new planning sought.[59] However, local and environmental protestors intensified their opposition. Five local landowners refused access to their lands and ended up in prison for contempt of court in 2005, these men being immediately dubbed 'the Rossport 5'. Another epic blame game had emerged.

It is also against this backdrop that one should situate the proposed Strategic Planning Infrastructure Bill of February 2006, which is likely to establish within An Bord Pleanála a new sub-unit to 'fast track' such developments and give them priority. The really problematic feature of the 'fast-tracking' debate is the implication that there should be no substantive appeal.[60] By sending planning permission straight to An Bord Pleanála first, that would alter the role of the Board, which usually provides an appeal mechanism on decisions by local governments. The only appeal left would be in fact on a procedural point of law to the High Court, for which leave must be sought. This is by no means an automatic right. Business lobbies have then seemingly achieved at least part of their agenda, of effectively restricting the scope of the planning system and not merely speeding things up.

Yet the real problems here were never really with the planning system. Political opposition was merely manifesting itself within the system. Notably, there was no alternative political forum to negotiate differences and reach a settlement other than via the planning or courts system. It should be pointed out that it is judicial appeals over planning decisions by An Bord Pleanála which cause the greatest delay, especially if they go all the way to the Supreme Court. Such litigation can add two years to the actual planning process, which can often be completed in a year. Indeed, the Board has a statutory obligation to decide most of its appeals within four weeks, and regularly does so. Finally, research by Ellis has noted that businesses themselves are responsible for a significant share of third party objections.[61] In conclusion, arguments for reform of the planning system along the lines of 'fast-tracking' are not without partisan and self-serving objectives. The core problem remains that there are intense political disputes over controversial environmental and planning issues that require primarily political resolution, rather than 'fast-tracking'.

One example of the political nature of environmental dispute lay in the waste sector. If planning policy was fast becoming a political minefield by 2005, the area of waste policy has descended into open warfare. By early 2001 the various regional waste plans, which included Danish style incineration, were in tatters. Several local county councils simply refused to vote for plans that included any incineration dimension. The response of the national government was to crudely bypass such opposition.[62] The legitimacy of local governments was checkmated by the legitimacy of the national government (re-elected in 2002). Legislation was simply passed which enabled the national minister to override the objections of local Councils wherever they had rejected incinerators. Planning requirements were also relaxed for new waste facilities.[63] Unelected city or county managers were empowered to advance plans for incinerators. Despite impressive local campaigns against incinerators, environmentalists had unquestionably lost that battle.

Yet waste policy continued to generate controversy. For example, from 2001 onwards a number of disturbing discoveries were made of large-scale and illegal waste dumps, first in county Wicklow and then later elsewhere in the country. Also uncovered were highly organized illegal waste smuggling gangs. These were bringing wastes to Northern Ireland and in some cases as far afield as Scotland. One reason for this was that a landfill levy had been introduced in 2002, and the costs of Irish landfilling had soared. Licensed landfill sites had little space anyhow and were predicted to reach capacity by 2007.[64]

The landfill levy marked a significant if belated experiment with so called 'green taxes'. The tax on plastic bags, already discussed comprehensively in Chapter One, was the second notable innovation of this type. Ireland was finally beginning to use such instruments, but other EU states had been experimenting with such taxes for much of the 1990s.

What was also innovative about such taxes was that their revenues were being retained for funding environmental improvements in the waste sector or for improvement of law enforcement capacity. A dedicated Environment Fund[65] was established to ensure such 'earmarking' by Irish authorities. Significantly, these revenues were also controlled by the minister responsible for environmental policy, thus reducing dependence on the Department of Finance.

On a critical note, one can point to the relatively low rate at which the landfill levy was set. The initial rate of €15 per tonne, together with the added stipulation that this may rise by no more than €5 per tonne per annum, were both relatively conservative levels of taxation. Consultants had recommended achieving a level of between €30 to €50 per tonne to be really effective.[66]

Yet taxes as a vital instrument in Irish environmental policy have by no means received wider acceptance. A revealing turning point was the decision to reject introducing a carbon tax in late 2004. This decision was taken despite Ireland's appalling record on greenhouse gases, and in blatant disregard for the National Climate Change Strategy (NCSS) of 2000. Although hedged with qualifications,[67] that strategy clearly indicated that green taxes and fiscal measures would have to be introduced, with tentative dates set for the years 2002 or 2003.[68]

The primary justification offered for rejecting a carbon tax was its likely ineffectualness, and reference was made to historically high oil prices of the period surrounding the US invasion of Iraq and beyond. Yet intense lobbying by IBEC and other businesses also explain much of this decision. Indeed, there are suggestions that the government seriously miscalculated the effects of a tax. It has now been estimated that a €20 per tonne CO_2 levy would have been likely to have reduced Irish emissions significantly.[69] Moreover, a 2005 report by the state's own 'think-tank', the Economic and Social Research Institute (ESRI), reiterated the case *for* a carbon tax. They were greeted with disbelief, even though that Institute has provided very convincing details on how such a tax could operate to reduce fiscal impacts on those with lower incomes.[70]

By way of contrast to such indecisiveness on taxes, Ireland began in 2004 to participate in an ambitious EU-wide emissions trading scheme. Although very complex, this scheme basically involves only large producers of greenhouse gases who are given a set quota for their emissions. If they exceed this they will have to buy excess emission permits from other EU-located large firms. However, if they emit less, they can actually sell their unused quotas for a profit, to other firms who need them.

While this initiative is not necessarily uncontroversial (environmentalists have alleged the allocated emission quotas are overly generous), what was striking here was the contrast in political leadership. This EU scheme for carbon emissions trading was dragging Ireland into the mainstream of modern environmental policy approaches to climate change. Without EU leadership, Irish participation in such a complex project was doubtful. But we have already seen that, when left with an issue where the EU cannot be involved (national taxes), there was no push factor to get the Irish government to innovate. On the contrary, and unlike other EU states, Ireland decided to close the door on any CO_2 tax. Yet emissions trading and a CO_2 tax are complementary. Smaller firms and other economic actors who are not big enough to join an EU emissions trading scheme can be brought into a regulatory tax system to reduce greenhouse gas emissions.

Ireland's political leadership was thus confirming its image as a state elite obsessed with economy *over* society, with growth *rather* than quality of life, and with a view of environmental policy as a perhaps necessary afterthought, to be done reluctantly. And only because the EU was there to tell the Irish political class that action needed to be taken.

CONCLUSIONS

The aim of this chapter has been to provide the reader with a narrative overview of how Irish environmental policy has developed. However, a number of wider lessons about Irish environmental policy can also be drawn. I suggest in this regard that three themes stand out: the adversarial style of Irish environmental policy; the vital importance of the EU; and the failure to develop a strategic rather than a reactive approach to environmental policy.

Irish environmental policy is pock-marked by extensive conflict. In fact, the style of Irish environmental policy appears to be getting *more* adversarial, not less. Consensus is rarely mentioned. At times it has become a 'dirty word' both for environmentalists who see in it a synonym for 'sell-out' and for government or businesses who interpret it as meaning 'time-delay'.

Litigation has emerged as the chief symptom of this visceral antipathy between environmentalists, developers, or the Irish state and its agencies. Indeed, I have argued here that a key feature of Irish environmental policy is that the Irish state has come to know environmentalists more as adversaries than as normal lobbying groups. An important and repeated problem has been the role of state agencies: are they independent regulators or government servants? And who can police state agencies who themselves are responsible for supposedly policing environmental problems?

Such an adversarial policy style is also reflective of a major imbalance of political power between environmentalists, government, and business. It is worth remembering that litigation is usually the last resort of social groups who feel they have little other negotiating or political power. In contrast, it is clear that organized farming and business interests can and do get a hearing from Irish governments as regards their concerns. The balance of interests between environment and development remains uneven. Indeed, environmentalists are still stuck with the image as marginal 'tweedy types'. That label was common for An Taisce in the early 1970s. It was still being bandied about in the first years of this century, as they challenged one-off rural housing to be met with condemnation for their alleged 'elitism'.

Even the original protest politics seen at Carnsore over the nuclear plans of 1979 has not died off. But neither has it matured into a professional national environmental lobby of real influence. It has instead fragmented into a more socially diverse pattern of localized and *ad hoc* protest. Successive Irish governments have responded to such protests by essentially ignoring them. Alternatively, they have attempted to treat the symptom by curbing the scope for litigation, or by entrusting more discretionary powers to national ministers who can simply impose policies. The national government has decided to force several controversial issues, such as waste incinerators or the Tara/M3 motorway. Such a style of decision-making is not much different from the rather crude views of the 1980s, that nothing should stand in the way of job creation. Despite all the glossy publications on 'sustainable development', official mindsets have not changed much.

Yet forcing through unpopular or controversial policies cannot be likely to lead to stable policy outcomes over time. The long-term costs of political resistance may be much greater and more uncertain than the short-term costs of negotiating with environmentalists and other interests. One particular uncertainty is whether the European Court of Justice (ECJ) will in future overturn certain controversial changes in Irish planning law, such as the innovation of charges for making objections, the fast-tracking proposal, or even how the 'polluter pays' principle has been applied.

It is also truly remarkable how Irish decision-makers have failed to draw analogies from the Irish industrial relations sector. Strike activity and unpredictable industrial actions have generally been reduced. Yet this is only because a complex machinery of dialogue and negotiation with trade unions and other social partners has been created. The stability this delivered was a vital ingredient in the making of the 'Celtic Tiger'.

Treating the symptom of litigation does not offer a cure, and it fails to address the underlying clash of conceptions of development that are lurking beneath conflicts as diverse as Wood Quay, Mullaghmore, Carrickmines, the Tara motorway, or the Rossport 5 controversy.

The last thirty years of Irish environmental policy have abysmally failed to achieve a style of decision-making which is more inclusive, consensual, and negotiated. Instead, Irish environmental policy remains stuck in a time warp of adversarial relations that will continue to pose serious problems.

A second strong theme evident here is the vital role of the EU. Some Irish environmentalists have been tempted to dismiss the importance of the EU in helping to protect Ireland's environment. They resent perhaps the idea that the EU somehow 'saved Ireland from itself' as regards environmental neglect. In fairness, one should note examples where other EU policies, such as the CAP, have directly led to increased water pollution or soil erosion. However, there can be no mistaking the strong and consistent push factor that the EU has provided for Irish governments to modernize environmental policy.

One can see this most clearly, for example, in the slow Irish experimentation with 'green taxes'. Ireland did more or less nothing in the late 1990s on that front, whereas other EU states were busy experimenting with such taxes then. Because the EU has no real competence on tax matters it cannot push the Irish on tax innovation. Yet it is interesting that two other forms of new environmental policy instrument (NEPI), emissions trading and the REPAK voluntary agreement, were both directly introduced in response to EU legislation.

Moreover, the very fact that EU environmental policies have the full force and authority of law is itself hugely important. EU laws are supreme over national law, albeit only on matters of EU competence. This has allowed the Commission to pursue the Irish authorities for improper implementation of environmental laws. It has given Irish environmentalists a regulatory watchdog who can scrutinize the gap between the Irish government's formal commitments in signing up to EU environmental laws and their actual practice. However, it was also surprising just how unmoved Irish authorities were by having a stack of Commission proceedings outstanding against them by the late 1990s. Action was often simply taken at the last minute.

In contrast, large-scale EU transfers have been vigorously embraced. Such funds have helped to modernize Irish sewerage infrastructure, to promote sustainable transport initiatives such as the LUAS trams, and to fund rural environmental schemes. The EU has also acted as a lifeline for the renewable energy sector in the face of relative uninterest by successive Irish governments in the late 1990s. The EU was even contributing almost one fifth of the total investment of the national development plan for 2000–6, a period when Ireland was, by some estimates, among the very wealthiest of EU states, in per capita terms.

It is interesting to speculate what the Irish authorities would have done without such transfers. One must also question what will happen in the future as Ireland no longer qualifies for EU funds. She will then have to finance environmental infrastructure exclusively from her own pockets. Will Irish governments be as generous?

There can be little doubt but that the EU has been vital in forcing the pace of change in Irish environmental policy. It has modernized the 'software' of Irish environmental policy content:

the laws, regulatory ideas, and concepts. Yet what the EU has *not* been able to change as much is the mindset and the governing culture of the Irish state with regard to seeing environmental policy as a lessor priority. Nor has the EU been able to change the institutional 'hardware' that much. The failure to develop An Foras Forbartha, its subsequent abolition, and then delays in establishing the EPA were all serious institutional shortcomings, about which the EU could do little.

The third strong theme that emerges here is that Ireland has failed to develop an approach to environmental policy that is fundamentally strategic in its conception. In particular, ecological modernization, as was discussed in the first chapter, has not taken hold. Such a strategy strives to replace the facile idea that high environmental standards are inimical to social and economic development. One does not have to sacrifice the environment for a strong economic performance.

Yet while environmental plans have emerged on paper since the 1990s, they have lacked ambition and have mostly gathered dust. It is true that integrated pollution prevention control (IPPC) licences have been introduced for larger industries. In theory, these compel firms to seek greater technical performance to reduce pollutants. However this innovation is mostly ghettoized in the industrial sector, whereas the construction, transport, energy, and agricultural sectors are all as significant a source of Irish environmental problems. Their activities typically do not require IPPC licences.

Most disappointingly, there has been no conscious attempt to choose a style of development which would be intrinsically more sustainable or just environmentally friendly. Unlike Denmark, where a domestic wind energy industry was supported for years, Irish authorities have done little to create a low environmental impact economy. Denmark has also invested heavily in domestic rail enhancements to balance motorways,[71] whereas Ireland is now merely upgrading rundown old stock.

Indeed, Ireland appears to be unable to learn from the mistakes of other EU states and not repeat them. For example, a more systematic approach to reducing pollution or waste in the first place has not been explored. Controversial and high cost incineration technology (a Danish example we might have ignored!), has been imposed in the teeth of significant protest.

Rather than exploring more fully the potential for public transport, Ireland has instead chosen to build a 1960s-style sprawling motorway infrastructure. There is no way that this can be considered sustainable development, given the low population densities outside Dublin. Deregulation of the national energy market has taken preference over nurturing a viable renewables sector.

After three decades of modern environmental policy, Ireland had unquestionably achieved development, but it can hardly be described as sustainable. What have we really to show for all those years? Many impressive laws and several intelligent and well thought out policies are obvious gains. The 'software' side of environmental policy has improved. It is not really the problem anymore. What remains weak is the institutional 'hardware' of the Irish state: the way government governs. In particular, what is wrong is a systematic failure to prioritize environmental concerns and manage them in a sophisticated strategic manner. We are sill muddling through as regards our environmental policies. The next chapter explores this institutional framework in more detail.

NOTES

1. See Fisheries (Consolidation) Act, 1959, Section 102.
2. See Blackwell, J. and Convery, F. (eds.) *Promise and Performance: Irish Environmental Policies Analysed* (Dublin: Resource and Environmental Policy Centre, University College Dublin, 1983); Scannell, Y. *The Law and Practice relating to Pollution Control in Ireland* (London: Graham and Trotman, 1982), p.62; Taylor, G. and Horan, A. 'From cats, dogs, parks and playgrounds to IPC licensing: policy learning and the evolution of environmental policy in Ireland', *British Journal of Politics & International Relations*, 3, 3 (2001), p.371.
3. An Foras Forbartha has sometimes been translated into English as the National Institute for Physical Planning and Construction Research; however, I have stuck to the closer meaning of the Gaelic used.
4. See, for example, the Control of Atmospheric Pollution Regulations, 1970, Statutory Instrument No. 156 of 1970.
5. See Fenlon, R.M. 'The Water Pollution Control Act: An evaluation', in J. Blackwell, and F. Convery (eds.), *Promise and Performance: Irish Environmental Policies Analysed* (Dublin: Resource and Environmental Policy Centre, University College Dublin, 1983), p.7. Note: some sources suggest part of its content was the product of a slow process of internal civil service review over a period of years. See Taylor and Horan, 'From cats, dogs, parks and playgrounds, etc.', p.371.

6. See Allen, R. *No Global: the People of Ireland versus the Multinationals* (London: Pluto Press, 2004), p.1.
7. There was a protest festival organized in the summer of 1978 but the festival in 1979 was bigger, better organized, and gained more attention.
8. Baker, S. 'The Nuclear Power Issue in Ireland; The role of the Irish anti Nuclear movement', *Irish Political Studies*, 3, 1988.
9. Technically, An Foras Forbartha was only disbanded with the passing of the 1992 EPA Act (see Article 32 of that Act). In practice it was *de facto* disbanded well before then and various staff regrouped into the Environmental Research Unit.
10. See Hederman, W. 'Battlefield Ireland', *Village Magazine*, 20–26 May 2005, pp.24–5.
11. See McDonald, F. *The Destruction of Dublin* (Dublin: Gill and MacMillan, 1985).
12. The regulation only came into effect in September 1990 and it was addressed exclusively to bituminous coals, meaning that non-smoking types of coal could be sold and some other types of fuels, such as peat. The ban was extended to the Cork and Limerick urban areas only in 2002. Peat was controversially not included, most likely because this was a domestically produced fuel and restrictions would have hit sales and employment. However, this was ostensibly justified on the grounds that peat has a lower set of emissions properties than coal.
13. Clinch, P.J. and McLoughlin, E. 'A Preliminary Analysis of the Ban on Bituminous Coal in Dublin', *Working Paper ESRS/01/08*, Dept. of Environment Studies, University College Dublin, September 2001. Available at: http://www.ucd.ie/pepweb/publications/workingpapers/
14. Clancy, L, Goodman, P. Sinclair, H. and Dockery, D.W. 'Effect of air-pollution control on death rates in Dublin, Ireland: an intervention study', *The Lancet*, 360, 19 October 2002, pp.1210–14.
15. These insights have been partly informed by the record of Irish attempts at pushing the Sellafield issue. See ENDS/Environmental News and Data Services, 'OSPAR row over nuclear reprocessing, slow progress on chemicals', *The ENDS Report*, 306, July 2000. OSPAR is a non-EU forum in which Ireland has raised the issue. OSPAR is the acronym used to describe the legal and diplomatic regimes established by both the Oslo and Paris conventions of 1972 and 1974. These agreements addressed dumping of pollutants into the North Atlantic and the North Sea by aircraft, ships, and from land based sources.
16. The terminology IPPC was used in the relevant 1996 EU Directive which made the approach mandatory for certain industries throughout the EU. It signals a more demanding approach than the earlier IPC licences. One difference is a greater focus on energy efficiency and scope for accidental emissions in audits. Reporting requirements were also increased. The standard which the licensing agency is expected to have regard to is that of 'best available techniques (BAT)', meaning best international practice but not necessarily state of the art technology in every case. The 1992 EPA Act used a weaker standard of 'Best Available technology Not Exceeding Excessive Cost' (BATNEEC). Ireland only fully met the IPPC Directive's terms with the Protection of the Environment Act, 2003.

17. OECD/ Organisation for Economic Co-operation and Development, *Environmental Performance Reviews – Ireland* (Paris: OECD, 2000), p.22.

18. See CPA/Combat Poverty Agency *Waste Collection Charges and Low Income Households* (Dublin: CPA, 2003); and CPA/Combat Poverty Agency and Fitzpatrick Associates, *Implementing a waiver system: guidelines for local authorities* (Dublin: CPA, 2005), pp.4–7. Available at: http://www.cpa.ie/publications/ImplementingAWaiverSystem_2005.pdf

19. There were also problems with private waste collectors refusing to accept waivers in Limerick city and, apparently, a plan by City Council officials to scarp waivers entirely. See Hanlon, K. 'Council discusses bin service row', *The Irish Times*, 17 August 2005; and Hanlon, K. 'Councillors and officials in row over free bin scheme', *The Irish Times*, 30 November 2004.

20. Under Article 52(3) of the Protection of the Environment Act 2003, a local authority is not *obliged* to grant waivers for those in hardship. The terminology used is that they 'may' grant such waivers. Note also that under Article 52(8) it is for a City or County Manager to decide the grant and scope of such waivers.

21. See 'Judgement reserved in waste disposal challenge', *The Irish Times*, 27 February 2003. Article 53(10a) of the Protection of the Environment Act 2003 allows for a manager to make orders that require waste for collection to have proof of payment of charges attached. In 2004 a High Court case decided that flat charges were consistent with the 'polluter pays' principle and otherwise lawful; however, there were at least two Circuit Court verdicts which decided flat waste charges were unlawful because they did not reflect the 'polluter pays' principle. As of March 2006, the Supreme Court was yet to rule on the legality of the flat charges for waste levied before 2005. See 'Bin Charges referred to the Supreme Court', *The Irish Times*, 21 March 2006; Carolan, M. 'Charge for domestic waste is deemed to be lawful', *The Irish Times*, 22 January 2004; and Fitzgerald, J. 'Council may have to refund €12.8m in refund levies', *The Irish Times*, 20 May 2005.

22. See, for example, McDonald, F. 'Bin charges are just part of 'polluter pays' policy, *The Irish Times*, 22 September 2003.

23. While endorsing the principle, De Sadeleer nonetheless admits it is somewhat vague and can contain neo-liberal overtones. See De Sadeleer, N. *Environmental Principles: From Political Slogans to Legal Rules* (Oxford: OUP, 2002), pp.59–60, and pp.21–59. Also see Larson, E.T. 'Why Environmental Liability Regimes in the United States, the European Community, and Japan have grown Synonymous with the Polluter Pays Principle', *Vanderbilt Journal of Transnational Law*, 38, 2 (2005), pp.541–677.

24. The Combat Poverty Agency was critical of the way that the 'polluter pays' principle has been applied in Ireland, which Fitzpatrick's associates described as becoming 'pay as you use'. See CPA and Fitzpatrick Associates, *Implementing a waiver system'*, etc.

25. It was not, strictly speaking, the very first environmental plan for Ireland. An *ad hoc* Environmental Council had presented such a plan in 1980, entitled 'A Policy for the Environment'. This had been largely ignored in the context of the severe economic and political crisis of the 1979–81 period.

26. A good example of this is S.I. No. 538 of 2001: European Communities (Environmental Impact Assessment) (Amendment) Regulations, 2001.

27. Doyle, A. 'Environmental Impact and Who Assesses What', *Irish Planning and Environmental Law Journal*, 5,1 (1998), pp.16–17.

28. Flynn B. 'Is supranational participation possible? The EU's attempt to enhance participation in Dublin's Transport Initiative', in F.H.J.M. Coenen, D. Huitema, and L.J. O'Toole, (eds.), *Participation and the quality of environmental decision-making* (Dordrecht, Kluwer, 1998), pp. 203–22.

29. For example, in 1996 the Irish government published its policy document, 'Renewable Energy: A Strategy for the Future'. At this stage, Irish government thinking was that renewables would be generating 5 per cent of electricity capacity by 2010, and 14 per cent by 2020.

30. These prices are at 1994–95 values. See CEC/Commission of the European Communities, *Implementation of Council Directive 91/271/EEC of 21 May 1991 Concerning Urban Waste Water Treatment as amended by Commission Directive 98/15/EC of 27 February 1998* (Luxembourg: Office of the Official Publications of the European Communities, 1999), p. 24.

31. According to the EEA, the difference between these varying levels of sewage treatment can be summarized as: 'Primary treatment (mechanical treatment technology) removes part of the suspended solid, while secondary treatment (biological treatment) uses aerobic or anaerobic micro-organisms to decompose most of the organic matter and retain some of the nutrients (around 20 – 30 per cent). Tertiary treatment (or advanced treatment technology) removes even more efficiently than secondary the organic matter. It generally includes phosphorus retention and in some cases nitrogen removal. Primary treatment alone will remove no ammonium whereas secondary (biological) treatment will remove around 75 per cent'. See EEA/European Environment Agency, *Indicator Fact Sheet WEU16 Urban Waste Water Treatment* (EEA: Copenhagen, 2004b), p.2.

32. Greece, by way of contrast, had 56.2 per cent connected to such plants in 2002, and in Portugal, 41.3 per cent of their population were connected to waste-water treatment in the same year. See OECD/Organisation for Economic Co-operation and Development, *Environmental Data Compendium, 2004* (Paris: OECD, 2005), Table 4b, p.76.

33. Fields, S./An Taisce, *Monitoring and Evaluation of the Rural Environmental Protection Scheme* (Dublin: An Taisce, 2002), p.43.

34. Ibid.

35. Grist, B. 'Wildlife legislation – The Rocky Road to special areas of conservation surveyed', *Irish Planning and Environmental Law Journal*, 4 (1997), pp.87–95.

36. Galligan, E. 'Case Notes', *Irish Planning and Environmental Law Journal*, 3 (1996), p.185.

37. This 'environmental operational programme' detailed spending on water and waste-water infrastructure at roughly €3.8 billion, although this was linked to meeting the obligations of the EU Urban Waste Water Directive. In other words, it was spending that was obligatory and part funded by the EU to 2005. To deal with the distinct problem of contamination of Irish rural drinking water wells, an additional €572 million was to be allocated.

Funding for coastal protection was a mere €52 million despite the fact that some 500 km of coastline was identified as requiring urgent attention. As regards sustainable energy some €225 million was allocated, but only €67 million was specifically for renewables, with almost half of that amount coming from the EU. A further €9.1 billion was to be spent on housing and €3 billion on healthcare. See GOI/Government of Ireland, *Ireland National Development Plan 2000–2006: Economic and Social Infrastructure Operational Programme* (Dublin: Government Stationery Office, 2000), pp.57, 61, 54, 69, and 2.

38. A number of measures were supposed to achieve the integration of environmental concerns with the NDP's objectives. The national sustainable development council, Comhar, was to be consulted prior to adoption. Environmental criteria were to be used in project selection. Environmental indicators and environmental representatives were also supposed to be included in the monitoring committee for the Economic and Social Operation Programme. Finally, there was some promise of the implementation of 'project level' EIAs, meaning *de facto* strategic environmental assessments. None of these measures are particularly convincing. See GOI, *Ireland National Development Plan 2000–2006,* p.11.

39. Newman, C. 'Heritage group is critical of economic goals in national plan', *The Irish Times,* 27 April 2000.

40. The exact levels of EU transfers from the European Regional Development Fund (which requires matching national funds) were as follows: roads (€530.22 million); public transport (€209.1 million); sustainable energy (€43.42 million); environmental infrastructure (€71.1 million). From the EU Cohesion Fund, the respective amounts were €231.2 million for roads, €55.8 million for public transport, and €280.35 million for environmental infrastructure. This quickly reveals that the share of EU funding for the environmental projects under the Irish NDP was the third highest level of aid, at 9.1 per cent. Other EU contributions were 11.2 per cent for roads, and 8.6 per cent for public transport. A level of 19.5 per cent for sustainable energy was the highest level of EU aid overall. See GOI, *Ireland National Development Plan 2000–2006,* p.4.

41. The NSS makes only minimal reference to achieving higher densities in settlement patterns. For example, it describes sustainable housing as *possibly* involving 'mixed-use and well-designed higher density development, particularly near town centres and public transport nodes like railway stations'. See GOI/Government of Ireland, *The National Spatial Strategy for Ireland, 2002–2020: People, Places and Potential* (Dublin: Government Stationery Office, 2001), p.103.

42. 'Doughnut cities', or sometimes termed 'edge cities', are two expressions used to describe the phenomenon whereby some American cities have grown in a way that involves extensive rather than intensive land use patterns. Their population density is low, and development spreads quickly to the outer fringes in a plethora of shopping malls and retail parks, especially whenever ring-roads have been built (as with Dublin's M50/Liffey–Valley and as proposed for Cork and Galway). The city centre

usually goes into relative decline. In such a city the car becomes the only realistic transport option.

43. The cost of building just a *single* km of motorway was estimated at an incredible €10 million in 2003 whereas in 1999 it was estimated at circa €5 million. Cost overruns were so large that by 2004 the National Roads Authority (NRA) was drawing up plans to raise funds for motorway construction by extensive tolling, which could yield as much as €300 million per annum. See O'Brien, T. 'NRA aims to raise €2 billion from new toll charges', *The Irish Times*, 15 April 2004.

44. Five new quality bus corridors were to be achieved and some 275 new buses bought. Rail investments were to be directed at purchasing just over 100 new rolling stock, completing the LUAS, and various other re-signalling projects that together were estimated to amount to €1.27billion.

45. By 2003 it was estimated that 64 km of new motorway had actually been built, 24 km of dual carriageway, and that a further 155 km of motorway was under construction. See O'Brien, T.'Brennan to accelerate motorway plans', *The Irish Times*, 13 August 2003.

46. Hederman, W. 'Battlefield Ireland'.

47. Dooley, C. 'Resistance in Kilkenny to motorway plan', *The Irish Times*, 21 July 2001.

48. The Heritage Council, the statutory authority responsible for Irelands landscape heritage, criticized the NDP during 1999–2000. They argued that it would increase the rate of archaeological heritage destruction, already running at roughly 10 per cent per decade, and would have a very large impact on the landscape. Equally, the Eastern Regional Fisheries Board warned that the hectic pace of motorway construction, and the fact that much of this was effectively expedited through specific legislation, all posed a risk to vulnerable small watercourses and eco-systems. Siggins, L. 'Motorways and housing developments add to strain on inland waterway system', *The Irish Times*, 23 July 2001.

49. O'Brien, T.'State agency warned of castle danger', *The Irish Times*, 18 August 2002.

50. For 2002, An Taisce made 300 appeals to An Bord Pleanála regarding local government planning permits, and were successful in 90 per cent of these cases. They also made 3,000 submissions to local governments as part of the initial planning process. See McDonald, F. 'Number of Bord Pleanála appeals queried', *The Irish Times*, 13 June 2003.

51. Hennessy, M. 'Fast-track planning body may face legal challenges', *The Irish Times*, 7 April 2004.

52. Sustainable development was written into the text of the Act as well, which is significant because it marks the first statutory definition of the term. The Planning and Development Act 2000 also allowed for Landscape Conservation Areas to be designated.

53. The Planning and Development Act 2000 actually allows for regional planning guidelines (Articles 21–27) and ministerial guidelines (Articles 28–31). The generic term 'strategic policy guidelines' (SPGs) appears to have evolved to cover both, however.

54. Lucey, A. 'An Taisce criticises one-off holiday homes', *The Irish Times*, 14 January 2005.
55. See, for example, McDonald, F. 'Planners despair as profit drives new housing policy', *The Irish Times*, 16 March 2004, and O'Brien, T. 'Almost 76,000 one-off houses constructed', *The Irish Times*, 7 November 2003.
56. See, for newspaper coverage and comment following this move Siggins, L. 'Housing row is more than a one-off', *The Irish Times*, 16 April 2005; McDonald, F. 'Roche tones down populist rhetoric', *The Irish Times*, 14 April 2005; McDonald, F. 'Roche defends housing policy', *The Irish Times*, 14 April 2005; Brennock, M. 'Greens and Labour voice strong concerns', *The Irish Times*, 14 April 2005; O'Brien, T. 'Warning of a high price to be paid for services to houses', *The Irish Times*, April 14, (2005b); and also Deegan, G. 'Clare County Council moves to dismantle house building restrictions', *The Irish Times*, 21 September 2005.
57. See, for example, Lucey, A. 'Planning Chief Denies Hidden Agenda Claims', *The Irish Times*, 15 December 2004.
58. Another criticism by developers was that third parties with no immediate interest in the planned activity could make objections under Irish planning law relatively easily whereas this was less common in some other EU planning systems. While this is partially true, other systems would have opportunities for planning hearings, inquiries and such like. Moreover, the international trend, as expressed in the Århus Convention of 1998, is clearly to widen the scope for participation in environmental and planning matters.
59. As of June 2006 the status of the project's planning was unclear. An Bord Pleanála had ruled just then on an appeal by An Taisce that the shore works associated with the plant required planning permission. See Siggins, L. 'Several key Shell Corrib work not authorised, board finds', *The Irish Times*, 2 June 2006.
60. For example, this is a major part of the argument made by Tom Flynn, B.L. See Flynn, T. *The Planning and Development (Strategic Infrastructure) Bill, 2006 – A Critical Analysis of its Implications For Environmental Law.* Paper given at the Fourth Law and the Environment Conference, Faculty Of Law, University College, Cork, Thursday 27 April 2006. Available at: http://www.ucc.ie/en/lawsite/eventsandnews/previousevents/environapr200 6/
61. The study undertaken by Ellis was for the year 1999 exclusively, so it provides a guide only. In that year 4.5 per cent of third party appellants were from the business sector, and about 70 per cent of that share were property developers themselves. By way of contrast, voluntary groups, which includes environmentalists such as An Taisce, comprised 3.7 per cent. The bulk of appellants were individuals (74.6 per cent) and residents' associations (10.7 per cent). Note that the category 'individuals' may contain some environmentalists operating in their personal capacity for legal reasons. See Ellis, G. 'Third Party Rights of Appeal in Planning: Reflections on the experience in the Republic of Ireland', *The Town Planning Review*, 73, 4 (2002), pp.453–4.

62. Section 22 of the original Waste Management Act 1996 was specifically amended through the Waste Management (Amendment) Act 2001 (Section 4), to allow the national Minister for Environment (etc.) to empower a City or County Manager to make a waste plan where an elected council had refused to, or was unable to do so. However, in legal terms the Protection of the Environment Act 2003 went even further. Under its Section 26(2)b, the making of a waste management plan becomes an executive function. That is a function which is at the discretion of a County or City Manager to exercise.

63. See Reid, L. 'Planning rules for waste projects to be eased', *The Irish Times*, 4 May 2005.

64. EPA/Environmental Protection Agency and Lehane, M., Le Bolloch, O. and Crawley, P. (eds.), *Environment in Focus 2002: key environmental indicators for Ireland* (Wexford: EPA, 2002a), p.vii.

65. In 2003 the Department of Finance suggested in their budgetary commentary that receipts from the Environmental Fund would be about €30 million per annum. See DoF/Department of Finance, *Budget 2003 Commentary*. Available at: http://www.budget.gov.ie/2003/esttabsEnviron.asp#Environ.

66. This implies that such a level cannot be reached until 2005, and perhaps much later given that it is at ministerial discretion to increase the rate. See DELG/Department of the Environment and Local Government, *Waste Management (Landfill Levy) Regulations 2002, Information Note and Guidance* (Dublin: DELG, 2002), pt.6.

67. These qualifications principally include, to name but a few: the maintenance of the stable economic environment and fiscal policies, allowing for advance notice, and providing policy certainty for industry and economic actors. DELG/Department of the Environment and Local Government, *National Climate Change Strategy Ireland* (Dublin: Government Stationery Office, 2000), p.27.

68. DELG, *National Climate Change Strategy Ireland*, pp.76, 26.

69. Raftery, M. 'We will pay for Carbon emissions', *The Irish Times*, 16 September 2004.

70. See next chapter for details.

71. For example, Denmark has spent heavily on upgrading the quality of its intercity rail fleet with modern IC3 trainsets introduced in 1990. These were manufactured in Denmark – a country without much of a tradition of locomotive engineering. The management structure of Danish state railways has also been comprehensively altered, with infrastructure now separated from passanger rail services and cargo rail privatized. Ireland has done none of these things as of 2006, even though they will be required under EU directives. Copenhagen has also built a small city metro which opened in 2002, and Denmark has ensured new rail links across the Öresund bridge to Sweden are alongside its motorways. Total transport investment was about 50 per cent for roads, with rail receiving specifically one sixth over the years 1990–2004. See Statistics Denmark, *Transport 2005* (Copenhagen: Statistics Denmark, 2005), pp.67, 90. Available at: www.dst.dk/transport2005

Chapter Four

Institutions, Instruments and Implementation: the weak points in Irish environmental policy

INTRODUCTION

Where are the critical weak points in Irish environmental policy, and why are these problem areas so deficient? These two questions inform this chapter. In order to provide a clear argument, I consider here just *three* aspects of governance that are vital for any successful environmental policy. These include: the *Institutional* capacity of state agencies, the *Implementation* of policy in practice, and the policy *Instruments* used by government (whether laws or taxes).

With regard to institutional weakness, this chapter examines just *two* specific cases. First, local governments in Ireland are structurally weak. This is fatal for any environmental policy because it is they who must execute most environmental laws in practice. This weakness has its roots in history. The Irish state has evolved as a highly centralized political system, with local governments controlled from Dublin. They are seen as pawns of national power and influence, rather than being allowed to develop as responsive and independent local governments in their own right. This breeds a culture of defensive governance.

Secondly, there is also a wider problem of regulatory independence, meaning whether environmental regulators can be trusted to be free from governmental pressure as they carry out their responsibilities. The foundation of the EPA has not really solved this profound problem, which also infects local governments and perhaps even An Bord Pleanála. As was discussed in the previous chapter, strategic planning guidelines and ministerial directives have compelled the Board to decide individual cases in the shadow of government policy advice.

With regard to the implementation of environmental policy, there has been controversy about just how bad the Irish record is. A closer examination of the Irish record over the years 2001–4 offered here reveals that Ireland had the *fifth* worst performance for the three main types of implementation problem analyzed by the European Commission. What is also evident is that Ireland's record is getting worse. By 2003, Ireland had a total of five negative verdicts of the European Court of Justice hanging over its head for non-implementation of EU environmental laws. Between 1993 and 1998 Ireland had none.

What is causing this woeful record? I point to an Irish local and national governance culture that is reactionary and proceduralist. Emphasis has been placed on merely working through the volume of EU legislation at a slow rate. The focus has all been upon the exercise of legal transposition: transferring EU Directives on paper into Irish legalese. Rather than anticipating problematic issues, the style has been to transpose right up close to deadlines. There has been little acceptance that enforcement of environmental laws involves moving from office-based paperwork to scientific and legal investigation on the ground. Political willpower to prioritize implementation has also been simply lacking.

Finally, with regard to policy instruments Ireland appears backward. 'Eco-taxes' have only recently been experimented with for landfills and plastic bags. Regressive charges have been imposed for household waste and electrical waste. Yet green taxes have been rejected for dealing with climate change, a more urgent issue. Ideological resistance to any tax experimentation is widespread. There is a failure to understand that such taxes can be introduced *without* very negative economic effects, especially upon those with lower incomes.

What has happened is that lobby groups have adopted a strategy of playing off one instrument against another. Voluntary agreements in particular are preferred by government and business over taxes, which remain under a cloud of ideological suspicion. What is not yet appreciated is that different instruments need to be combined to reinforce each other. It should not be a game of 'pick and choose', which is what is happening.

Innovative emissions-trading has been introduced to deal with the climate change issue, but only because of EU leadership. In any event, the Irish scheme has been uninspiring. The level of emissions reduction promised is low. Participants have been treated very favourably. Several million euro that could have been raised by the government selling 5 per cent of emission permits went unrealized. In any event, Irish firms have already breached their emissions limits for 2005[1] and the market for permits has proven very volatile. Ireland then remains mostly stuck with her laws, poorly enforced, with but a few policy experiments on the margins.

'HARDWARE PROBLEMS':
WEAK IRISH ENVIRONMENTAL INSTITUTIONS

Any successful environmental policy requires capable state institutions. That seemingly innocuous claim has been among the most consistent finding that political science accounts of environmental policy have revealed. The institutional dimension can make for the success or failure of any environmental policy, even where the basic scientific issues are well understood, or if there is plenty of finance and popular support. Within the jargon of political science, institutions simply 'matter'. They are the vital foundations upon which any environmental policy must rest.

Weak local environmental governance.

Arguably the most pivotal institutions for Irish environmental policy are local governments.[2] It is they who have carried the burden of enforcing and applying much of the body of EU and Irish environmental laws. They also retain basic regulatory functions, such as granting initial planning permission, checking water quality, or first inspections of pollution incidents. Yet Ireland's thirty-nine city, borough and county councils[3] must rank among the poorest specimens of local governance within western Europe. They lack much by way of fiscal or legal autonomy.

Almost half their funding is directly disbursed by national government.[4] The Irish Constitution did not even bother with a section on local government until amended in 1999. Traditionally, they have been politically policed by the Cabinet in Dublin,[5] principally through the DEHLG. This centralization grew stronger with the evolution of the Irish County/City Manager system since the 1930s. These 'managers' are in effect unelected technocratic prefects, chosen by national ministers from within the ranks of the local civil service cadres. They unquestionably exercise considerable power over the elected but part-time councillors.

Indeed, there are several examples of appointed County or City Managers embarking on open conflict with elected councillors over environmental and planning matters. In many cases, managers have been able to overrule both the elected councillors[6] or the Council's professional planning staff. Even when considering an application for planning permission on lands which have been designated as ecologically sensitive under EU laws, it is merely *discretionary* upon a manager (rather than mandatory) to consider expert advice on heritage matters.

More generally, there is in Ireland a systematic distrust of local elected representative democracy per se. It is little surprise that there has been a growing trend to use national legislation to remove the scope for local councillors to decide environmental issues. County Managers were granted the power to impose waste charges under the Protection of the Environment Act, 2003.[7] Enabling legislation was also passed in 2001 and 2003,[8] which allowed County or City Managers themselves to make local waste plans. These included incineration, even where local councillors had explicitly voted to reject that option. This was the case in Cork, Galway, and Dublin City Councils.[9]

Another reason why it has been so easy for national government to centralize environmental powers into the hands of managers is that councillors have often proved woeful at taking decisions, especially on the zoning of land for planning. Systematic planning corruption over rezonings was uncovered in the 1990s, and this has done the most to erode popular belief in having *elected* representatives take vital decisions.[10] Even where corruption has not been involved, Ireland's clientelist[11] local political culture has played havoc with a wider public interest. Councillors have frequently[12] voted to rezone lands against the expert advice of council planners or other staff, usually because of local political lobbying. And such rezonings cannot be appealed to An Bord Pleanála.

The result is often a bizarre legal stand-off between the 'executive functions' of the manager and council staff, versus the so-called 'reserved functions' of the councillors.[13] For example, this happened in Killarney in 2006[14] where councillors voted to rezone a hotel site 1.9 miles *outside* the town centre, as a 'town centre'. This was a classic form of 'doughnut' sprawl guaranteed to undermine a compact sustainable urban centre. It was also contrary to the town's own master development plan. The Town Manager subsequently refused to act on this rezoning motion. However, councillors can attempt to compel a manager to act, under Section 140 of the Local Government Act 2001.[15] Unfortunately, this power has been used in a number of controversial rezoning cases. In just one example from 2004, over sixty such motions were placed before the Kerry County Manager in a single month.[16] Councillors also retain the right to vote for the delisting of buildings of heritage value, another power which has been abused.[17]

In all of these cases, leaving the decision with the councillors has certainly *not* guaranteed the best environmental outcome. Yet it does not logically follow that the same discretionary powers should be simply handed over to unelected managers. Indeed, what seems badly needed is the basing of any sensitive planning or environment decisions on detailed expert evidence and objective transparent criteria, which are amenable to scrutiny. The problem is a general one of allowing too many important decisions to be taken in a far too discretionary way, rather than based on evidence or objective standards.

Aside from a lack of belief in the very idea of local government, another problem has been resources. Money and personnel for local government were limited, at least until the mid-1990s. In most cases, environmental issues were managed day to day by a chief environmental officer, lately styled Directors of Environmental Services. Many would be civil engineers, even though a background in environmental and planning law or the natural sciences, would both seem more suitable.

By the end of the 1990s, the cumulative volume and complexity of Irish and EU environmental legislation had become a serious issue. A survey[18] undertaken of the time devoted to EU environmental policy by senior local government officials has revealed that some 43 per cent of the respondents estimated they were spending more than three working days per month on implementing EU laws.

In the past the 'environment' brief was essentially assumed to be about running the local landfill dump, municipal waste collection, and the sewerage or wastewater system. Enforcement and regulation were not seen as the key activities at all. The mindset was not oriented towards the concept of 'regulating' the local environment.

For example, in the long-running saga involving complaints about various chemicals plants in Cork harbour, it was clear that Cork Council's enforcement capacity was then very limited. It was reliant on individual initiative rather than a solid institutional system for oversight. After literally thousands of complaints, a series of relatively small-scale legal actions were taken.[19] The sad reality was that the paradigm of Irish local government on environmental questions was simply one of technical management.

There was a belief in eventually 'engineering away' problems with new sewage plants or waste infrastructure. Solutions would be found through technical modernization, but phased in over time. That same civil engineering world-view also explains how incineration was so uncritically accepted as a waste management 'solution' in the late 1990s. Given the predominance of civil engineers in key local government environmental jobs, it was not surprising. The idea of having a strong legal enforcement ethos was rare. Some councils have only recently hired dedicated environmental or planning enforcement officers. For example, only in 2004 did Dublin Councils agree to establish a dedicated five-person environmental enforcement unit.[20] Nor were Irish local governments given detailed rules to follow on *how* they were supposed to enforce environmental standards. By way of contrast, Danish local governments have to meet a minimum number of environmental inspections per annum.[21] Nothing like this exists in Ireland.

Since 2004 Irish local governments are obligated to record how many environmental complaints they receive and how many investigations and prosecutions they carry out. In 2004, they investigated 44,964 cases of pollution. They instigated enforcement proceedings (although not necessarily prosecutions) in 7,260 cases: just 16 per cent. No commentary was provided about the vast majority of cases where no enforcement measures were taken. Presumably a great many of these were bogus or trivial complaints. Yet could *all* 84 per cent of the cases not followed up be trivial?[22]

With regard to planning enforcement complaints, Irish local governments investigated a total of 10,176 cases in 2004. Of these, 16 per cent were dismissed, and only 7.4 per cent were prosecuted. The majority received merely warning letters or enforcement notices.[23] Wide discrepancies have also emerged between the numbers of initial planning permissions granted by some local governments but subsequently reversed by An Bord Pleanála.[24] The performance of the thirty-four City and County Councils local governments on waste management was also revealed for 2004. On average, just 19.4 per cent of household waste was recycled and 79.6 per cent was landfilled, but there were again very wide variations in performance.[25]

Specialist environmental regulatory expertise remains limited. For example, pollution-related health concerns were (and still are) simply passed on to local Health Services Executives'[26] statutory medical officers, who typically have no background in assessing toxicological risks associated with various forms of complex pollution. Since the founding of the EPA in 1993 there has been a tendency for local councils to refer complex scientific matters to the EPA. Yet the relationship between the concerns of the local oriented councils and the nationally oriented EPA have not always married well.

Although pollution licensing was effectively handed over to the EPA since 1993, planning permission was kept separate and the preserve of local councils. Apparently, the rationale was to keep neat administrative boundaries, and not burden the EPA with planning matters. But this meant local concerns and knowledge were not always given due priority in EPA licensing. Nor could local governments attach environmental conditions to any planning permit, and appellants couldn't raise environmental issues before An Bord Pleanála.[27] Since 2000 they can do so, but the Board and local governments are still not allowed attach environmental conditions to their planning decisions. In practice this is nonsense, as planning and environmental issues are inexorably linked. The outcome has been a time-wasting administrative hurdle for both environmentalists and those seeking EPA licenses, as they follow a twin-track planning and environment authorization process. An integrated single environment and planning permit solution would seem both logically feasible and preferable.

Finally, the absence of strong fiscal powers has also led to a weakness in capacity for local environmental governance in Ireland. The long running saga of 'water/waste' charges in Ireland has already been recounted in the last chapter. The result today is that local governments have to squeeze as much revenue as they possibly can from what becomes a regressive flat tax on waste alone. They are not free to impose taxes or charges on water consumption, nor on traffic congestion, nor on other environmental 'bads'.

The problem of regulatory independence

Perhaps the most serious weakness evident in Irish local councils has been a conflict of interest between their role as local referees over planning and their wider agenda as promoters of local economic development. They build roads, and new housing, and refurbish public spaces and other physical infrastructure. Up until the early 1990s they did such activities effectively without any planning permission and under ministerial supervision. Since then, their developments must go through a very minimalist procedure of basically conferring with other state agencies such as the Heritage Council or the EPA, and the submission of a written report to councillors, who have some rights to either refuse go-ahead or demand changes.[28] This is effectively a system of 'self-permission' even if appeal by third parties is possible to Bord Pleanála.

This observation neatly brings to the fore the problem of regulatory independence. According to Allen, heavy but informal political pressure would often be placed upon local council staff in the 1970s and 1980s to drop environment or safety objections over any proposed factory.[29] Local councils have also run appalling landfills, sometimes without, or in contravention of, planning permission. There remains speculation about the extent of *de facto* collusion in illegal waste dumping practices, although this has been proven in at least one European Court of Justice (ECJ) case.[30]

Giving planning permission requires expertise balanced by common sense, basic procedural fairness and transparency, but above all, complete independence. Under the current set-up of Irish local governance, it should be obvious that the latter condition cannot be assured. Council planners will be under the direction of the all powerful City or County Manager. This is not an institutional set-up conducive to ensuring that planning or environmental regulation is free from serious conflicts of interests, or the threat of political or administrative manipulation.

It is worth recalling that one rationale for the creation of the EPA in 1993 was precisely that local governments had lost credibility as environmental regulators: they were, far too often, serious polluters themselves. A separation of powers was called for. It is intriguing that the logic of a separation of powers had not been extended to the local level of planning permission or environmental inspection.

In fact, 'regulatory independence' has proved very controversial for the EPA itself. Environmentalists allege it is simply too lenient and favourable to industry in granting licences and its inspection regime. In contrast, Shipan has argued that the Irish EPA should be regarded as perhaps *more* independent than most other European environmental agencies.[31] However, his approach may be criticized as lacking qualitative detail.[32] Measuring regulatory independence as a formal institutional attribute, as he does, is one thing. But regulatory independence is not merely a function of formal legal powers. It is as much a matter of institutional reputation. If any regulator loses its reputation for independence, this can be fatal. It might then be better to suggest that while the Irish EPA should be regarded as formally free from obvious political manipulation, the evolution of its informal reputation has been problematic. Shipan's relatively benign view is not shared by Irish environmentalists, nor by all academics. For example, the accounts provided by Taylor are highly critical of the agency's style of working.[33]

The EPA has spent the first decade of its existence overly obsessed with the technicalities of Integrated Pollution Prevention Control (IPPC) licensing. Only recently has it begun to orient itself towards a general environmental policing role, which is what Ireland badly needs. Yet even Shipan notes that 'over the last several years, we see evidence of a small, but steady, drop in monitoring and enforcement activities, once the number of licences is controlled for'.[34]

It should be remembered that if IPPC licensing is to live up to its promise, it requires proactive agency outreach with target firms to get them to push continually for reduced emissions. That should mean more inspections, visits, and monitoring, not less. It is not prudent to have the state's leading environmental watchdog undertaking less scrutiny of the permits it issues.

The performance of the EPA since 2003 with regard to inspection has been mixed. The number of audits undertaken in 2005 was lower than either 2004 or 2003, as were the number of inspections. The number of monitoring inspections fell significantly in 2005, compared with years 2001–4, while the levels of notification of non-compliance have on average increased during the period 2001–5. This suggests problems with licence compliance. While the EPA has placed great stress on increased prosecutions in 2004–5, even in 2001 the agency was able to sustain a dozen or more cases. Their prosecution rate has at best then doubled. Activities which have unquestionably expanded greatly are the investigation and auditing of local governments' environmental functions. Table 4.1 provides details of this data, although in many cases it is qualified by divergent reporting practices from year to year.

Facts and figures aside, the subjective reputation of the agency with environmentalists has unquestionably worsened. Most Irish environmentalists are openly sceptical about the agency. One mainstream environmentalist described the EPA to me as 'just a pollution licensing outfit'. Key personnel changes have furthered their doubts. First, Dr Mary Kelly, a noted environmental policy expert, was appointed Director-General of the agency from 2002. Previously she had a high profile stance as the head of the environmental lobbyist team for the Irish business and employers representative group, IBEC. During her role in that position, she established a track record of opposition to carbon taxes and even offered a cautious defence of the controversial US decision not to ratify the Kyoto agreement.[35] Then, in July 2004, a former employee of Indaver Ireland, a Belgian waste management company, was appointed by the government as a

TABLE 4.1 OVERVIEW OF EPA REGULATORY ACTIVITIES FOR THE YEARS 2001–2005.

	2001	2002	2003	2004	2005
IPC/IPPC licences granted	48	39	40	41	29
Waste licences granted	35	30	36	33	26
No. of audits (both IPC/IPCC & Waste)	59**	126**	191	274	173
No. of inspections (both IPC/IPCC & Waste)	445**	597**	854	867	703
No. of complaints (both IPC/IPCC & Waste)	1,737*	1,273*	1,047	1,077	1,123
No. of monitoring inspections (both IPC/IPCC & Waste)	1,126**	1,096	1,224***	1,136	675
No. of notifications of non-compliance issued (both IPC/IPCC & Waste)	296**	496	653	718	619
No. of prosecutions undertaken	13**	11	20	17	20
No. of convictions secured	12**			16	16
No. of cases pending				22	12
No. of audits of local govt. activities		4****	25****	50	22
No. of investigations of local govts.				281	244

Notes:

* These figures for complaints relate to IPC/IPPC licences only, and they also include complaints submitted by both the public and the licensee themselves. Later EPA data do not make that distinction and they include complaints on waste licences.

** These figures are for IPC/IPCC licences only, therefore comparison is limited with later years.

*** In 2003 this category is referred to as 'Emission Monitoring Visits'. The terminology is not repeated in other years. I have assumed it is similar to 'monitoring visits' provided for in other years.

**** These figures relate to audits of water pollution activities only.

Source: EPA(2001), EPA(2002c), EPA(2003a), EPA(2004f), EPA(2005j).

director of the EPA. It was this same company that would be granted controversial licences for incinerators in Cork harbour and Meath in 2005. It must be noted that, in all details concerning these licence applications, this individual has *not* been involved in consideration of the cases,[36] and there is no suggestion that she has ever acted improperly. However, environmentalists construed her appointment as placing an advocate for incineration into the very heart of the independent environmental regulator. The Green Party called for her appointment to be stopped.[37]

Perhaps a more substantive turning point for the reputation of the Irish EPA with the wider public was the so-called 'Askeaton Inquiry' into unexplained animal and alleged human health problems in the Shannon estuary. The site is near a large aluminium smelting plant and a coal-fired electricity station. The EPA's scientists in their final report, issued in 2001, were inconclusive, but controversially ruled out any link involving industrial pollution.[38]

This report was viewed by local farmers as a whitewash, and noted international scientists challenged some of its methodological aspects.[39] From the EPA's perspective, the entire Askeaton controversy was something of a burden it had not sought: a complex six-year multi-agency[40] inquiry with heated political lobbying and debate. Askeaton reinforced an institutional culture within the EPA, which believed they should primarily focus on permitting and not try to act as an environmental 'fire brigade' for disputes that inevitably become politicized.

Unfortunately, an environmental 'fire-brigade' with real authority, wide expertise, and an unquestioned reputation is exactly what Ireland badly needed. One commentator summed up well at least part of the problem at the heart of the Askeaton saga by arguing: 'The greatest failure of the affair, however, is not the lack of answers but the lack of response by officials to the earliest complaints from the farmers. Concerns about animal illness arose in Askeaton in the late 1980s and can be documented as far back as the early 1990s'.[41] The EPA was functioning by 1993, so just what was it doing to engage with such public complaints and why did it take until 2001 to produce an inconclusive report? Even in July 2005 Cork harbour suffered a serious pollution incident, which the EPA was yet again very slow to respond to adequately.[42]

Another anomaly is the curious provision whereby the EPA hears appeals upon its own preliminary decisions to grant IPPC or waste licences.[43] For example, in October 2004 the EPA issued a draft waste management permit to Indaver Ireland for the operation of a hazardous waste incinerator in Cork harbour. When this was challenged by local environmentalists, their concerns were adjudicated upon by the EPA itself! Padraig Larkin, a Director-General of the EPA, even admitted this situation was 'somewhat unusual'.[44]

One other deficiency of the agency is an apparent weakness in medico-toxicological expertise as part of its licensing procedures. The EPA is in fact statutorily bound to consider waste licences with regard to human health, but the question is whether it has the required expertise to do this. During the hearings for the two incinerators at Cork harbour, repeated medical evidence was advanced.[45] The final report of the oral hearing mostly disposed of such arguments, by reliance on general studies which suggest modern incinerators should be safe, if operating correctly to latest EU emissions standards.[46] Given Cork harbour's existing concentration of chemical firms, what was more at issue were the site-specific risks. In the end the EPA decided, based on highly technical and statistical evidence, that any further air emissions would be within EU limits and the absorptive capacity of the harbour environment.[47]

In November 2005 licences for both the Cork harbour and Meath incinerators were issued. Some stringent conditions were attached, such as a monitoring frequency in excess of what is demanded under EU legislation. However, the consideration given to risks arising from mixing of wastes, and the need for its sorting and classification, was basically left to be resolved at a later stage between the EPA and Indaver.[48] One of the big fears of anti-incineration activists was that a general mixed waste stream would end up being burned, containing some potentially harmful materials.

Moreover, Director-General Kelly herself had previously written to the Minister for Health in 2003 to explain that the EPA was *not* equipped to provide baseline health assessments of subsequent risks posed by incinerators to local populations. She therefore requested his Department to become involved in assuaging fears and undertaking research.[49] A Health Research Board (HRB) report on health risks associated with incinerators and landfills had earlier become available. Its findings were not as clear-cut as supporters or detractors of incinerators would have liked, but it did note that safety was strongly related to site-specific issues, how plants were managed, and that health monitoring should be a capacity that authorities should have both before and after the operation of any incinerator.[50] In the final report of the oral hearing it was noted that a health monitoring capability was only beginning to be put in place.[51] In fact, no specialist medico-toxicological unit exists within the EPA and much was made of this point by objectors to the incinerators.[52]

Any fair assessment of the Irish EPA cannot be that it is just a 'front' for Irish business to allow them lax pollution permits. Nonetheless, there clearly are serious problems in the way the EPA has evolved. Since 1993, it has mostly seen itself as a technical agency for working with industry to deliver a technical permitting system, together with some scientific backup for local and national government. Its language and mindset was that of the laboratory natural sciences. What it seems to be tortuously evolving towards is a more responsive environmental policing agency. Such an agency will have to develop a much greater accent on legal expertise, regulatory economics, and political science insights on compliance.

The problem is that such change may be too slow, and far too late to alter the reputation of the agency. Significantly, the Green Party have called for major reform of the EPA, making this a key demand for entry into any future coalition.[53] In particular, they have argued that future directors might come from the ranks of environmental NGOs rather than waste businesses.

IRELAND'S IMPLEMENTATION RECORD: A GROWING CRISIS

In the closing days of September 2005, it was reported that Ireland was facing large EU fines, of circa €21,600 per day. Ireland had not followed-up on a European court decision some years earlier, which had found that Ireland had failed to implement properly the important Environmental Impact Assessment (EIA) directives, with respect to peat cuttings.[54] This one event captures how woeful Ireland's implementation of environmental policy has become, and it is indicative of a numbing complacency among Irish political decision-makers. In other EU states, such a story would be front-page news. In Ireland, it was greeted with muted disdain and consigned to the middle pages.

In fact, the implementation and enforcement of environmental policy has been consistently revealed in academic evaluations to be one critical variable that simply makes or breaks the success of environmental measures. After all, it matters little how good an environmental law is on paper, or how well designed a particular scheme is in theory. If they are both ignored on the ground, they are worthless. However, it should be obvious that implementation of any set of environmental laws is never 100 per cent. All states experience problems, many of which are routine delays and glitches, or simply honest mistakes.

The implementation of EU environmental laws has been a very serious problem for nearly *all* member states. Environmental laws are consistently the biggest single problem area for the EU, perhaps accounting for as much as 40 per cent of all court cases initiated by the Commission.[55] Typically, these involve cases where directives are either transposed into national law too late, poorly, or sometimes not at all. Yet most complaints seldom end up in litigation with the Commission: as little as 15 per cent. Finally, the problem of implementation also relates to basic Irish statute laws and regulations as well.

How bad is Ireland's implementation of environmental policy?

How bad is the Irish record on implementation of environmental laws? That question has generated heated debate within the Irish media.[56] Both the Commission and Irish environmentalists have produced assessments of the Irish performance that place Ireland among the very worst offenders.[57] Yet is Ireland's track record here exceptionally bad?

Ireland is, generally speaking, not the very worst offender. A larger volume of more persistent cases of poor implementation in the environment sector can be linked to states like Belgium, France, Italy, or Spain. However, Ireland has become consistently worse at the implementation of EU environmental laws over the last decade. Her cases of non-compliance are also getting to be of a much more serious type. From being a well *below* average offender, Ireland has risen to become an *above* average offender. Also, the relationship with the Commission staff responsible for ensuring that member states apply EU laws has become adversarial, fraught and, at times, openly hostile.[58]

Yet complacency reigns in the face of this growing problem. When challenged about Ireland's implementation record, many civil servants simply repeat the mantra: 'we are not the worst'. Another line taken is to assert that problems are mainly a thing of the past.[59] To silence critics Irish authorities have also lately taken to trotting out the statistic that Ireland has 'a transposition rate of 98 per cent'.[60]

However, the measure of 'transposition' is merely a count of the number of EU laws that have been formally converted into the Irish legal system as required under EU law for any one year. It is a crude quantitative measure of paper shuffling and rubber-stamping. It does not measure the *quality* of that exact legal transposition. In several important European Court cases, this was revealed to be seriously deficient in Ireland, most notably with regard to EIAs or waste permits. Anyhow, nearly all EU states can now point to transposition figures in the high 80–90 per cent range.[61]

Notwithstanding problems interpreting data,[62] better measures of Ireland's implementation can be gleaned from a variety of Commission sources. These reveal a picture of a country that has steadily worsened in its ability to implement EU environmental laws.

For example, Chart 4.1 below measures cases of *serious* implementation problems for the environment sector. It also compares Ireland's performance over the period 1993–2003 with that of a peer group (Portugal, Greece and Denmark), as well as the EU average. What is being measured here are incidences of where a member state has not yet responded to a negative verdict of the ECJ, after they have been prosecuted by the Commission for a serious implementation failure. This is a good measure of implementation problems, assuming that only the most serious cases go all the way to court, because it captures over a long period of time the most important rather than the trivial cases.

Chart 4.1 clearly shows Ireland rising from an almost perfect zero score for most of the 1990s, to actually having, by 2003, some five verdicts of the ECJ hanging over it. In that year Ireland also reached the EU average level, so it is true this table does not place Ireland among the worst offenders (France, Belgium, Germany and Italy would all stand out in that category). However, it is noticeable how the Irish performance has steadily worsened. Ireland, originally nowhere near as bad as Portugal or Greece in the early 1990s, had by 2003 exceeded their ranking.

An understanding of the *quality* of legal transposition is also needed, rather than a crude count of how many directives have been processed. The tables below, based on an official Commission

CHART 4.1 NUMBER OF ECJ VERDICTS PER ANNUM OUTSTANDING AGAINST MEMBER
STATES ON ENVIRONMENTAL ISSUES, 1993–03.

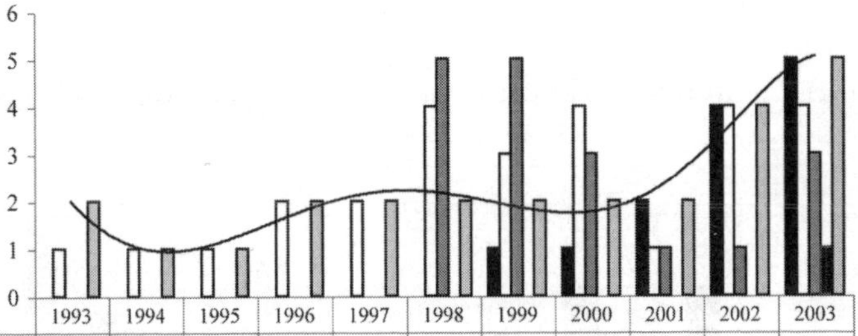

	1993	1994	1995	1996	1997	1998	1999	2000	2001	2002	2003
■ Ireland	0	0	0	0	0	0	1	1	2	4	5
☐ Greece	1	1	1	2	2	4	3	4	1	4	4
▨ Portugal	0	0	0	0	0	5	5	3	1	1	3
■ Denmark	0	0	0	0	0	0	0	0	0	0	1
☐ EU AV	2	1	1	2	2	2	2	2	2	4	5

■ Ireland	☐ Greece	▨ Portugal
■ Denmark	▨ EU AV	—— Poly. (EU AV)

Source: CEC (2004), CEC (2003), CEC (2002a), CEC (2001), CEC (2000b), CEC 1999a), CEC (1998),
CEC (1997), CEC (1996), CEC (1995), CEC (1994).

scoreboard produced annually since 2001, provide us with some
measure of this.

These record *three* different types of implementation problem,
of varying seriousness. The first are simple non–communication
cases, where a member state fails to transpose on time an
environmental law and therefore does not formally communicate
to the Commission exactly how it has put the directive into
effect. The second problem is non-conformity between an EU
environmental directive and domestic legal measures. In some
cases, such a mismatch may not be very serious. Yet it can
occasionally involve deliberate watering down of a national law
to avoid the full rigour of an EU environmental law. The third
measure records cases of 'bad application'. These describe a
situation where an EU environmental directive has been properly
transposed into the national legal system on paper, but in reality
it is being wrongly applied by national authorities or *de facto*
ignored. It provides a measure of the more *serious* implementation problems.

With respect to the simple cases of non-communication, Chart
4.2 reveals Ireland's recent performance as just average, almost
literally. Greece, by way of comparison, appears systematically
above average in having this type of problem.

CHART 4.2 NUMBER OF ANNUAL ENVIRONMENTAL NON-COMMUNICATION CASES
FOR SELECTED EU STATES 2001–4.

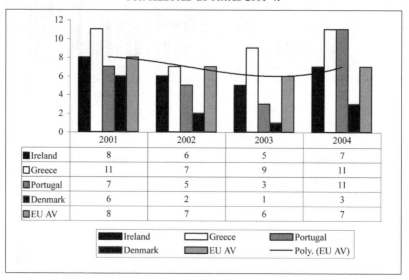

	2001	2002	2003	2004
■ Ireland	8	6	5	7
□ Greece	11	7	9	11
■ Portugal	7	5	3	11
■ Denmark	6	2	1	3
■ EU AV	8	7	6	7

Sources: CEC (1999b), CEC (2000a), CEC (2002b), CEC (2003b), CEC (2004d).

CHART 4.3 NO. OF ANNUAL CASES OF NON-CONFORMITY WITH EU
ENVIRONMENTAL LAWS FOR SELECTED MEMBER STATES 2001–2004.

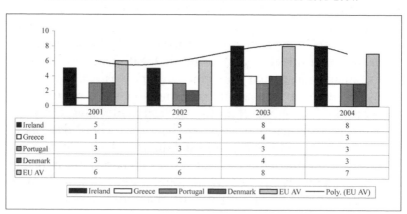

	2001	2002	2003	2004
■ Ireland	5	5	8	8
□ Greece	1	3	4	3
■ Portugal	3	3	3	3
■ Denmark	3	2	4	3
□ EU AV	6	6	8	7

Source: CEC (1999b), CEC (2000a), CEC (2002b), CEC (2003b), CEC (2004d).

CHART 4.4 NUMBER OF ANNUAL CASES OF BAD APPLICATION OF EU
ENVIRONMENTAL LAWS 2001–2004, FOR SELECTED EU COUNTRIES.

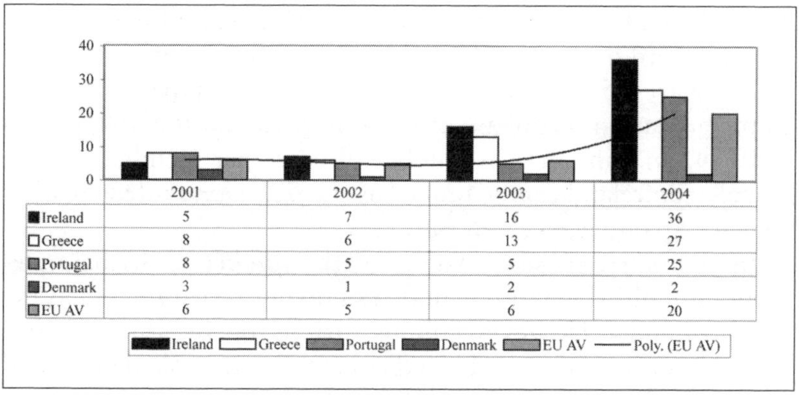

	2001	2002	2003	2004
■ Ireland	5	7	16	36
□ Greece	8	6	13	27
▨ Portugal	8	5	5	25
■ Denmark	3	1	2	2
▨ EU AV	6	5	6	20

Legend: ▨ Ireland □ Greece ▨ Portugal ■ Denmark ▨ EU AV ——— Poly. (EU AV)

Source: CEC (1999b), CEC (2000a), CEC (2002b), CEC (2003b), CEC (2004d).

CHART 4.5 AVERAGE NUMBER OF ALL CASES OF NON-COMMUNICATION, NON-
CONFORMITY AND BAD APPLICATION OF ENVIRONMENTAL LAWS, PER ANNUM FOR
EACH MEMBER STATE (2001–2004).

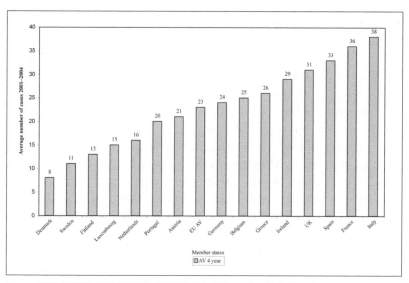

Source: CEC (1999b), CEC (2000a), CEC (2002b), CEC 2003b), CEC (2004d).

However, Chart 4.3 reveals that Ireland during the period
2001–4, had a steadily worsening record with regard to cases of
non-conformity. Even within the last two years up to 2004,
Ireland has either met or exceeded the general EU average.

Chart 4.4 shows that Ireland's cases of bad application, which are serious, have steadily increased. Between 2002 and 2004, Ireland significantly *exceeded* the EU average and had a much worse record than either Greece or Portugal to boot.

As Chart 4.5 shows, when all three different types of cases of implementation problem are taken together for the period 2001–4, and an average number of cases per member state is calculated, Ireland can be ranked as the *fifth worst* offender, after the UK, Spain, France and Italy.[63]

In summary, these measures of the *quality* of Irish implementation of EU environmental laws do not reveal Ireland as the worst offender. However, coming fifth in the assessment above must be considered a terrible indictment. It is notable that Ireland appears to have a worse record than her peer group of Portugal, Greece and Denmark. In relative and comparative terms there can be no question but that Ireland is faring badly.

Finally, how should one evaluate the Irish performance with respect to implementing and enforcing domestic legislation, rather than EU environmental laws? In practice it is hard to distinguish between the two categories, as much of domestic environmental law is now enacted to implement EU directives. Irish authorities do not generally publish statistics on the number of cases of implementation problems. Nonetheless, one can glean an impression of serious problems, and again a distinct sense of complacency, feeding into a slowly dawning crisis.

The uncovering since 2001 of several illegal waste sites exposed the lax state of Irish environmental law enforcement. The major scandal here involved dumps in Wicklow, where perhaps as much as 600,000 tonnes of waste from construction and even hospitals was secretly buried. The EPA has estimated that at least twenty-five illegal landfill and fifteen illegal waste handling yards existed in 2005, although the agency believed that large-scale dumping such as in Wicklow was no longer occurring. About 21 per cent of Irish households were also not availing of any waste collection service in 2003, with their waste presumably being disposed of irregularly as well.[64] Another trend has been well organized waste smuggling networks exporting waste to Northern Ireland and even Scotland.[65] In one ECJ case, Limerick City Council was found to have persistently and illegally dumped waste on sensitive wetlands in flagrant breach of European and Irish law.[66]

One independent source of information on the state of Irish implementation of environmental laws is the office of the Irish Ombudsman. As many as 27 per cent of her complaints now relate to planning and environmental matters and she has been very critical of local governments failing to sufficiently enforce planning and environmental laws. Her analysis is that there remains an apparent lack of willpower, organization, leadership, or a sense of urgency to tackle illegal developments. She has noted that official Irish departmental (DEHLG) statistics reveal that for the year 2002, only 436 out of 1,710 planning enforcement orders were complied with: barely a quarter.[67] Chart 4.6 provides details on planning enforcement actions and convictions secured. There have been strange variations in the volume of planning enforcement activities in recent years, and the actual number of convictions has declined since 2001.

CHART 4.6 NUMBER OF PLANNING ENFORCEMENT PROCEEDINGS INITIATED BY IRISH LOCAL GOVERNMENTS, AND NUMBER OF CASES RESULTING IN CONVICTION, 1993–2004.

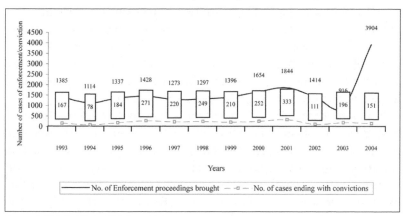

Source: DEHLG (2004a), DELG (1998a).

A proceduralist and reactionary implementation culture

Why is Ireland getting worse at implementing environmental policy? One frequently cited answer by many interviewees[68] was that there was no political prioritization placed upon environmental questions. The environment was not and is still not seen as being important enough. For example, one interviewee noted that in Denmark or other EU countries, warning letters from the Commission regarding some implementation problem would provoke searching parliamentary questions. It would be seen as politically significant. Not in Ireland.

Two other negative aspects of Ireland's administrative culture are also culprits: a *proceduralist* and a *reactionary* administrative style of working. The first of these problems is a culture of *proceduralism*. This involves a fixation upon the paper-based procedures involved with implementation. EU directives have to be turned into Irish ministerial regulations or statute laws. This means in practice there is little energy left for actually enforcing these regulations. The *substantive* issues of implementation are left less explored while the procedures and formalities take up the bulk of effort.

The second problem is a *reactionary* style: Irish administrative staff are continually playing catch up with the huge volume of EU legislation. EU directives are often left on the 'back-burner' until the last moment. There is then a mad rush to meet the deadline in a flurry of activity.[69] There are few examples of prioritizing the most important directives for early transposition and enforcement, although the major Water Framework Directive of 2000 has arguably received good handling so far.[70] This culture comes straight from the 'top down': a lack of political direction and leadership at the very highest levels is to blame.

It is true that a lack of awareness among the administrative and political class may help excuse the poor implementation record of the 1980s. At that time, the then Department of the Environment and Local Government was simply sending out administrative circulars to notify local governments about the existence of some new EU directive. Rulings by the ECJ in the later 1980s made it clear that this practice was unsatisfactory, because such measures lacked the force of law. 'Lack of awareness' used as an excuse cannot be credible post 2000, when Ireland has had twenty-seven years of experience with EU environmental laws and procedures.

The greatest implementation failure has been with the Habitats and Birds Directives. These have proven incredibly difficult in nearly every member state. However, in Ireland, property rights and land ownership are very emotive. More simply, Irish farmers constitute a powerful constituency. They initiated a number of highly successful campaigns to have both directives implemented gradually. One academic assessment put things rather bluntly: 'Buying off the (Irish) farmers was the key to unlocking the transposition process.'[71]

Problems here were also institutional. Responsibility for these EU nature and biodiversity laws was uneasily divided between rival departments in the 1990s. The result was a tussle for dominance in their implementation between the powerful Department of Agriculture and the weak and new Arts, Culture and the Gaeltacht Department.

In the middle of all of this was the weak 'cinderalla' national heritage agency, Dúchas. They faced incredible political pressure. If they speeded up the process of legal designation of ecologically sensitive lands, their political masters would face heavy lobbying from farmers and landowners. If they slowed down, this would and did lead to habitats loss, and conflict with environmentalists and the Commission. In the end, Dúchas became 'pig in the middle'. It was the butt of criticism from every quarter. Morale sank, and the agency retreated to a defensive posture.[72] It was no surprise when in 2003 Dúchas was effectively abolished and its staff and personnel incorporated into the DEHLG. This was a move which was widely interpreted as placing the issues of land designations under firmer political control.[73] Once again one can question such a move on the grounds of regulatory independence. Should personnel tasked with the sensitive and highly technical job of designating lands which are ecologically sensitive under EU laws be under such direct ministerial supervision, or should they be in a separate agency?

A persistent failure was also a weak legal basis for designations. This was critical, because a court case in 1994 had declared earlier Irish scientific designations of habitats to be an unconstitutional interference with property rights. What was needed was a dedicated comprehensive Act of the Oireachtas, for example a new Biodiversity or Habitats Act. What Dúchas got were dribs and drabs of *ad hoc* regulations instead.

For example, by the end of the 1990s Irish authorities had cobbled together a mechanism by which, both informally and formally, landowners could challenge their designation. They could have it removed or modified. The *formal* appeals board for this, while generally agreeing to reach decisions scientifically, was an organization not distinct from the machinery of the civil service. Nor was it based on a proper statutory footing.

Environmentalists complained that the *informal* process of consultation was basically unsound because it lacked transparency. It was turning into an *ad hoc* negotiation with landowners, to reduce the extent of protected lands.[74] As if to confirm such worries, the Ombudsman found in 2005 that Dúchas staff in 1999 had made a designation required under EU environmental law to protect birds in a way that lacked proper legal authority. It also excluded fifty acres of land from designation that was to be used by Dublin port authorities for landfill, following *informal* discussions with them.[75]

Yet such institutional weakness in implementation was widespread. At the heart of this was, once again, poor local governance. For example, applications for waste permits from local governments during the mid 1990s were taking on average over two years. Some took as long as four years, revealing one reason why illegal dumping grew in the 1990s.[76] Eventually, after being prodded by the Commission, Ireland admitted her administrative and institutional failures with regard to implementation. The Office of Environmental Enforcement (OEE) was established in 2003, but within the national EPA. This was to offer a dedicated national environmental enforcement agency and one that would police local governments as much as firms.[77]

There has been a notable upsurge in prosecution and investigative activity (detailed in Table 4.1). There has even been structured collaboration with specialist Irish Garda policing units. By 2002, County Council staff together with Gardaí could be found in roadside checkpoints to prevent illegal waste smuggling. A number of local governments were finally prosecuted by the OEE in 2005, a major institutional turning point.[78]

However, Liam Reid, a journalist who has extensively covered the illegal waste traffic story for years, has argued that these measures are still basically not enough: 'The current enforcement system is patchy at best and has proved inadequate to deal with this waste trafficking. The prosecutions have been sporadic, with at most modest fines in the District Courts, nothing to deter illegal operators who can get to share profits of €4,000 per load.'[79]

It is true that fines are typically low: not one of the local governments prosecuted in 2005 had to pay more than €10,000 in fines or costs. The derisory nature of the fines was also evident in the case of an operator of an illegal waste dump in County Wexford, who at District Court level was fined on three counts a grand total of €900. Even including the costs of legal representation here, this is still a paltry fine for a repeat offender.[80] In 2006 the EPA eventually succeeded in imposing its highest ever fine of €42,329 through a court action. This was for a prosecution against a Clare-based pharmaceutical company after admitting they had been responsible for an incredible *eleven* breaches of their IPPC licence.[81] Considering that fines of up to €15 million have been made possible in recent legislation, this reveals that industrial polluters do not pay very much.

It is also worrying that it took until 2005 for the Irish Minister for the Environment to issue policy directives which clarified what exactly local governments should do when they uncovered illegal waste dumping, such as removing it from residential areas and imposing liability for costs on landowners.[82] This directive was vital, because the only financial deterrent that would really scare those responsible for illegal waste dumps would be paying the full costs of remediation. That this policy was not in place until 2005 speaks volumes in itself.

In truth, the approach of (belatedly) getting tough with polluters through a legal crackdown armed with small fines is not entirely convincing. It is part of the reactionary regulatory culture I describe here. Legal prosecutions are in reality an admission of failure, as by that stage environmental damage has often been done. It usually takes a very long time for a court case to produce a verdict. For example, the time period from a citizen's complaint to the European Commission and thence to a court verdict from the ECJ in Luxembourg can be at least five years and up to a decade. What is needed is clearly a greater preventative effort, including preventative legal instruments such as wider use of injunctions.

Legal enforcement will always be required, but to achieve the most successful implementation of environmental policies requires consensual behaviour and, not infrequently, major financial support. It is notable how this was forthcoming for the politically powerful and savvy farming/landowner sector in the case of Habitats/Birds. Yet a historic absence of funding for local governments has been at the root of their many problems in waste management.

THE INSTRUMENT MIX: TOO FEW 'NEPIS'

As regards the policy instrument mix, Ireland has simply been too slow and too timid in experimenting with a range of new environmental policy instruments (NEPIs). Such NEPIs include green taxes, charges, negotiated environmental agreements with industry, pollution emissions trading, and a host of other detailed schemes.[83] While NEPIs are no panacea, it is clear that a *range* of sophisticated and modern environmental policy tools are necessary. Overdependence on traditional law is no longer tenable, especially if there are serious problems in implementing and enforcing laws.

But once again complacency is at the centre of events. Ireland appears to adopt NEPIs only when pushed to do so by the EU. Left to their own initiative, Irish policy-makers usually favour simpler and much cruder responses: a belief in legislating or else simply engineering away the problem.

Ireland's lukewarm uptake of eco-taxes: an ideological impediment to reform?

More specifically, Ireland seems to be very weak in the area of exploring green or ecological taxes. By way of contrast, the Nordic states have been experimenting with these since the early 1990s. Green taxes are now quite mainstream across Europe and their success is widely acknowledged.[84] However, the Irish domestic political scene is biased against introducing any truly significant green taxes. There have been taxes or charges on plastic bags, landfills and, more recently, waste electrical equipment. Yet a more strategic use of such taxes has been shunned. Indeed, as Chart 4.7 shows, the share of broadly defined environmental taxes as a percentage of GDP has actually fallen in Ireland between 1995 and 2002. Significantly, all the peer group countries of Greece, Portugal, and especially Denmark, have a higher share of such taxes. The Danes have actually *increased* their share of environmental taxes.

Industry lobbies, led principally by IBEC, have adopted a consistently strident line of argument *against* the imposition of any eco-taxes on energy. When an EU CO_2 tax was mooted in the 1990s, it was opposed by IBEC. The introduction of such a

CHART 4.7 ENVIRONMENTAL TAXES AS A PERCENTAGE OF GDP 1995–2002.

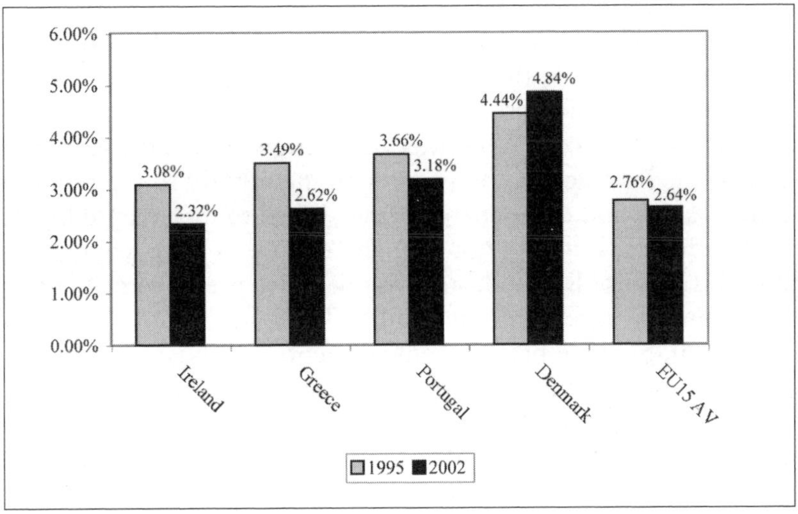

Source: Eurostat (2005), p.170.

fiscal instrument was eventually promised in a government National Climate Change Strategy (NCCS) of the late 1990s. According to the time-scale set out in that document, it was supposed to have been introduced in the budget of 2002.[85] After intense lobbying,[86] the proposed CO_2 tax was shelved indefinitely in September 2004. The rationale offered was that historically high oil prices were having similar effects or that the predicted reductions were likely to be small in scale.[87]

The case for a CO_2 tax was in truth never seriously considered. For example, emission reductions depend on the level at which any CO_2 tax operates over time, and most models of such a tax would have increased the rate on a phased basis. So initial gains might be modest, but later reductions, as an economy adjusts, would be larger. According to the Economic and Social Research Institute (ESRI), reductions in the order of 40 per cent could have been achieved.[88] Sustainable Energy Ireland (SEI), the Irish government's own expert energy conservation agency, also pointed out that further CO_2 reductions would have followed in the wake of the tax, through additional voluntary schemes which they were planning to introduce with industrial firms. These schemes would have helped firms reduce their tax liability and thus achieve even greater reductions.[89] In conclusion, Ireland refused to introduce a perfectly sensible tax measure, mainly due to lobbying and ideological bias.

Interestingly, the argument for a CO_2 tax refused to go away. In September 2005, the official state economic think-tank, the ESRI, published a controversial report advocating yet again the need for a CO_2 tax.[90] What was also intriguing was the generally hostile media reaction, pointing with incredulity to the report's timing, as oil and other energy prices soared to then record highs.

Another reason why not so many eco-taxes have been introduced is because Irish industrial lobbies have preferred negotiated or voluntary agreements instead.[91] These are agreements of a contractual nature between governments and business sectors. The parties undertake to perform certain environmental tasks or attain specified targets by a given date. The idea is that such agreements are more flexible than laws. Most environmental policy experts agree the effectiveness of such approaches have been very mixed, although there is no fundamental reason why they cannot deliver real benefits. This is especially the case if such agreements are properly designed and entered into seriously by the participants.

However, what has happened in Ireland is that voluntary agreements have become an alternative to eco-taxes rather than a complement. For example, during the 2004 debate over whether Ireland would introduce a CO_2 tax, the chief executive of Enterprise Ireland was critical of a proposed carbon tax on 'competitiveness' grounds. He suggested instead a negotiated agreement would be better, which of course would be purely voluntary for participants, unlike a tax.[92] Traditionally, IBEC have favoured voluntary approaches over green taxes.[93] In 2006, another voluntary agreement was negotiated between IBEC and the government, after a brief debate on introducing a levy on chewing gum to cover the costs of related littering.[94]

Other smaller schemes have included a voluntary phosphate detergents phase-out[95] and a farm plastic recycling scheme. The latter was working well, but has since encountered problems in collection of plastics for recycling. Its rules were therefore revised.[96] Two more recent voluntary agreements have concerned Construction and Demolition Material (CDM) waste and one on solid fuels. Both are too recent to be properly evaluated at this time.

The most significant voluntary agreement is the REPAK scheme for packaging waste. At first glance it appears very successful. Reports in May 2006 indicated that REPAK was recycling close to 66 per cent of packaging waste, and before that they had met their recycling targets for 2000 and 2005. Yet it was also acknowledged that much of this was being shipped to Northern Ireland, China, Spain or Scotland.[97] In any event, REPAK represents 65 per cent of the waste packaging stream. While that is impressive in theory, a persistent problem has been that eligible firms refused to join REPAK or to submit their own waste management plans to local governments.[98] As of April 2006, the EPA admitted that 280 non-compliant firms had been identified.[99]

As was shown in Chapter Two, of greater concern is that packaging waste volumes keep rising (except for 2004) as surely as REPAK gets better at recycling, The European Environment Agency (EEA), commenting on the Irish REPAK model, noted: 'Prevention and reduction of packaging amounts are not included . . . (and there was) an apparent loophole in the system, as major producers can pay waste contractors a price equivalent to recycle the amount of packaging they supplied in the previous quarter and never have to accept packaging waste back from customers or the public.'[100] One wonders would an Irish tax on packaging waste not have achieved the same results, faster, and with fewer evaders?

Unfortunately, tax has been stigmatized as a 'bad word' within Irish politics, and the official fiscal policies of the last decade have been geared towards successive major tax reductions: between 1995 and 2004 the tax burden was reduced from 33.1 per cent of Irish GDP to 30.2 per cent, well below the EU average of 39.3 per cent.[101] In theory this should mean there is more scope for new taxes. In practice the ideological realm of politics acts as an impediment.

This is not just a problem among policy elites who may hold neo-liberal views. The general Irish population appear hostile to taxes per se. Clinch and Dunne have examined why eco-taxes have not emerged in Ireland and, based on focus group research, they noted:

> People were suspicious and distrustful of the government in relation to tax policy. Most people felt they were already overtaxed and that if an extra tax were put on energy they

would be sceptical that it would be recycled . . . [and] an increase in the price level and higher inflation was a big fear. The participants were of the belief that bigger companies would simply pass on any increase in their taxes onto them, the consumers, and be able to write off most of it in a way that the ordinary taxpayer would not.[102]

In an earlier survey, respondents indicated that they supported environmental taxes in principle, but only 20 per cent admitted they would be prepared to pay more themselves.[103]

In fact, public support for eco-taxes might be more nuanced than is realized. Much depends on how they are presented, justified, and designed. A 2004 Eurobarometer survey of attitudes to environmental questions revealed that only 8 per cent of Irish respondents thought 'making everyone pay more in taxes' would be an effective policy response, whereas 35 per cent endorsed '*only* taxing those who cause environmental problems'.[104] These findings were almost exactly in keeping with the EU average level of support. However, they do not suggest anything other than lukewarm support for highly targeted fiscal measures. The 'tax' word is still a taboo.

Yet the idea that 'eco-taxes' must entail negative income effects is not at all valid. A 2001 EU-funded consultancy study of eco-taxes in Europe pointed to few concerns about income effects and indeed noted that exemptions were often granted far too leniently to placate interest groups worried about losses.[105] The Combat Poverty Agency (CPA), while concerned about the impacts of a CO_2 tax on low-income groups, also noted there were feasible policy measures available to offset such risks.[106] In fact, the ESRI have detailed how any CO_2 tax could be implemented in a way that would be more or less revenue neutral.[107] More importantly, they have also argued that such a tax could be introduced gradually, in a way that would not hit those on lower incomes hardest. Any criticisms that such green taxes must hurt the poor are unjustified.[108] As regards the macroeconomic effect of a CO_2 tax, the ESRI indicated that competitiveness losses associated with such a tax were not likely.[109] Indeed, the Nordic states, who have pioneered green taxes, are typically ranked among the most innovative, competitive, and egalitarian societies in the world. Green taxes can, if cleverly devised and executed, have positive economic effects on job creation, innovation, or savings.

There is actually, then, a logical case for what could be called 'eco-competitiveness' through green taxes. But this would be a policy of preaching virtue. Wider ideological resistance to the very idea of any eco-tax must first be overcome. In fact, a balanced debate is missing in Ireland, and it is one reason perhaps why Irish innovation with green taxes have been so disappointing. In its place has evolved a very crude debate about excessive taxation, when in fact Ireland has comparatively low taxes.

The 'eco-tax' innovations that have emerged then have been either marginal or stealthy in their style. This is understandable given public and elite views on tax. As the landfill levy and plastic bag tax have been discussed in previous chapters, this chapter avoids repeating any detailed observations about them. However, it should be emphasized that, while they appear to be generating meaningful revenue, they are quite conservative measures from an environmental perspective. For example, why just have a tax on plastic bags: why not upon all forms of non-biodegradable or non-reusable packaging? And why just tax landfills without taxing waste generation and sources of waste in the first place?

Irish eco-taxes remain small-scale and camouflaged. For example, in the late summer of 2005, a so-called 'Visible Environmental Management Charge' (VEMC) on electrical appliances and 'white goods' was imposed. This particular innovation was undertaken to comply with ambitious EU directives on waste electrical and electronic equipment (WEEE).[110] However, it must be stressed that the precise design of the charging scheme has been entirely developed by the Irish authorities themselves. Even though the EU is likely to be blamed for a new 'stealth tax', the legislation in question does not in fact specify how member states should implement charges or taxes to cover recycling of such goods. It merely demands that consumers can return their electrical goods to the point of sale for recycling, along with other obligations of a general nature. The situation is made more complex by the decision of some producers to simply absorb the cost, for example Irish based computer manufacturers, whereas most electrical goods retailers decided to pass it on to the consumer.[111]

There can be little doubt that this is a highly controversial environmental tax. Its effect is that of a regressive tax upon ordinary consumers. In fact, the intention of the EU's WEEE Directive was supposed to ensure that such recycling costs would be internalized by producers and retailers.[112] As Dermott Jewell of the Irish Consumers' Association argued: 'It is obvious the consumer is now being asked to cover the cost of the producers' waste, which is not what the polluter pays principle is about.'[113] Once again the nebulous 'polluter pays' principle was at the heart of the matter.

Leaving it to the market: the brave new world of Irish carbon emissions trading.

One of the biggest innovations in Irish environmental policy in recent years has been the arrival of emissions trading. In fact, the Irish Emissions Trading Scheme (ETS) is just a small part of a general EU-wide initiative, revealing how innovation has been encouraged by Brussels' leadership. Emissions trading appears at first glance to be a radical departure.

At its simplest, ETS allows firms to legally produce emissions (or pollution) up to a certain level: a 'cap' in the jargon. This is usually expressed in permits per tonne of a given gas. In the case of the Irish ETS it is tonnes of CO_2 equivalent. The level of a cap for each firm is usually based on their average historic baseline level of annual emissions, together with projected emissions, minus a certain amount to ensure pollution overall is reduced.[114] If the firm produces less than their set level ('cap') per annum, expressed in the number of permits per tonne, then they can sell their unused permits to other firms who have produced more emissions than they have permits for. Alternatively they might choose to 'bank' their spare permits for next year. At the end of each 'trading' year, all firms must either meet their 'cap' or buy extra permits to cover any extra emissions. Failure to do this results in a heavy fine and the entire system requires good monitoring from an environmental agency.

The EU ETS approach has allowed for a very wide degree of national autonomy in how each state designs and implements their own national ETS, called in the jargon a 'national allocation plan' (NAP). How has Ireland coped? Ireland's NAP has been unambitious. Firstly, one should note that the Irish ETS is really very small within an overall EU-wide context: only 106 Irish companies and institutions at 120 different large sites are covered, whereas within an EU context some 14,000 installations participate.

Secondly, criticisms were voiced by environmentalists about the process by which CO_2 permits were allocated. The consultation and public participation process was limited and grudging, especially at the initial stage.[115] A second round of refining allocations was made open to public comment. However, the detailed participation by environmentalists was absent at this stage, whereas the EPA held closed workshops with firms and bodies that were to be given permits.

The more substantive criticism has been that the Irish authorities were excessively lenient with large industrial firms, who are the main target of the EU ETS initiative. Other sectors of the economy are simply not covered. Leniency was expressed in two ways. Firstly, the Irish permit allowances given out to firms have been too generous. Secondly, why were these simply given away for free, when recipient firms could later sell these permits for money?

Environmentalists were certainly quick to allege that the Irish NAP as part of the EU ETS was something of a 'giveaway' on both counts.[116] In the first draft version of the NAP prepared by the Irish EPA in February of 2004, the participants collectively would have been allowed produce 22.5 million tonnes of CO_2 equivalent per annum between 2005 and 2008. This in effect would have meant a net *increase* on their prior level of emissions by as much as 0.2 million tonnes. However, this proved unacceptable to the European Commission. Irish environmentalists argued that the level should be no more than 17 million tonnes per annum, a much more ambitious level.

Eventually, a revised version of the Irish NAP was approved by the Commission in July 2004 with an annual total NAP of 19.2 million tonnes per annum.[117] The final Irish NAP, brought into force in March 2005, actually sets the level of reductions at a threshold of at least 97 per cent of projected emissions for the participants collectively, in other words a 3 per cent cut overall.[118]

However, the level of reductions sought from large industrial firms should have been higher, especially given the decision taken in September 2004 not to introduce a CO_2 tax. In any event, Irish participants within the ETS have not meet their annual target of 19.2 million tonnes. They have actually exceeded this substantially by producing circa 22.3 million tonnes.[119] The ETS scheme, in its first year, was simply not working.

The second area of controversy was the decision to make only very limited use of an auctioning of permits to firms. Under the Irish NAP, only some 502,201 tonnes will be auctioned to cover administration costs. This works out at just 0.75 per cent of the total NAP. Subsequently, the EPA claim that the amount involved will be up to 1 per cent of the NAP, and indeed a first auction was held in January 2006.[120] The remaining 99 per cent of permits have been given away free.

In fact, the EU common legal rules on ETS *precluded* any large-scale auction: only 5 per cent of permits could be distributed this way. The thinking here appears to have been basically one of political expediency. In order to get the scheme up and running and buy goodwill from industry, any large-scale auctioning of permits was set aside. However, this flies in the face of most expert economic analysis, which suggests that auctions of permits are an important way of ensuring any ETS initiative is truly effective.[121]

Even if the Irish authorities could have auctioned only 5 per cent of the permits, one wonders why they did not do so. Why was only a minimalist level of 1 per cent opted for? Other EU states have auctioned their full 5 per cent allowance, for example Denmark.[122] In fact, if just 5 per cent of the final existing allocation was auctioned at December 2004 prices of €10 per tonne, this could have yielded over €30 million for the government.[123] Finally, the issue of auctioning has not gone away. For the period 2008–12, auctioning of permits by each national authority will be permissible up to an increased level of 10 per cent.[124]

However, the real secret at the heart of Ireland's experiment with carbon emissions trading is not that it represents a 'giveaway' to big industrial firms operating in Ireland. Instead, what many commentators have failed to appreciate is that ETS will provide Irish governments with a politically easy way of 'buying' CO_2 reductions. By January 2005 the Irish Department of the Environment confirmed that it had revised its estimates, and would be likely to spend €185 million between 2008 and

2012 on carbon permits to reduce Ireland's emissions from 67 million tonnes to 60 million.[125]

Such a strategy is not cost free and indeed could be very risky if the price of CO_2 permits is volatile or soars. In fact, such volatility is already evident. The price of a permit had risen from below €7 in January 2005 to €22 by July of that year: a tripling of prices in less than a year.[126] The January 2006 EPA auction revealed prices of €26 per permit. However, in April 2006 prices crashed downwards, on foot of emissions data that showed there would be a surplus of permits. Too many EU countries had issued too many permits in an attempt to be generous with their big industries.[127]

Unfortunately, this approach plays a big part of where Ireland now finds itself headed after abandoning a CO_2 tax. The implications of such permit price volatility are that the Irish taxpayer is exposed to an uncertain cost. At least with a domestic CO_2 tax we would have had much more control and say over the distribution and scale of the costs involved.

The fairness of this approach would also seem wanting. The costs of such a strategy will be met from general taxation rather than from the sectors of the economy and society that are actually causing a disproportionate amount of our CO_2 emissions. One should remember that the sectors that are responsible for a greater share of Irish greenhouse emissions are chiefly transport, energy and agriculture. Yet *all* taxpayers will pay for buying CO_2 permits from general taxation. This is patently unfair.

CONCLUSIONS

Institutions, implementation and instruments matter for environmental policy. If any one of these elements is wanting, the quality of environmental policy is placed in doubt. This chapter has detailed, across these three headings, exactly where and how serious problems exist. One should be clear that this is not to recount a litany of who is to blame. In fact, this book argues we should stop seeing Irish environmental policies as mainly the responsibility of key persons, parties, or groups. The problems are deeper than this. They are institutionalized. Unfortunately, institutional reform will take time, thought, and real political leadership to deliver. There is no quick fix. This is one message this chapter offers.

However, there are other insights. One of these is the inter-relatedness of the three aspects of institutions, implementation, and instruments. Very often a weakness in one area spills over into undermining some other area. For example, weak Irish local government structures increased implementation problems. One can also see that if legal implementation is such a problem, serious consideration of using tax instruments is justified, rather than waiting around for the slow grind of justice at district court level. That is a recipe for continued failure. Therefore, the three headings, while distinct, are strongly linked. Progress on one heading requires progress on another.

Finally, common themes which have already been signalled throughout this book are evident in this chapter as well. The reek of complacency abounds and envelops any meaningful discussion on CO_2 taxes. Ireland has ditched CO_2 taxes, meaning she must depend even more on emissions trading. This implies ordinary taxpayers will pay more for meeting Ireland's demanding Kyoto obligations. An entire section of the political elite have simply given up on local government. The stock response to any sign of weakness or difficulty is to hand power to either City/County Managers under ministerial direction or to the EPA.

Complacency is also clear with regard to Ireland's experience in implementing environmental laws. A mediocre track record has been allowed to cascade into the status of a serious offender. Ireland is now being placed routinely in the dock, quite literally, in the guise of the European Court of Justice in Luxembourg. For the first time she faces the dubious distinction of being fined for not applying EU environmental laws properly. Complacency is also discernible more subtly in the story on emissions trading and eco-taxes.

Yet again, in this chapter the EU as a political entity emerges as a progressive force, steering, prodding and pushing the lukewarm Irish authorities towards a more sophisticated type of environmental policy. It was EU pressure that led to the establishment of the Office of Environment Enforcement: a rare example of 'hardware' changes at Brussels' behest. It is also within an EU framework that Ireland has begun to experiment with emissions trading, and it is from EU origins that one can trace the basic model for the REPAK packaging waste agreement as well. Yet a final puzzle remains perhaps unanswered here: how can Irish complacency on environmental matters be unseated other than through jolts of EU leadership? The next chapter embarks on providing something of an answer and maps out a reform agenda much informed by the arguments made here.

NOTES

1. O'Brien. T. 'Ireland exceeds quota for harmful emissions', *The Irish Times*, 16 May 2006. Under the EU Emission Trading Scheme (ETS), the Irish annual emissions quota was 19,238,190 tonnes of CO_2. In 2005 Irish emissions from large firms or institutions participating in the scheme were 22,397,678 tonnes.
2. I prefer to use the term local governments rather than local authorities where possible throughout this text.
3. Since the Local Government Act 2001, City and Borough Corporations have been renamed 'Councils'. Urban District Councils and Town Councils became Town Councils. As of 2006 there were twenty-nine County Councils (three covering Dublin alone), five City Councils, five Borough Councils, and seventy-five much smaller Town Councils. There are also eight regions, and two regional assemblies. These are not regional governments in the sense understood in continental Europe. They are more delegated planning bodies, staffed by appointed (not elected) councillors, seconded local government and civil service personnel, plus some new staff.
4. The sources for income for Irish local governments in 2002 could be divided into four principal headings: Central Government dedicated grants (28 per cent), a special Local Government Fund which provides bloc grants from the national government (19 per cent), rates on commercial premises (24 per cent), and charges for provision of services (29 per cent). One can quickly see here that almost half their income is directly controlled by the national government. A growing revenue stream in recent years are planning development levies. See LGMSB/Local Government Management Services Board, *Service Indicators in Local Authorities 2004. Report to the Minister for Environment, Heritage and Local Government. June 2005* (Dublin: LGMSB, 2005), p.12.
5. For general literature describing the centralized, if not authoritarian, nature of Irish local governance, see Daly, M.E. *The Buffer State: The History of the roots of the Department of the Environment* (Dublin: IPA/ Institute of Public Administration, 1997); Knox, C. and Haslem, R. 'Local government', in Collins, N. (ed.) *Political Issues in Ireland Today* (Manchester: MUP, 1999) pp.55–69; Callanan, M. and Keogan, J.F. *Local Government in Ireland: Inside Out* (Dublin: IPA/Institute of Public Administration,

2003); and Daly, M.E. (ed.) *County and Town: One Hundred Years of Local Government in Ireland* (Dublin: Institute of Public Administration, 2001).

6. The precise way this often would happen is as follows. A County or City Manager would claim before councillors that a matter was an 'executive function' and not a reserved function (see fn.13 below for an explanation). More subtly, where councillors vote to endorse in principle a course of action by a manager, the later execution of that policy could be claimed by a manager to be an executive function.

7. McDonald, F. 'Bin charges are just part of "polluter pays" policy', *The Irish Times*, 22 September 2003. The relevant provision which made setting a waste charge and grating waivers an executive function (one for a manager to make) is Article 52(8) of the Protection of the Environment Act 2003. Local councillors in Dublin City Council retaliated to that move by threatening to refuse to vote for the Council budget in 2004. See Kelly, O. 'Dublin Council may fall unless city manager changes waste charges', *The Irish Times*, 29 November 2004. Such rows also occurred in Tralee Urban District Council and Sligo County Council.

8. Section 4 of the Waste Management (Amendment) Act 2001 (Section 4), altered the previous Section 22 of the Waste management Act 1996 to allow the national Minister for the Environment to empower a manager to make a waste plan where an elected Council had refused or was unable to do so. The Protection of the Environment Act 2003, under its Section 26(2)b, further clarified the power of a County/City Manager to make any future waste plan, by declaring such to be an executive function.

9. See, for example, Kelly, O. 'Manager to proceed with plan for waste incinerator', *The Irish Times*, 16 September 2004. In that case, city councillors voted by a majority of thirty-two to five, against an incinerator. For Galway, see Siggins, L. 'Council rejects plan for Galway city incinerator', *The Irish Times*, 12 October 2004. For Cork, see Roche, B. 'Council rejects incinerator for Cork', *The Irish Times*, 29 November 2005.

10. See Humphreys, J. 'File on Waterford council official for DPP', *The Irish Times*, 30 November 2005. Note, however, that the high profile corruption case and conviction against a former assistant City Manager for Dublin was quashed in 2004. See Cullen, P. 'Redmond conviction for corruption quashed', *The Irish Times*, 29 July 2004.

11. By clientelism I mean a sociological phenomenon whereby voters give their votes to certain specified politicians, out of the expectation that they themselves will receive direct tangible benefits from the election of that particular politician. These benefits could be the securing of planning permission, a medical card, etc. For some specific examples related to listed buildings, see McDonald, F. 'At the heart of our towns', *The Irish Times*, 11 November 2000.

12. Aside from the example, discussed below, of Killarney (2006), rezoning in opposition to the expert advice of council planners was also undertaken in the following cases: in Meath a flood plain was rezoned for housing (2005); near the Battle of the Boyne site in Louth (2004); in Galway City

over the rezoning of industrial land to commercial use facilitating retail malls (2004) and perhaps most notorious of all in Wicklow, where seventeen rezonings were undertaken by councillors in the course of an eighteen hour meeting, all against the advice of the council planners. See O'Brien, T. 'Council rezones flood plain for housing', *The Irish Times*, 26 July 2005; Keogh, E. 'Anger at rezoning of area near site of battle', *The Irish Times*, 24 May 2004; Siggins, L. 'Council rejects plan for Galway city incinerator', and Reid, L. 'The Garden of Ireland', *The Irish Times*, 9 September 2004.

13. Under Irish local government law the presumption is that unless a matter is expressly defined as a reserved function for local councillors to decide (by vote), the matter is an executive function, which can be decided at the discretion of the manager. Article 149(4) of the Local Government Act, 2001 states clearly: 'Every function of a local authority which is not a reserved function is, for the purposes of this Act, an executive function of such local authority.'

14. Lucey, A. 'Killarney councillors vote for rezoning', *The Irish Times*, 8 March 2006, and Lucey, A. 'Killarney manager not to act on rezoning motion', *The Irish Times*, 5 April 2006.

15. City or County Managers will often refuse to follow an Article 140 motion on grounds that to do so would be illegal by reference to some other norm. Often expert legal advice is sought in such cases. Article 178 of the Planning and Development Act, 2000 prohibits any local authority from 'effecting' any development which is in material contravention of the development plan.

16. See for example, Lucey, A. 'An Taisce criticises one-off holiday homes', *The Irish Times*, 14 January 2005, and Deegan, G. 'An Taisce seeks change on planning', *The Irish Times*, 6 May 2004. This provision could be very simply tightened up to prevent abuse by modifying the text of Section 140(7), which details that at least one third of all councillors must vote for the measure. That could be simply changed to two-thirds (66.6 per cent), which would require very broad political support to be sustained.

17. See Lucey, A. 'Councillors delist Valentia house to allow development', *The Irish Times*, 22 September 2004. In this case the delisting was against the advice of the council's own planners, and independent advice. Note that council planners themselves can propose mass de-listings of such buildings as part of county or city development. As many as 500 were proposed to be de-listed for the latest Dublin City Development Plan (2006–2011).

18. This survey was undertaken by myself and Mr Brian Dawson during autumn 2003, as part of the Higher Education Agency/HEA funded research project, 'SE-3 and Implementing EU environmental policy, etc.', at the Environmental Change Institute, NUI, Galway. About 38 per cent of the respondents suggested they were spending 1–3 days per month on implementing EU environmental laws, 6 per cent answered they were working full time on the issue, and 13 per cent suggested they were spending less than one full working day. The officials surveyed were County/City Managers and Directors of Environmental Services.

19. Allen, R. *No Global: The People of Ireland Versus the Multinationals* (London: Pluto Press), pp.111, 116

20. This unit was supposed to double to ten by 2005. See Reid, L. 'Dublin taskforce to illegal waste activity', *The Irish Times*, 10 June 2004.

21. This is the so-called 'minimum agreement' negotiated between the Danish Ministries for Environment & Energy and Local Government in 1999. It requires that 50 per cent of larger firms are inspected each year in every municipality, and for smaller plants or firms 50 per cent over the previous and existing year. This performance is supervised by the Danish Environmental Protection Agency. In cases where this target is not met, the matter is investigated by the minister, who may then set legally binding targets for inspections. There is some evidence that this reform has led to an increase in the frequency of environmental inspections in municipalities where it was previously lower than average. See Krarup, S. 'Danish Municipalities' Monitoring Efforts', AKF Working Paper Denmark 1 February 2006, pp.17–19. Available at: http://www.akf.dk/udgivelser/workingpaper/2006/pdf/01 monitoring effort.pdf/

22. LGMSB, *Service Indicators in Local Authorities 2004*, pp.61–2.

23. LGMSB, *Service Indicators in Local Authorities 2004*, pp.126–7.

24. See McDonald, F. 'Number of Bord Pleanála appeals queried', *The Irish Times*, June 13, (2003b).

25. LGMSB, *Service Indicators in Local Authorities 2004*, p.146, Table 19.2. Some idea of the variation in performance over waste management can be seen by comparing councils' recycling rates. Good performers were: Galway City (49.5 per cent), Waterford City (47 per cent), and Cork County Councils (36.6 per cent). Poor performers were Cork City (2.55 per cent), Mayo County (2.5 per cent), and Kildare County Councils (7.2 per cent).

26. Ireland had until 2004 a network of regional health boards. Since 2005 a national Health Service Executive has emerged to replace this, although regional sub-groupings exist for the delivery of services.

27. A good example of how the artificial division between environmental and planning matters has worked badly in practice can be seen in a 1998 case involving a proposed cement factory. In this case, which went on appeal to An Bord Pleanála, the latter ruled that they would not even listen to evidence that the plant's emissions would increase national CO_2 emissions, because this was an environmental concern for the EPA's IPPC process. See McDonald, F. 'CO_2 emissions not an issue in hearing', *The Irish Times*, 7 July 1998.

28. See Planning and Development Act, 2000, Article 179.

29. Allen, R. *No Global: The People of Ireland Versus the Multinationals*, pp.238, 4.

30. Murtagh, P. 'EU may be about to judge us wanting on the environment – yet again', *The Irish Times*, 30 May 2005.

31. Shipan, C.R. *Independence and the Irish Environmental Protection Agency: a comparative assessment.* Working Paper of the Policy Institute, Trinity College Dublin, December 16 (Dublin: The Policy Institute, TCD,

2005), p.25. Available at: http://www.policyinstitute.tcd.ie/working_papers/PIWP08%20-%20Shipan.pdf

32. Shipan uses a scoring mechanism whereby he ranks the Irish EPA across a number of functional dimensions. These include: whether agency heads can be fired easily by politicians; whether agency board members can be appointed or removed by politicians easily; the answerability to parliament of the agency; whether their budget is autonomous; the regulatory powers the agency enjoys. It is important to note that his work was a preliminary study.

33. See Taylor, G. *Conserving the Emerald Tiger: The Politics of Environmental Regulation in Ireland* (Galway: Arlen House, 2001), pp.95–7; Taylor, G. 'Conserving the Emerald Tiger: the politics of Environmental Regulation in Ireland', *Environmental Politics*, 7, 4 (1998), pp.55–74; and Taylor, G. 'Environmental Democracy, Oral Hearings and Public Registers in Ireland: Methinks thou do'st protest too much', *Irish Planning and Environmental Law Journal*, 5, 4 (1998a), pp.143–51.

34. Shipan, *Independence and the Irish Environmental Protection Agency: a comparative assessment*, p.27.

35. It is important to note here that no critic of the EPA has questioned her professional competence or qualifications for the position, and, as Director-General of the EPA she has expressed regret that the Irish government abandoned the proposed CO_2 tax in 2004.

36. Pocock, I. 'Director of EPA is excluded from vote', *The Irish Times*, August 27, (2004).

37. Beesley, A. 'Green Party calls for appointment of new EPA director to be terminated', *The Irish Times*, 28 August 2004.

38. The EPA report was published in August 2001, after national cabinet approval and over six years of research by the EPA. Controversially, it ruled out industrial pollution related to animal deaths on twenty-seven farms. Instead, it suggested farming practices and nutritional deficiencies may be to blame. The report also denies there are any significant human health problems in the area connected with pollution, although it does admit there is slightly increased risk of death from respiratory illness for children under 14 years. The cost of this report was estimated at €5.3 million in 2002 prices.

39. For accounts of the critique of the EPA's final report on animal deaths and alleged human health problems at Askeaton, see O'Dowd, F. 'EPA's Askeaton report slated', *The Sunday Business Post*, 2 December 2001; Ahlstrom, D. 'Valid questions raised on EPA's methods', *The Irish Times*, 21 November 2002; Deegan, G. 'Farmers welcome new report on deaths of animals', *The Irish Times*, 21 November 2002; Healy, A. 'Geologist questions Askeaton report', *The Irish Times*, 19 January 2004. The most substantial critique of the EPA's report for Askeaton was provided in November 2002, in an independent report commissioned by the IFA, and led by Prof. Brian Alloway (University College London). While this was not conclusive either as to a source of pollution, it suggested that industrial pollution could *not* be ruled out. In particular, Prof. Alloway noted that the

EPA's methodology was flawed because it omitted testing for some pollutants that might be associated with industrial pollution from nearby heavy industrial plant.

40. The specific mechanics of the report were made much more complex by the necessity to include many other state agencies: the local health board, the Department of Agriculture's veterinary laboratory, and the Irish farm advisory service, Teagasc.

41. Ahlstrom, D. 'Investigation set up too late to provide answers', *The Irish Times*, 10 August 2001.

42. See McDonald, F. 'Policing the waste land', *The Irish Times*, 3 September 2005. He describes how 255 tonnes of caustic soda was released into the harbour from the Glaxo Smith Kline plant. According to McDonald, one EPA director admitted that the agency should have been more proactive and there has been an undertaking to provide public warnings much faster via the EPA website.

43. See Environmental Protection Agency Act, 1992, Article 85 (6).

44. The exact quotes from Deputy Director Padraig Larkin as reported by Barry Roche, Southern Correspondent for the Irish Times, were: 'It is somewhat unusual in law to have a body that makes the first decision making the decision on appeal', and 'Ideally, we would prefer that an appeal wasn't back to ourselves, but that is the law'. Roche, B. 'Appeals process flawed, says EPA', *The Irish Times*, 6 August 2005.

45. See Roche, B. 'Medical evidence cited by objectors', *The Irish Times*, 2 March 2005 and Roche, B. 'Opponents may take legal action to block incinerator', *The Irish Times*, 26 November 2005. A CHASE (Cork Harbour Alliance for a Safe Environment) spokeswoman claimed that during the oral hearings expert medical evidence was not engaged with adequately. See footnotes below for an evaluation of the EPA's approach.

46. EPA/Environmental Protection Agency, *Report on Objections and Oral Hearing. Indaver (Ringaskiddy) Waste Licence Register 186–01*. Volume 1. Main Report and Recommendations (Wexford: EPA, 2005b), pp.91– 123. Available at http://www.epa.ie/Licensing/WasteLicensing/OralHearings/186–1IndaverOralHearingReport/

47. While the precautionary principle was considered and rejected as grounds for licence refusal in general terms, its consideration in the inspector's report did not specifically apply it to the uncertainties appertaining to this site-specific context of imposing further emissions in a zone such as Cork harbour. See EPA, *Report on Objections and Oral Hearing. Indaver (Ringaskiddy)*, Point 4.4.2.6, pp.220–5.

48. O'Brien, T. 'Licences given for waste plants in Cork, Meath', *The Irish Times*, 26 November 2005. On the issue of waste handling, see EPA, *Report on Objections and Oral Hearing. Indaver (Ringaskiddy)*, Condition 8.2.3, p.369.

49. See Kelly, M. 'Baseline Health Data', Letter to Michael Kelly, Secretary General Department of Health and Children, 25 March 2003, available at: http://www.epa.ie/Licensing/WasteLicensing/OralHearings/186–1IndaverOralHearingReport/.

50. See HRB/Health Research Board, *Environmental Effects of Landfilling and Incineration of Waste – A Literature Review* (Dublin: HRB, 2003), available at http://www.hrb.ie/publications/. While this report pointed out that there was no conclusive evidence, to date, associating incinerators with cancer clusters, it also noted that such evidence was methodologically hard to prove anyhow. In other words, ultimately we are dealing with regulating uncertainty rather than risk. And the HRB team did note that: 'There is some evidence that incinerator emissions may be associated with respiratory morbidity. Acute and chronic respiratory symptoms are associated with incinerator emissions.' See HRB, *Environmental Effects*, etc., p. 6. Again this should be qualified by the need for further research. One point that does come across from the HRB study is that the health impacts of incinerators depend very much on whether they are of old or new technology, how they are operated, and what waste is burned. In other words, the public health uncertainty/risk is a function of site-specific and local population factors as much as an intrinsic feature of incineration per se. The HRB report was, in summary, inconclusive about health risks, but very useful nonetheless. However, why was it only made available in 2003, when incinerators had featured in waste management plans since 1998? And why were the EPA not working with the HRB much earlier on this precise topic given that they had offered reports of dioxin levels in the 1990s as a way to assuage public fears?

51. EPA, *Report on Objections and Oral Hearing. Indaver (Ringaskiddy)*, Point 4.1.2, p.98.

52. Keogh, E. 'Ability of EPA to handle incinerator hearing queried', *The Irish Times*, 3 March 2005.

53. See Reid, L. 'Greens call for reform of EPA', *The Irish Times*, 16 March 2006.

54. See 'EU imposes €21,600 fine in peat extraction row', *Irish Independent*, Friday, 30 September 2005. However, a subsequent report in the *Irish Times* in early October claimed that the Commission Office in Dublin suggested that Ireland was unlikely to face the fine in question as the Irish authorities had belatedly taken some action to meet the Commission's requests to comply with the Court verdict.

55. For the year 2002, it was estimated that breaches of environmental laws accounted for over 40 per cent of Commission infringement proceedings that ended up being referred to the European Court of Justice. About 38 per cent of all complaints were about an alleged poor implementation of EU environmental laws. Source: CEC/Commission of the European Communities, *20th Annual Report on Monitoring the Application of Community Law*, 2002, COM(2003) 669 final 21.11.2003 (Luxembourg: Office for Official Publications of the European Communities, 2003).

56. See Staunton, D. 'Ireland accused of breaching EU rules on health environment', *The Irish Times*, 12 April 2005; Staunton, D. 'EU censures Ireland over illegal dumping', *The Irish Times*, 27 April 2005; Staunton, D. 'State in breach of EU environmental law', *The Irish Times*, 14 July 2004; McDonald, F. 'Running up a big bill for our rotten track record', *The Irish*

Times, 17 July 2004; Pocock, I. 'Slurry hits the fan', *The Irish Times*, 22 May 2004; Raftery, M. 'Not a record to boast of', *The Irish Times*, 1 July 2004.

57. For example, a 2004 report by the Commission placed Ireland alongside France, Italy, Spain and Greece as serious offenders with either many environmental laws simply not transposed or only poorly so. See Wall, M. 'Ireland's poor record cited on implementing environmental laws', *The Irish Times*, 20 August 2004. Another 2004 report, commissioned by the Irish Green Party through one of their MEPs, Patricia McKenna, argued that Ireland had 'the second highest number of environmental infringement cases after Spain.' See: McKenna, P. and Clerkin, S. *Ireland's Compliance with EU environmental law*. A report Commissioned for Patricia McKenna MEP (1999–2004), June (2004), p.3. Available at http://www.greenparty.ie/en/content/download/946/6403/filecompliance report pmckenna-sml.pdf

58. In 2005, the Irish Minister for the environment openly complained that the Commission initiated legal proceedings without informing him first. See Chapter One.

59. O'Brien, T. 'EU criticism on waste rejected as outdated', *The Irish Times*, 24 September 2004.

60. Wall, M. 'Ireland's poor record'.

61. It is true that in 2003 Ireland's transposition rate for environmental directives was 98.3 per cent. However, what is often not said is that for that year *no* state had a rate below 90 per cent and only one state dropped below 95 per cent (Greece). What seems like an exceptional Irish performance is really then just slightly above average. Indeed, several states had either the same or a higher rate of transposition than Ireland in 2003: Belgium, Denmark, Austria, the UK, Sweden, Finland, and Luxembourg. Equally, one should note that the 2002 Report on the Monitoring of the Application of Community Law reveals that, for environment related directives, Ireland had a much less impressive transposition rate of 91 per cent. Transposition rates before those years are tabulated in a way that makes it difficult to give an overall assessment for the environment sector. The data is simply too fragmented.

62. There are a series of five special reports on the application of EU environmental laws, covering the years 1996–7 to 2004. However, it is only lately (2001–4), that the Commission have finally provided a transparent 'scoreboard' of each member state's efforts in the environmental sector. Because the Commission collect and present data according to the types of Commission enforcement activity (warning letters, reasoned opinions, and the type of infringement), the result is that the overall picture is very fragmented. The Commission also has a habit of taking individual complaints and rolling a number of similar ones into an aggregate complaint dossier. This means there can be an underestimation in Commission data of the actual number of instances of breaches of environmental law.

63. These findings are quite different from the report on compliance with EU environmental law (2004) commissioned by Green MEP Patricia

McKenna. That report suggested that Ireland had the second worst level of bad application cases for the years 1998, 2000, 2002. However, I could not find evidence to sustain that view. The Commission provided 'scoreboard' tables in the relevant annual surveys on the implementation of environmental law 2001–4, which reveals that this assertion is only correct for the year 2003. Other *second* worst offenders over those years were, respectively, Belgium (2001), Belgium and France (jointly 2002), and Spain (2004).

64. See EPA/Environmental Protection Agency, Press Release: 'The Nature and Extent of Unauthorised Waste Activity in Ireland', Thursday, 15 September, (Wexford: EPA, 2005c).

65. O'Brien, T. 'An Taisce to sue State over dumping', *The Irish Times*, 14 December 2004; Reid, L. 'Illegal NI dumps had waste from South', *The Irish Times*, 3 February 2004; Reid, L. 'EU ruling due on Ireland's illegal dumping', *The Irish Times*, 17 September 2004.

66. Murtagh, 'EU may be about to judge us wanting on the environment-yet again'. This case detailed a litany of examples where local governments themselves were dumping waste without permits. It also describes a disturbing case where the EPA effectively absolved Limerick City Council (then a Corporation) from the need to have a waste permit for such actions, arguing that the activity was 'waste recovery'. This argument was rejected out of hand by the European Court, and the Limerick case was firmly categorized as serious illegal waste dumping activity.

67. Reid, L. 'Ombudsman criticises lack of enforcement of planning laws', *The Irish Times*, 28 April 2004.

68. This section in particular draws heavily on interviews conducted by myself and Mr Brian Dawson with many local government and environmental policy actors between October and December 2003. This research was conducted as part of a Higher Education Agency/HEA funded research project, 'SE-3 – Implementing EU environmental policy, etc.', at the Environmental Change Institute (ECI), NUI, Galway.

69. For example, with regard to the Habitats and Birds Directives, Ireland stood out as being late in giving its list of definitive sites. In 2000, Irish environmentalists were claiming that the actual number of sites worth protecting was much more than the Irish government was offering to the Commission – almost 600 instead of 364. See Laffan, B. and O'Mahony, J. 'Mis-fit, politicisation and Europeanisation: the implementation of the Habitats Directive in Ireland', *OEUE Occasional Paper*, 1.3, (September, 2004), pp.14, 19. Available at: www.oeue.net/papers/ireland-implementationofthehab.pdf

70. Flynn B. and Kröger, L. 'Can Policy Learning Really Improve Implementation? Evidence From Irish Responses to the Water Framework Directive', *European Environment*, 13, 3, (2003), pp.150–63.

71. Laffan and O'Mahony, 'Mis-fit, politicisation and Europeanisation', etc., p.12.

72. For example, they became very reluctant to engage in wide public consultation, having witnessed how public meetings became shouting

matches against their harried staff. Also, there were not unfounded fears that consultation could alert landowners to impending designations. In some cases this could trigger destruction of vital habitats as owners sought to take pre-emptive action, a trend very common in the cases of quarries or drainage projects.

73. For a sample of the mostly negative media commentary, see McDonald, F. 'Break-up of Dúchas may be unlawful', *The Irish Times*, 23 April 2003; Viney, M. 'Brooding on the politics of conservation', *The Irish Times*, 10 May 2003; Editor/Irish Times, 'End of Dúchas', *The Irish Times*, 28 April 2003: and Battersby, E., 'Knocking down Dúchas', *The Irish Times*, 19 April 2003.

74. Laffan and O'Mahony, 'Mis-fit, politicisation, and Europeanisation', etc., pp.19–20.

75. McDonald, F. 'Order for bird protection area made without authority', *The Irish Times*, 27 May 2005.

76. Staunton, D. 'EU censures Ireland over illegal dumping'.

77. McDonald, F. 'Policing the waste land'.

78. These include: Offaly County Council, for breach of its waste licence in September 2005. See EPA/Environmental Protection Agency, Press Release: 'EPA Prosecutes Offaly County Council', Thursday, 29 September (Wexford: EPA, 2005). Total fines and costs imposed were circa €7,000. Also prosecuted was Roscommon County Council in July 2005, again related to waste. Costs and fines came to €9,250. See EPA/Environmental Protection Agency, Press Release: 'EPA Prosecutes Roscommon County Council', Tuesday, August 2, (Wexford: EPA, 2005e). Very serious charges were laid against Waterford County Council in June 2005 for waste management irregularities. These were referred to the Director of Public Prosecutions and jurisdiction was to go to a higher court. See EPA/Environmental Protection Agency, Press Release: 'Judge Refuses Jurisdiction in EPA Court Cases Against Waterford County Council and Waterford City Council', Friday, June 10, (Wexford: EPA, 2005f). Cavan County Council was prosecuted by the OEE for poor operation of a landfill. Fines and costs totalled circa €7,900. See EPA/Environmental Protection Agency, Press Release: 'EPA Prosecutes Cavan County Council', Friday, December 9 (Wexford, EPA, 2005g).

79. Reid. L. 'Illegal dumping controls are still rubbish', *The Irish Times*, 9 September 2004.

80. Murtagh, 'EU may be about to judge us wanting on the environment-yet again'.

81. Deegan, G. 'Investigation urged into health patterns after firm is fined', *The Irish Times*, 16 February 2006.

82. Reid, L. 'Planning rules for waste projects to be eased', *The Irish Times*, 4 May 2005.

83. For an introduction to the general literature on NEPIs, see Jordan, A., Wurzul, R.K.W., and Zito, A.R. (eds.), *'New' Instruments of Environmental Governance? National Experiences and Prospects* (London: Frank Cass, 2003); Bailey, I. *New Environmental Policy Instruments in the European*

Union: Politics, Economics and the Implementation of the Packaging Waste Directive (Aldershot (UK): Ashgate, 2003); Helm, D. (ed.), *Environmental Policy: Objectives, Instruments and Implementation* (Oxford: OUP, 2000); Hatch, M. (ed.), *Environmental Policy-making: Assessing the use of alternative policy-making instruments* (New York: State University of New York Press, 2005).

84. See EEA/European Environment Agency. *Environmental taxes – Recent developments in tools for integration. Environmental issue report No 18* (Copenhagen: EEA, 2000). Available at: http://reports.eea.eu.int/ Environmental Issues No 18/en/tab content RLR; and ECOTEC Research and Consulting (et al.), *Study on the Economic and Environmental Implications of the Use of Environmental Taxes and Charges in the European Union and its Member States* (Brussels: ECOTEC, April, 2001). Available at: http://ec.europa.eu/environment/enveco/taxation/ch1t4 overview.pdf

85. See DELG/Department of the Environment and Local Government *National Climate Change Strategy Ireland* (Dublin: Government Stationery Office, 2000), pp.27 and 155.

86. For example, there was intense lobbying by the Irish dairy industry, who wished to close some of their old large plants and transfer the CO_2 emissions from these old plants to new plants – a move the EPA resisted. See Hennessy, M. 'Changes can be made to carbon plan, says EPA', *The Irish Times*, 11 June 2004 and Taylor, C. 'Carbon tax could lead to job losses – industries', *The Irish Times*, 18 February 2004.

87. It has been suggested that the initial rate for an Irish CO_2 tax might have been €7.50 per tonne which could have returned a revenue stream in the order of €250 million. The estimated reductions were predicted as being between 0.5 million and 0.75 million tones each year, which does not seem much, given that official policy is to reduce CO_2 levels by 9 million tonnes per annum. See Taylor, C. 'Cabinet abandons plan to introduce carbon tax', *The Irish Times*, 10 September 2004.

88. The ESRI suggested a 40 per cent reduction was possible if the rate of tax was set at €20 per tonne of CO_2 rather than the suggested €7.50 per tonne. See Bergin, A., Fitzgerald, J. and Kearney, I. *The Macro-Economic Effects of Using Fiscal Instruments to Reduce Greenhouse Gas Emissions (2001-EEP/DS8-M1) Final Report: A Report by the Economic and Social Research Institute, prepared for the Environmental Protection Agency* (EPA: Wexford, 2004), p.30. Available online at: http://www.esri.ie/. See also Taylor, C. 'Proposed carbon tax could benefit poorer households', *The Irish Times*, 22 July 2004.

89. Such reductions were estimated as being in the order of an additional 1.8 million tonnes of CO_2 over a three-year period during the operation of the proposed tax, which would work out at an additional 600,000 tonnes per annum, effectively doubling the cautious government estimate of a likely yield of 500,000 tonnes of carbon reduced per annum. See Reid, L. 'Putting a price on the main cause of global warming', *The Irish Times*, 31 December 2004.

90. See Bergin, A., Fitzgerald, J., Keeney, M., McCarthy, N., O'Malley, E., and Scott, S. *Aspects of Irish Energy Policy*. Policy Research Series No. 57, September 2005 (Dublin: ESRI, 2005), p.6.

91. For literature on voluntary or negotiated agreements see Börkey P, and Lévêque, F. 'Voluntary Approaches for Environmental Protection in the European Union – A Survey', *European Environment: The Journal of European Environmental Policy*, 10,1 (2000), pp.35–54 and OECD/ Organisation for Economic Co-operation and Development, *Voluntary Approaches for Environmental Policy: An assessment* (Paris: OECD, 2000a).

92. Taylor, C. 'Enterprise Ireland chief calls for flexibility on carbon taxation', *The Irish Times*, 27 January 2004.

93. IBEC/Irish Business and Employers Confederation, *IBEC Environmental Policy* (Dublin: IBEC, 1997), pp.7.1–7.5, and IBEC/Irish Business and Employers Confederation. 'Cool heads needed to move forward on Climate Change', IBEC Press Release, 11 April 2001. Available at: http://www.ibec.ie/ibec/buspolicies/buspolciesdoclib3.nsf/

94. See DEHLG/Department of Environment, Heritage and Local Government, Press Release: 'Breakthrough on Chewing Gum. Roche Announces €7 million Industry-Funded Programme', 26 January 2006. Available at http://www.environ.ie/

95. Since 1999 an agreement by the Irish Detergents and Allied Products Association (IDAPA) has been in place, aiming to phase out phosphate-based domestic laundry washing powders. See ENDS/Environmental Data Services (1999), 'Phosphate detergent phase-out in Ireland', *The ENDS Report*, 299, December 1999

96. See Flynn, B. 'Voluntary environmental policy instruments: Two Irish success stories', *European Environment: The Journal of European Environmental Policy*, 12, 1 (2002), pp.1–12; and DEHLG/Department of Environment, Heritage and Local Government, Press Release: 'Farm Plastics Recycling: Revised Scheme Will Improve Service To Farmers', 3 May 2006. Available at http://www.environ.ie/

97. O'Brien, T. 'Ireland now recycling 66 per cent of used packaging', *The Irish Times*, 22 May 2006.

98. Estimates by REPAK itself, of non-compliant firms who had not joined REPAK nor notified local governments of their waste plans, were as high as 1,050 in 2001 and were still at a level of 700 by 2004. See EEA/ European Environment Agency, *Sustainable Use and Management of Natural Resources: EEA Report No.9/2005* (EEA: Copenhagen, 2005), pp.42–3.

99. The majority of these have since joined REPAK, although thirty-nine chose not to and thirty-seven were still not compliant. See EPA/Environmental Protection Agency, 'Improvements in the Enforcement of the Packaging Waste Regulations', EPA Newsletter, April (Wexford: EPA, 2006b), p.12. Available   at: http://www.epa.ie/NewsCentre/Newsletter/epaNewsApril2006/FileUpload, 9451,en.pdf

100. Ibid.

101. Smyth, J. 'Tax rate among EU's lowest', *The Irish Times*, 18 May 2006.

102. See Clinch, P. and Dunne, L. 'A Theory of Impediments to Environmental Tax Reform', *Environmental Studies Research Series Working Papers*, ESRS 01/14, UCD/ University College Dublin, (Dublin: Dept. of Environmental Studies, UCD, 2001), pp.11, 13. Available at: http://www.ucd.ie/pepweb/publications/workingpapers/

103. In 2000, some 66 per cent of respondents of a DELG survey said they were in favour of putting up taxes on things harmful to the environment. However, when they were asked would they individually be prepared to pay more tax, only 20 per cent were willing. DELG/Department of Environment and Local Government and Drury Research, *Attitudes and Actions: A National Survey on the Environment*, April 2000, (Dublin: DELG, 2000), pp.11–12.

104. Eurobarometer/Commission of the European Communities, *Special Eurobarometer 217: the attitudes of European citizens towards the environment* (Luxembourg: Eurobarometer, 2005), question 15, p.83.

105. ECOTEC Research and Consulting (et al.), *Study on the Economic and Environmental Implications of the Use of Environmental Taxes and Charges in the European Union and its Member States*.

106. CPA/Combat Poverty Agency, *Submission to the Department of Finance on the introduction of a Carbon Energy Tax* (Dublin, CPA, 2003). Available at: http://www.cpa.ie/publications/submissions/2003 Sub CarbonTax.pdf

107. These studies have suggested that a CO_2 tax set at €20 per tonne would likely produce emissions reductions in the region of 40 per cent. The average cost of this per household would have likely been circa €250 and would have led to a 0.6 per cent increase in consumer prices at 2004 values. The ESRI suggest that, for low income families, an extension of the existing social welfare fuel allowance scheme, together with targeted income tax cuts, would easily cover any extra burdens and might actually leave them better off. See Taylor, C. 'Proposed carbon tax could benefit poorer households', *The Irish Times*, 22 July 2004.

108. For example, the evaluation carried out in 2000 by the European Environment Agency (EEA) on the subject of environmental taxes noted that 'careful design of new taxes or tax modifications can reduce or remove such equity problems'. See EEA, *Environmental taxes – Recent developments in tools for integration*. In the Netherlands, their national CO_2 tax is implemented in a way that means that low income consumers have a tax free allowance for natural gas and electricity to meet their basic needs. Moreover, they are exempt from waste collection and sewage taxes at the municipal level as well (ibid.). With regard to Irish evidence, the ESRI's major study of CO_2 taxes suggested that just over one fifth of revenues would be required to provide compensation for regressive effects. See Bergin, A. et al., *The Macro-Economic Effects of Using Fiscal Instruments to Reduce Greenhouse Gas*, pp.30–1. Another study concluded that almost 90 per cent of those likely to be adversely impacted by a CO_2 tax could be feasibly compensated within existing social welfare and tax systems. See Scott, S. and Eakins, J. *Carbon*

Taxes: Which Households Gain or Lose? (2001-EEP/DS7-M1). *Final Report*. *A Report prepared for the Environmental Protection Agency by the Economic and Social Research Institute* (Dublin: ESRI, 2004), p.20. Available at: http://www.esri.ie/

109. The most important ESRI study into the CO_2 tax noted that: 'The economic cost of this tax would be quite small. In particular, if the additional revenue were used to fund a reduction in taxes on labour – income tax or social insurance contributions – it would actually produce a small increase in output and employment in the medium term.' See Bergin et al., *The Macro-Economic Effects of Using Fiscal Instruments to Reduce Greenhouse Gas*, p.30–1.

110. There are two directives on WEEE. The main one is Directive 2002/96/EC and a second one was made law in 2003 (Directive 2003/108/EC), which amends Article 9 of the previous directive to moderate the obligations for industrial WEEE.

111. What is also revealing is that the new charges are subject to VAT, or sales tax, which means the Irish exchequer gets its own small cut. Strictly speaking, this has nothing to do with covering the costs of recycling white goods. Nor is it transparent how the varying rates of the charge have been calculated to cover the true economic cost of recycling from point of sale.

112. In the directive in question (Directive 2002/96/EC), the 12th recital makes the principle of producer responsibility clear. It is also expressed in Articles 2, 5, and 8 of that directive. None of the articles of this directive gives member states permission to allow producers to recoup their financial arrangements from consumers.

113. Quoted in O'Brien, T. 'Recycling price rise on electrical goods', *The Irish Times*, 13 August 2005.

114. EPA/Environmental Protection Agency, *National Allocation Methodology* (Wexford: EPA, 2004c). Available at http://www.epa.ie/Licensing/EmissionsTrading/NationalAllocationPlan/finalmethodology/

115. Finnegan, P./GRIAN, *Recommendations On Ireland's Draft National Allocation Plan 2005–7*, 10 March 2004 (Dublin, GRIAN, 2004), pp.5–6. Available at http://www.grian.net or http://www.grian.ie/Policy/CarbonTax.htm

116. Ibid. and see CANE/Climate Action Network Europe (2005), *Qu Quo Vadis, EU ETS? Is the EU's key climate policy tool headed in the right direction? CAN Europe position paper on EU ETS Phase 2 (2008–12)* (Brussels: CANE, 2005). Available at www.climnet.org.

117. In July of 2004 the European Commission eventually approved Ireland's National Allocation Plan for Carbon Emissions trading 2005–2007, although only after the Irish government had agreed to cut the level of CO_2 by 180,000 tonnes per annum. Also agreed was that unused permits for planned developments could not be used for existing facilities. See Staunton, D. 'State in breach of EU environmental law'.

118. EPA, *National Allocation Methodology*, p.2.

119. O'Brien. T. 'Ireland exceeds quota for harmful emissions', *The Irish Times*, 16 May 2006.

120. EPA/Environmental Protection Agency, 'EPA Holds First EU Auction for Emissions Trading', *EPA NEWS*, April, (2006d), p.1.

121. A recent scholarly review of the American experience of emissions trading in general concluded: 'The overall efficiency of allowance trading would be increased and the social cost of regulation reduced, perhaps substantially, if emission allowances were distributed initially through a revenue-raising auction.' See Burtraw, D., Evans, D.A. Krupnick, A., Palmer, K. and Toth, R. 'Economics of Pollution Trading for SO_2 and NOx', *Annual Review of Environmental Resources*, Vol. 30 (2005), p.281. See also Goulder, L. *Environmental Policy Making in Economies with Prior Tax Distortions* (Cheltenham: Edward Elgar, 2002).

122. CEC/Commission of the European Communities, *Commission Decision of 7 July 2004 concerning the national allocation plan for the allocation of greenhouse gas emission allowances notified by Denmark in accordance with Directive 2003/87/EC of the European Parliament and of the Council*, C (2004) 2515/6 final 07.07.2004 (Luxembourg: Office for Official Publications of the European Communities, 2004a).

123. I arrive at this figure as follows: 5 per cent of 66,960,000 Mt (the final cap in the Irish NAP) is 3,348,000 Mt. If sold at the average futures market price for December 2004 of €10 per tonne, this could have yielded €33,480,000 in 2005.

124. CANE, *Qu Quo Vadis, EU ETS?*, p.5.

125. Editor/Irish Times, 'Failure on Kyoto', *The Irish Times*, 25 June 2005.

126. See Ryan, E. 'Action on climate change makes sense', *The Irish Times*, 18 February 2005 and Oliver, E. 'B of I to facilitate emissions trading', *The Irish Times*, 23 May 2005.

127. Morrison, K. 'Emissions trade prices drop again', *The Financial Times*, 27 April 2006, and Kay, J. 'Key to Carbon trading is to keep it simple', *The Financial Times*, 8 May 2006.

Chapter Five

Beyond The 'Blame Game': A Reform Agenda For Irish Environmental Policy

INTRODUCTION

How can Ireland move away from a blame game style of environmental policy and politics? This chapter changes style in terms of the book's overall argument. From being descriptive it is now time to be prescriptive. However, such a question is too broad to answer in anything other than a limited way here. In particular, this chapter does not systematically consider reform of policy instruments: the 'software 'side of environmental policy.[1] To narrow the discussion to a manageable scale, a few concrete reform suggestions are offered. These have the merit of being tangible for the reader, even if they can only be sketched out here. This chapter is *not* then a precise 'blueprint' for reform, rather an argument about what types of reform are possible.

Those qualifications aside, the need for an overhaul of Irish environmental policy is urgent. The case for such a comprehensive reform is set out here over two distinct sections. Firstly, 'hardware' reform of environmental *institutions* is argued for. Secondly, reform of the overarching *strategies* for environment policy is examined. Within each of these sections a number of specific cases are offered of how innovation could proceed.

The most important area for reform would be to improve the overarching strategies for environmental policy. Ireland is weakest on a strategic vision of environmental issues. Introducing an ecological modernization approach would be beneficial.

Making sustainable development a tangible and meaningful concept is also badly needed. Currently, it is a much abused cliché. Unfortunately, putting environmental policy strategies into place is not easy. Unless made tangible, they tend to be nebulous and merely rhetorical. Strategic approaches can also be demanding where they reach controversial conclusions. For example, should Ireland reject nuclear energy? Following the logic of sustainable development, this chapter argues we definitely should. But not all commentators would be likely to agree. Keeping options open has its appeal, and rejecting nuclear energy would not be an easy choice. It implies we need to invest massively in costly and less proven renewable energies, in alternative fuels for vehicles, and even in 'clean coal'. All of these stark choices imply great difficulty in first agreeing reform, never mind executing it. Yet adopting strategic approaches to Irish environment policy should not be shirked.

The other institutional reforms advocated here are more straightforward. They are certainly not wildly radical. However, they would demand considerable political leadership, legislative time, and significant financing. Nonetheless, they are definitely feasible within the lifetime of a single government. Most of the examples stay within the existing framework of institutions and laws, rather than suggest something entirely novel. There is also a sense that institutional reform is more tangible than agreeing strategies for environmental policy. For all of these reasons, transforming institutions is likely to be a good place to begin, building up a momentum for wider reform later. Yet what exact reforms would be both desirable and feasible?

Upgrading the 'Hardware': The Case for Institutional Reform

Over previous chapters, a serious mismatch between the 'software' of Irish environmental policy content and the clanking institutional 'hardware' has been described. That gap must be plugged. The EU has modernized Irish environmental laws and regulatory thinking, but the institutional dimension has only been poorly reformed. For this reason, arguments about institutional reform constitute a major part of this chapter.

Exploring environmental partnership.

A first priority should be that environmentalists must be brought in from the cold. They should be invited into the evolving national partnership institutions, which have been an important factor in transforming Irish industrial relations and macro-economic policy. Environmentalists are a notable omission from existing social partnership. No environmentalists are members of the National Economic and Social Council (NESC), a 'think tank' which undertakes research and stimulates debate on partnership approaches. Nor do any environmentalists sit on the National Economic and Social Forum (NESF), a more advisory body.

There is a national environmental partnership forum, Comhar. However, this amounts to environmentalists intermittently meeting up with each other and agreeing that serious problems exist. They are not allowed to negotiate with those forces in society who are creating some of those environmental problems. Institutionally, Comhar is a marginal entity, even if its contribution has been laudable.

In fact, the Irish state has mostly failed to engage with environmentalists or take them very seriously. Dialogue, when it has been attempted, has sometimes failed miserably. For example, in the late 1990s consultation with environmentalists over genetically modified foods broke down entirely. A lack of genuine and meaningful participation by environmentalists in the national biodiversity plan (2002) has also been a source of real frustration and anger. More recently, environmental NGOs (ENGOs) were deeply shocked when in January 2006 a new advisory committee for the Environmental Protection Agency (EPA) was nominated by Minister Roche. It had just one environmental NGO representative, but two from farming groups (IFA, ICMSA)[2] and one from business (IBEC).[3]

The truth is that the Irish state can get away with this treatment because environmentalists are weak politically. They would never treat the Irish Farmers Association (IFA) the same way. If one asks why they are weak, it is tempting to fall back on the stock answer that Irish people don't really care about the environment: the 'Irish are not Swedes' argument. This ignores the institutional dimension. It also forgets that public opinion is changing, and is not always a reliable guide to policy outcomes or how people vote.[4]

One surer reason why the IFA are stronger is because their interests are immediate economic ones: the income of farmers. By way of contrast, An Taisce and other ENGOs must focus on a very wide public good of environmental protection. Yet in reality environmental issues are vital lifestyle issues which do impact directly on people's health, work, quality of life and, sometimes, upon their income.

One goal for Irish environmentalists might be to repackage their campaigns away from arguing *against* threats to Ireland's environment and more towards lobbying *for* tangible benefits in their (environmental) quality of life. For example, the focus could be on commuting, a major drain on many people's time. Better housing and spatial management policies (whose aim should be compact cities and towns), would reverse growing commuting trends in the first place. In other cases, commuting can be made more sustainable by a focus on trains and buses, especially if their quality and reliability is much enhanced. Environmentalists must make the shift from being *advocates* against environmental threats to being also advocates *for* sustainable infrastructure.

Campaigning on health and safety risks associated with pollution or incineration is a notable feature of the local environmental movements that have emerged. However, it is not clear if such 'risk based' campaigns are that politically savvy. For a start, it ghettoizes debate. A political conflict over what type of development should be encouraged pivots upon an ultimately complex scientific disputation between experts and counter-experts about what should be permissible. From having a wide debate about what type of transport, energy, or waste management systems we want (or could have), the entire focus becomes: is this safe or not? In fairness some of the anti-incineration campaigns have tried to widen the debate about how waste in society should be dealt with in general. In practice, the pressing nature of the alleged health risks usually predominate.

That narrows the political 'field of play'. Tactically it ordains that the struggle will take place on unforgiving ground: the contested science of risk. Ordinary voters are very likely to be reasonably confused and turned off by endless expert/counter expert allegations. Such a style of activism is reactive rather than proactive. It is all about the pollution issues at hand and thinks less about the institutional dimension of how these issues will be decided.

But institutions matter. For example, one feature which has made the IFA very influential is its institutional sophistication. It was astute enough in the 1970s to hire expert economists to master the obscurities of the CAP.[5] It established full-time offices in Brussels and Dublin. It understood the importance of working the local, national, and Brussels levels of political influence. There was no point just applying pressure at one level alone.

Irish environmentalists, by way of contrast, are weak nationally and fragmented locally. Currently there is a thin national tier of environmental NGOs (described in Table 5.1). They are accompanied by literally dozens of very active, but essentially local, environmental campaigners. These are usually very *ad hoc* in their organization. This weak national but strong local level of mobilization is something distinctive about Ireland. Allen, in his account of Irish environmentalism, recounts basically a litany of small-scale *local* campaigns.[6]

TABLE 5.1 IRELAND'S MAIN NATIONAL LEVEL ENVIRONMENTALIST GROUPS
(NOTE: this does not list all organizations)

I. An Taisce/The National Trust for Ireland:
Founded in 1948, membership is now circa 5,000, with twenty local branches outside Dublin. About seventeen full-time members of staff are employed. It does not see itself as a protest group as such, but rather as an expert lobby and public interest group. Other environmentalists tend to see it as more moderate and less radical, despite the criticism received for its campaign on one-off rural housing. Under Irish planning law it is granted a statutory right of comment on proposed developments, and this has tended to draw the organization into focus on planning matters. Its core activity is lodging planning objections and litigation, although it does classic policy lobbying work as well. Expertise has been developed in habitats and also on urban transport, to complement the original focus on listed buildings and bad planning. See http://www.antaisce.org/

II. Birdlife Ireland:
As its name implies, this is the national organization for ornithologists in Ireland, and from this base the organization has developed considerable expertise on environmental matters. Membership is circa 10,000 with twenty national branches. Fifteen full time staff are employed. Once again, however, the focus is quite narrow – mainly on habitats and their quality. However, this organisation is extremely professional and often has scientific studies to back up its claims. Moreover, it is tied into strong international and UK networks which have funding and expertise. For these reasons it has been widely respected. It has also participated in actual conservation work by providing field staff to work locally with farmers, in particular to save the Corncrake. See http://www.birdwatchireland.ie

III. Coastwatch Ireland:
Established by Karen Dubsky in the late 1980s as a network of activists. It has been very influential and active on the issue of coastal pollution. They have uncovered a number of very serious pollution problems, and have been very proactive in either bringing

complaints to the European Commission or helping local environmental groups do so. See http://www.coastwatch.org/

IV. Earthwatch/Friends of the Earth, Ireland:

An internationally networked group first established in the early 1980s with a focus in Munster, but later an office was opened in Dublin. Operating under the name 'Earthwatch' during the 1990s, they dissolved in late 2003 due to lack of funds. The group was refounded in October 2004 as Friends of the Earth, Ireland, with an all-Ireland focus, including Northern Ireland. It appears to operate as a federal type system, with some six smaller local affiliates in various parts of the island. It has run campaigns on climate change, waste, water, and wildlife. It is seen as a more radical and protest oriented type environmentalist organization, with a notable anti-incineration stance. See http://www.foe.ie

V. Friends of the Irish Environment (FIE):

Based in Allihies, west Cork, this is really a small information network rather than a classic lobbying organization. It produces an excellent internet-based bulletin of environmental news. The focus of the organization is to monitor the implementation of environmental laws, and uncover irregularities in this. It has a special area of expertise on questions of forestry, and a growing expertise on questions of the marine environment. See http://www.friendsoftheirishenvironment.org/

VI. FEASTA/The Foundation for the Economics of Sustainability:

A radical economic think-tank founded in 1998, it seeks to challenge conventional economic assessments of the 'Celtic Tiger' era. FEASTA have run workshops and several lecture series as well as producing a number of publications. They have developed a particular interest in questions of energy supply, but rural housing and climate change issues have also been addressed. They have appeared before Oireachtas committees on several occasions, but do not appear to lobby in the traditional manner. See http://feasta.org

VII. Irish Peatland Conservation Council (IPCC):

Founded in 1982, this is the most expert group on Irish peatland conservation. It has developed considerable expertise on the various habitats and nature designation controversies. See: http://www.ipcc.ie/

VIII. VOICE/Voice of Irish Concern for the Environment:

A general environmental lobby and educational environmentalist group established in the late 1990s as a registered charity, in the aftermath of the closure of Greenpeace Ireland in 1996. The group is mainly Dublin based, and is now small. It has run campaigns on fluoridation, genetically modified foods, and forestry. See http://www.voice.buz.org/

IX. Irish Wildlife Trust:

A smaller conservation organization whose focus is as much on educational activity as it is on protest. They also engage in lobbying. Their speciality is mainly on land conservation, biodiversity, and habitats protection. In recent years it has run campaigns to protect badgers from culling, conserve hedgerows, and wetlands. See http://www.iwt.ie/

Ireland has no shortage of volunteers who turn up to fight the many disparate local 'bush fires' of environmental protest. Yet there are far too few players at the Dublin and Brussels policy-making stage who can spot trends well in advance.[7] At that level they can pre-empt the worst environmental policy compromises before they become established policy. If they are really good, they can actually set agendas.

Is this weakness at the national lobbying level because Irish environmentalists disdain 'suits and ties' politics for the stark moralistic certainties of local environmental protest? Such a mindset does exist. For example, Allen has argued that 'a green movement . . . based on grassroots autonomous assembly would be a powerful force against globalisation'.[8] Such prescriptions are naïve. A smattering of community-based campaigns on their own are unlikely to have sufficient social power to stop unwanted environmental policies.

The reality is that political power is concentrated and institutionalized. It is true that some political power is a function of the wider legitimacy of ideas and opinions held among mass society. If any government loses its credibility on a given issue among the wider electorate, it may have to abandon controversial plans. Local environmental campaigns can and do play a part in challenging official government policies this way. Sometimes they can unseat the power of the state in the realm of opinion and ideas. They win the argument.

Yet governments, even when they lose the argument, may simply choose to steamroller ahead. This is easier to do when faced with the diffuse and weakly held opinions of mass society, especially where voters are so often simply led to a point of utter confusion over issues such as waste incineration or planning concerns. Imposing policies through institutionalized power has been a repeated feature: Wood Quay, the Tara motorway, Glen of the Downs, Carrickmines, and the 'incineration wars' were all examples. In every case environmentalists mobilised, usually *locally*. They often won the arguments. Yet *national* policymakers embedded in the key institutional decision-making positions of the state had the scope to impose their will. Incineration in Ireland was politically defeated *locally*. Yet, it was ultimately decided *nationally* and imposed by simple legislative changes. Local environmentalists were outflanked.

The track record of success for *local* environmental campaigns is then mixed. The obvious point is that any local level campaign requires also national level co-ordination and strategic action to be effective.[9] Moreover, national and EU level lobbying has greater scope to be proactive rather than reactive. The aim should be to modify the text of laws and to change government policy *before* they become fixed.

Unfortunately, at the national level, the number and type of environmentalist organizations is limited, suggesting there is no ready agent to play the role of a national umbrella group. The foremost candidate would have to be An Taisce, Ireland's oldest and largest environmental group, with over 5,000 members. This organization has become much more professional, and has tried to broaden its focus. Yet it remains very much specialized on the issues of planning, or urban and rural heritage conservation. In effect it has become a planning 'fire brigade'. Other national level lobby groups (see Table 5.1) are either very specialized or just far too small to play such a role. Some have even disappeared: Greenpeace Ireland closed down in the late 1990s. Earthwatch went bankrupt in 2003 and had to be reconstituted as Friends of the Earth (Ireland) a year later.

In summary, what seems needed is something akin to an 'environmental IFA', at least in terms of its organizational professionalism, focus, and style. In fairness, the absence of such a body is not the fault of Irish environmentalists. The Irish state has never encouraged such a modernization, whereas it has actually encouraged such trends in the trade union sector. The formation of the large SIPTU[10] union in the late 1980s was encouraged by generous state funding incentives. It was simply in the public interest to have fewer but better organized and disciplined trade unions. Recent budgets have also provided tax allowances for trade union membership.

Yet the level of state financial support provided to Irish environmentalists is simply not adequate. For example, while some €500,000 was made available in 2005 for environmental projects under a local partnership awards scheme, this fell far short of what is needed. Most of this money is parcelled out in dribs and drabs, and only to very local groups for environmental awareness raising activity. A dedicated but very small 'core funding' scheme has been in place since 2001. This involves a disparate group of twenty-three different national environmental groups, who clubbed together after negotiations with the Department of Environment, Heritage and Local Government (DEHLG). They established a centralized funding/disbursement vehicle: the Environmental (Ecological) NGOs Core Funding Ltd (EENGOCF).

However, in 2004 the EENGOCF received only €185,000, and in 2005 this was actually slightly reduced to €180,000.[11] By the time this is sub-divided for each group, the amounts involved are very small. One estimate provided by an EENGOCF researcher was that this fund was meeting no more than 5 per cent of the expenses of the larger environmental NGOs. Also clearly unsatisfactory is the need to negotiate with the DEHLG each year for the subvention, rather than have a multi-annual financial framework. That would allow ENGOs to plan their organizational development more rationally.

This level of financial support compares poorly with what the Irish state offers to other civil society groups. Environmental lobbies in other EU states typically receive much more. In 2004 for example, the European Environmental Bureau (EEB), a federation of national ENGOs, received about 50 per cent of its funding from the European Commission and another 25 per cent from national governments.[12] Dutch environmental groups receive guaranteed funding from their national lottery, and the Dutch environment ministry has a generous funding programme. This has allowed Dutch ENGOs to becoming not just more vocal, but more expert in what they lobby for and against.

Without guaranteed and large-scale funding, Irish environmental groups are forever destined to live a precarious existence. Such funding would also enable environmental groups to move beyond just protest mode. However, it should be very clear that protest will always have to remain a key tool held in reserve. Yet secure funding would permit them to explore policy agenda-setting, multi-level lobbying (simultaneously in Brussels, Dublin, and locally), and eventually join negotiations over policy details with government and industry.

One should be clear that endorsement of greater public funding for environmentalists and their entry into a partnership approach does not mean that environmentalists must submit to some cosy consensus view. Consensus is not necessarily the end goal of partnership. Rather its aim is to move conflict onto the stage of negotiation. Yet negotiation with the powerful groups in society is impossible without first having built up an institutional base. This is why state support for environmentalists would be vital.

If sensible rules are followed, public funding need not run the risk of co-option. For example, such funding could be under the supervision of the relevant Oireachtas committee, rather than left to potentially partisan ministerial *largesse*. It could also be limited to a certain set level of each organizations' income, say perhaps no more than one third. Such mechanisms are common enough in other EU states, and have helped tremendously in furthering the effectiveness of their environmentalist lobbies. Moves in this direction seem a more plausible way of breaking out of what has become one of the sharpest points of the 'blame game' over Irish environmental policy.

Ensuring Regulatory Independence

Regulatory independence is a key concept that must be central to any genuine institutional reform. Ensuring that principle is upheld requires very specific reforms of local government, the EPA, and An Bord Pleanála.

Firstly, a unique argument is made here for significant changes in Irish local governance. Independent environmental and planning inspectors should be established, but distinct from the local authority bureaucracy. These statutory officers could administer both the planning permit and zoning process in full independence. A separate local environmental inspectorate could provide a basic and local field level enforcement unit, working to an agreed schedule of inspections, with oversight from the national EPA or Office of Environmental Enforcement (OEE).

The rationale for the creation of a cadre of independent environmental and planning inspectors lies with the separation of powers principle. Regulators, as referees, should be as free as is practicable of partisan political direction or conflicts of interest. Unfortunately, that logic has not been applied to the local level. There is no reason why it cannot be. Existing dedicated environmental enforcement staff, together with the local planning office, could easily be taken out of the hands of the local government entirely, which in reality means the supervision of the County or City Manager.

Each council area[13] could then have a statutory planning inspector and a separate environmental inspector. At a stroke, such a bold move would mean planning and local environmental issues would be free from any alleged or real conflicts of interest with the activities of local governments themselves. Establishing such distinctive posts would also raise the profile of the job involved, whereas now such staff toil relatively anonymously. Ideally, this change should also remove the ability for councillors to rezone lands in order to court votes. The planning inspector would decide specific zoning cases. However, it is obvious that no executive planning inspector should have complete discretion on zoning.

They would follow the land-use guidelines as set out in city or county development plans. Specific zoning decisions would be justified on expert planning criteria. Inspectors would have to explain how their decision would give effect to the general planning goals as decided by the elected councillors in development plans. Therefore, politicians would continue to set the *general* planning objectives. However, the execution of policy in *particular* cases would be carried out by a planning inspector.

It might be objected that this would lead to a network of isolated individuals who would lack adequate resources to do their job properly. Yet legislation could specify the establishment of a minimum number of staff. Another important qualification should be to set down an agreed minimum schedule of enforcement activity per annum for each inspector to undertake. It could also be specified that staff would have a background in relevant regulatory training and expertise, such as planning or environmental law. Ring-fenced funding instruments to guarantee financial independence for core funding would be necessary. These could be programmed to rise in line with inflation. The ability to charge fees for planning permission and environmental inspections would also help in that regard.

If there were concerns that new planning and environmental inspectors would be isolated with regard to their role, there are simple precautions. National level networking could be undertaken through annual conferences. A joint training centre or programme would help. There might also be scope to explore a structured exchange of views with An Bord Pleanála. Local environmental enforcement inspectors could be networked together under the auspices of the national Office for Environmental Enforcement (OEE), which currently resides within the EPA.

The EPA itself requires urgent reform to guarantee not just its regulatory independence, but the appearance that it is so. Too much discretion is left to the Minister for the Environment or the government of the day. It is *they* who appoint members to the EPA's twelve-strong advisory committee, its powerful director-General, and the other Directors (see Table 5.2).[14] Only one of the twelve advisory committee members need be from an environmentalist organization.[15] The funding base of the EPA should be made more independent and less at the discretion of government ministers of the day.[16] Under its current set-up, the Minister for the Environment has potentially wide powers to direct the EPA to take action on a range of activities.[17] There is no reason why some of these powers should not also be available to the relevant Oireachtas committee.

TABLE 5.2 BOARD OF DIRECTORS AND ADVISORY COMMITTEE OF THE EPA
(As of May 2006)

BOARD OF DIRECTORS
Note: Formal titles (Dr, Ms, etc.) have *not* been used.

Mary Kelly
(Director General)
Padraic Larkin
(Deputy Director General and Director of Office of Licensing and Guidance)
Larry Stapleton
(Director of Office of Environmental Assessment)
Laura Burke
(Director of Office of Communications and Corporate Services)
Dara Lynott
(Director of Office of Environmental Enforcement)

ADVISORY COMMITTEE
Note the third advisory committee ended its term in March 2004. The fourth advisory committee was not appointed until March 2006.

Sean Byrne *(Honorary secretary, Wicklow Uplands Council)**
Marion Byron *(IBEC)*
John Buckley *(Auctioneer, Killarney, Co. Kerry)**
Willie Callaghan *(Association of Municipal Authorities in Ireland)*
Carmel Dawson *(Irish Countrywomen's Association)*
John Dillon *(farmer and ex president of Irish Farmers Association)**
Donal Harte *(farmer and Irish Creamery Milk Suppliers Association)*
Mary Kelly *(Director General of the EPA and ex-officio member)*
Jeanne Meldon *(environmental consultant and Fáilte Ireland – State Tourist Board)*
Irene Sweeney *(community representative, Arklow, Co. Wicklow)**
John Sweeny *(Royal Irish Academy)*
Katherine Walsh *(Institute of Engineers of Ireland)*

---

*Denotes a ministerial appointment

In general, a greater say should be given to the Oireachtas as a whole, operating through committee oversight.[18] In particular, new legislation should specify that advisory committee members and directors should be objectively expert or qualified on environmental matters: currently the minister decides this as a matter of their opinion. Appointments could be nominated by the minister after receiving independent advice, but then confirmed through an Oireachtas committee hearing. Selection of candidates from the corporate sector must be balanced by appointments from the third-level scientific community, and especially from established environmental NGOs. The bigger issue is to continue reorienting the EPA away from merely being a licensing body to becoming a more proactive enforcer.

In fact there is an argument for separating the Office of Environmental Enforcement (OEE) from the EPA proper. Originally, when the OEE was being mooted in response to Commission pressure, such a move was seriously considered. However, it appears that Department of Finance cost concerns forced the new entity to remain within the EPA structure. Given the way the EPA has evolved, a distinctive OEE might seem prudent. Rather than wait around for the EPA to undergo a culture shift from permitting to environmental policing, why not just separate the two and let them specialize in what each does best?

Under this model the EPA would still focus on permitting, and indeed it would continue to inspect IPPC and waste permits. It would also provide a high-level laboratory back-up for national and local governments. It should also increase its fast response capability to citizens' reports of pollution.

However, the OEE would be free to get on with a general environmental inspection and enforcement programme (not just of licences). They could also be more responsive to public complaints and worries. Crucially, a separate OEE would also be able to scrutinize the EPA's own inspection duties to make sure they were not being too lenient on firms, a repeated allegation by environmentalists. It could have an oversight role, then, on IPPC and waste licensing as administered by the EPA.

The real justification here for such a separation would be to guard against 'agency capture'. This is the phenomenon whereby regulatory agencies can become too close with the licensees they regulate. It will be recalled that environmentalists have alleged that the EPA is too pro-industry in its outlook. Creating a distinct environmental policing agency in the guise of the OEE would avoid putting 'all the eggs in one basket' in this respect.

Much more problematic is the issue of An Bord Pleanála, which has come under sustained criticism from developers, politicians, and environmentalists alike. The existing agenda is one of 'fast-tracking' for national infrastructure. Unfortunately, existing government plans will be unlikely to do much to improve things. The proposed national infrastructure panel within An Bord Pleanála will effectively mean there is no substantive appeal process. All major infrastructure development will go straight to them, with only a limited judicial review remaining afterwards on questions of law.

A very different version of 'fast tracking' is suggested here. An Environmental and Planning Court, modelled on positive examples from Australia and New Zealand, should be considered. This could be a specialized division of the High Court, styled as a Planning and Environmental Law Court. It has worked well in New Zealand and three Australian common-law jurisdictions.[19] It would not be therefore out of keeping with our legal system and there is an Irish precedent as well. A Commercial Court, as a division of the High Court but operating under different rules, has been established since 2004. It appears to be working well. For example it was dealing with cases within eleven weeks on average by 2006.[20] By speeding access to the courts, it would then address the fact that delays are more often in the legal system rather than in the actual planning process. It would also provide a substantive appeal process on original local government planning decisions. Complete independence in deciding such appeals would be reinforced with the safeguards of judicial procedure.

In this model, planning permission would continue to be sought from local governments, as is normal. However, appeals of these decisions would go straight to this new court rather than to An Bord Pleanála. The only other courts of appeal would be either the Irish Supreme Court or the European Court of Justice (ECJ), on points of law.

Yet why do we need a new court as such, and how would it interact with An Bord Pleanála? It will be recalled that strategic planning guidelines (SPGs), as provided for under the Planning and Development Act 2000, have had a major effect in how the Board reaches decisions. In practice they have operated as strongly persuasive directives that the board are obliged to 'have regard to'. Strictly speaking, they do leave the Board with some discretion. The problem is that in practice they have diminished the Board's regulatory freedom. SPGs subtly shift the identity of the Board from being a national planning referee to becoming the government's own head planning inspector, obliged to make decisions which meet *its* directives. The Board becomes just another organ of government, rather than a separate arm of the state. Once again, the separation of powers principle appears here as a critical concept.

An Bord Pleanála should be clear about what it is. Either it is a quasi-judicial body that offers independent evaluation and adjudication over planning proposals or it is an executive agency of government whose job is to implement their planning policies.[21] One body cannot do both of these tasks. Therefore, the simplest reform would be to split the functions of the existing planning board along those lines. What is now a semi-judicial role within An Bord Pleanála should be made a fully judicial function of a new court.

This approach would copper-fasten the role of independent adjudication over any planning proposal. It would ensure that the local government level gets a first say in the process, something which the proposed strategic infrastructure 'fast-tracking' Bill reduces for major projects. However, crucial to its success would be major changes in rules of procedure as regards the handling of evidence. Judges empanelled for such a court should be statutorily mandated to adopt a more inquisitorial mode of judicial practice. The goal should be to get judges to examine the substance of the proposed development in the round, and not just whether the letter of the law as regards procedure had been followed. That means some evaluation of expert scientific argument.

Another function which an Environmental and Planning Court could have would be to act as an appeal body for IPPC and waste licences granted or refused by the EPA. It will be recalled that, currently, the EPA both grants preliminary licences and acts as the appellate body as well. In doing this, an Environmental and Planning Court would certainly need to be equipped to weigh scientific evidence and not merely consider procedural evidence.

It might be better if An Bord Pleanála were to become an executive agency, leaving its quasi-judicial functions to specialist judges. Alternatively, if it were felt that the volume of cases would be too much for a court to handle cost-effectively, a division of labour could be worked out. Cases involving national infra-structure, designated ecological areas, or listed buildings, should all go automatically to the Environmental and Planning Court. More routine appeals could continue to be handled by the Board.

Serious consideration should also be given to developing a proper national spatial planning agency. It is possible that An Bord Pleanála could be oriented in that direction, especially if its appeals function were wound down. This would involve design-ing, steering, and implementing a coherent planning policy for national and local governments, and not merely adjudicating on planning appeals. Another future role for the Board could be increased checking that planning laws are being properly applied by local governments – an oversight function. A serious weakness with the existing configuration of Bord Pleanála is that it is not oriented to operate as an enforcement agency over the planning conditions it mandates. These are often flouted.

Improving implementation

The implementation of environmental policy is clearly another area that needs attention. Much of the above menu of institu-tional reforms would go a considerable way towards improving the institutional capacity to implement and enforce environmental laws. However, other reforms would have merit as well.

The political responsibility for implementation and enforcement of environmental laws is currently opaque. Existing ministers for environment and local government either blame previous incum-bents, other government departments, or even local governments. That sort of 'blame game' leads nowhere.

One innovation could be the creation of a junior ministerial post with responsibility for implementation and enforcement of environmental laws; a 'minister for implementation'.[22] This person would have a remit to bring together senior civil service grades and local government officials to prioritize difficult cases and, above all, to anticipate problems before they become serious.

They could act as an information broker within the maze of government. Such an office would also confer political leadership for this vital issue upon one identifiable individual. This minister would, of course, have to be answerable to the Oireachtas. However, it would not be fair to create such a post without conferring some concrete powers and resources upon the office holder.

That means either some legal powers of coercion (perhaps directed at local authorities) or, more optimistically, control over a small discretionary implementation fund, in the region of several million euro. These funds could allow for research into particularly problematic areas of implementation and pilot projects to resolve problems.

In any event, the key point here is that high-level political responsibility should be taken within national government for tackling the worst implementation log-jams. That task is far too important to be left to ordinary line ministers. They are simply too busy with other agendas. Moreover, it would make sense given that implementation problems frequently cross over the supposedly neat boundaries of existing government departments.

But funding will also be vital for successful implementation. To be effective, implementation requires a mixed formula of 'carrot and stick'. That means financial resources have to be found for side-payments to those who can be broadly identified as deserving of them during the implementation process. The danger, of course, is that such a scenario quickly ends up degenerating into something of a 'bribe' logic to ensure acceptance for what is, after all, simply the law. The 'polluter pays' principle once again arises here, but its use is inappropriate. In the case of EU ecologically sensitive areas designations, which is the single biggest implementation problem facing the Irish authorities, it risks labelling landowners as 'polluters'. In fact, the issue often turns on the question of their potential future development rights of designated lands.

One way forward would be to offer more proactive *investments* in environmental technologies rather than doling out lump-sum *compensation*. These targeted investments would be just like grants that are commonly provided for industrial firms to research, develop, and install cleaner production technologies. There is considerable scope to apply classic ecological modernization strategies here. If applied intelligently, such investment funding would provide a *substantive* rather than *procedural* solution to implementation problems. For example, advances in mapping technologies and computers would also allow for 'smarter' applications of fertilizers at field level. The serious problem of contamination of rural drinking water supplies could even be addressed by requiring new homes in rural areas to have their own 'state of the art' active filtration systems, or other novel approaches to water sanitation.

Excessive animal manure wastes could be profitably used for energy generation on-farm and off. In 2005, the EPA released a very important discussion document on the scope for centralized anaerobic digestion plants as a means of solving much of Ireland's farm waste problems.[23] It was greeted mostly with indifference by policy-makers. Yet in light of the furore over the Nitrates Directive, it is amazing that more government support for such technologies is not forthcoming. In fact, by 2006, proposals for new anaerobic digestion plants were facing local opposition at the planning stage, in part because of poor location.[24] There is a need for government leadership and legislation to establish where exactly such plants should be located and what limits should be set as to their scale.

Doubtless there would be some things that grants for technology and investments could not solve. For example, quarrying of designated habitats is a type of activity that will almost inevitably destroy the habitat in question. In that case, one has to manage intelligently the demand for the product in question: aggregates, gravel, or stone. Some countries apply an aggregates tax for that purpose.[25] Ireland, unsurprisingly, does not, although it should be considered.

Alternatively, there may even be merit in paying landowners to become, where they are willing, much more proactive managers of key biodiversity zones. The 'compensation culture' of past schemes should be ended. A shift should be made to paying farmers a significant regular income for providing specific nature protection services, basic field-level ecological monitoring and, in some cases, active habitat creation and maintenance.[26] A flaw with the existing REPS programme is that it is simply not targeted enough: many participants are smaller farmers who pose few environmental threats. What is needed is a fiscal instrument which is very focused on the designated ecologically sensitive lands under EU directives. For example, since 2005, the UK has experimented with 'environmental stewardship' payments. These combine targeting, but are also open to a wider pool of farmers, and have tiered payments according to the quality of additional environmental protection the farmer provides.[27]

While the above measures are all about 'resourced implementation', there is still a need for a forceful application of environmental law. Already the creation of the OEE is a move in the right direction. Yet it could be enhanced even further, especially considering that in the waste sector there is a persistent problem of organized illegal activity. What is needed is a proper environmental policing capability, as, for example, has been used effectively by specialist units of the Italian police forces against illegal waste gangs.[28] Co-operation with the Irish police, the Gardaí, has been undertaken in the past and legislation allows for this. At one stage there were suggestions of systematic liaison with the Criminal Assets Bureau to seize the illicit earnings of illegal waste gangs.[29] Such links should be made a permanent and integral feature of the OEE. It would then become in effect a joint policing agency, not unlike the successful Criminal Assets Bureau.

The level of fines imposed should be increased, but this is not straightforward. In particular it would seem necessary to stipulate through legislation that mandatory higher fines be imposed. While the maximum fines set out in most environmental legislation are quite high in theory, in practice they are not imposed. The real problem is that, at District Court level, judges are very reluctant to impose larger fines without the benefit of a jury trial which is undertaken in the higher courts. A few recent prosecutions have been referred by the district judges to the higher courts via referral to the Director of Public Prosecutions (DPP). Yet for the OEE, taking District Court prosecutions are faster and simpler. If the OEE hopes to routinely secure convictions with much higher fines, they will have to develop considerable in-house litigation expertise to win in Circuit and even High Court trials.

Finally, there are other institutional reforms that could much reinforce environmental policy implementation. Two organizations not previously mentioned in much detail have been the Heritage Council and Sustainable Energy Ireland (SEI). Both are essentially advisory and research entities, meaning their formal powers for policy execution are restricted. Their levels of funding and staffing are also quite limited.[30] This is unfortunate, because they both have been successful environmental institutions and they have considerable future promise. With very limited resources they have sustained a tempo of environment-related activities which is impressive. For example, the Heritage Council have part-funded a network of twenty-four local government heritage officers (by end of 2004), which has built up the capacity of local governments to understand heritage issues in a broader way. They have also lobbied hard for funding for a national biological records centre.

The thinking of both organizations on environmental questions is usually ambitious and progressive. They deserve greater resources, enhanced formal powers, and a much bigger say. Once again, changes should be made to ensure their independence. A particularly important point, given conflict within the Heritage Council between its chairperson and council members (some of whom resigned), should be to ensure that only persons with objective experience, qualifications, or a track record of involvement in heritage and environment matters should be appointed to its governing structures. Currently, the very unsatisfactory situation exists whereby any Minister for the Environment (etc.) may appoint a member to the council, or to one of its committees, 'who, in the *opinion* of the minister, has an interest in, or knowledge or experience of, or in relation to, the national heritage'.[31] Environmental regulation is far too important to be left to the vagaries of ministerial opinion.

In fact, things would be much improved if both the Heritage Council and SEI were given a role for delivery of policy in a more authoritative way, and not merely left to advise government. For example, rather than merge Dúchas into the DEHLG, the much more obvious thing to have done would have been to assign those staff to the Heritage Council and give them the role of independently classifying, consulting, and designating sensitive ecological lands on a scientific basis, free from direct ministerial supervision. Equally, SEI could be given control of a very substantial funding instrument to subsidize the growth of the renewables sector. Currently, it only funds research and pilot projects. If Ireland is really serious about seeing renewable energy expand, then control of funding to effect such a transformation must be handed over to an agency which has the expertise and the belief in such technologies.

No single innovation here would be enough on its own to improve implementation. Yet, taken together, these measures could mark a significant breakthrough from the existing situation. Now a 'blame game' dominates the implementation question. If we are ever to break away from that, a range of very pragmatic and positive measures will have to be tried.

STRATEGIES FOR A BETTER ENVIRONMENT

A strategic dimension for Irish environmental policy has been a weak point in the past. There has been a failure to unite various measures into a coherent vision. Rhetoric about sustainable development has been common, but little tangible action has followed. Ecological modernization approaches have not been explored or debated to any depth, even though the approach has been widely used in other European countries.

Ireland needs to articulate its own coherent approach to sustainable development and ecological modernization. If seriously engaged with, these strategies each offer an insight into the exact type of ambitious environmental policies Ireland requires. In other words they provide the signposts for where we should be heading.

Making Sustainable development decisive: the case of energy

The problem with sustainable development as a strategic way of looking at environmental questions is that it has become a cliché. At times it appears to be a meaningless feel-good formula. All political parties are seemingly in favour of it. Environmentalists, farmers, quarry owners, property developers, waste contractors, civil servants, city managers, teachers, and school children will all happily quote it. The Irish government has produced several glossy and thick publications purporting to set out Ireland's commitment to sustainable development. Inside these, one finds general environmental policy promises that are already in place, and many fine aspirational statements (which cost nothing). Unfortunately, sustainable development has become something of a meaningless buzzword, abused with ubiquity and vacuity in equal measure. It urgently needs to be rescued as a concept if it is to offer any guidance.

In fact, sustainable development does mean something specific, even quite stark.[32] For one thing, it argues for a type of environmental policy that takes the very long-term view. Environmental policy measures should then be ambitious, proactive, and strategic, rather than reactive and small-scale. Long-term here means *at least* several generations. The standard definition is that sustainable development should 'meet the needs of the present without compromising the ability of future generations to meet their own needs'.[33]

Yet this formulation is odd. How can we literally pass on today's resources to future generations? Our known oil reserves will end in less than one hundred years. Conversely, essential natural resources alter as technology innovates. New resources are discovered all the time. Why then worry about leaving resources for posterity? And how can we make choices today for future generations, whose life conditions we can only guess at? At this juncture, some have been tempted to conclude that sustainable development is well-meaning nonsense.

But it is not at all nonsensical. For example, we can reasonably guess that human basic needs will not be likely to change so much. There will clearly be a need for land/territory, for basic nutritional needs to be met, for clean plentiful water supplies, etc. These are not banal insights. Sustainable development invites us to return to the basics in environmental policy. It asks what are the really essential resources to protect? In practice this would reorient our priorities towards ensuring water sources are ample and clean, that natural biodiversity (which cannot be replaced) is well protected, and that complex soil systems are secured.[34]

None of these issues typically receive the priority they deserve in Irish environmental policy. Indeed, it is revealing that providing reliable supplies of clean water is something which Ireland is today having difficulty achieving. A significant portion of Irish rural drinking schemes are contaminated. The town of Ennis, in Clare, experienced a tap water drinking ban for weeks in 2005 due to serious contamination. From a sustainable development perspective, this is a symptom that something is seriously remiss. For a state that cannot first ensure plentiful clean drinking water, fancy emissions trading schemes are very much beside the point. One message of sustainable development is 'get the basics right'. Put this way, sustainable development becomes suddenly tangible. It offers us a concrete framework by which to prioritize what needs to be done.

There is a second great merit in thinking about what future generations could legitimately expect from us. It quickly reveals that we must make hard choices. Environmental policy cannot continue to be seen as a type of policy where everyone can be pleased: a 'win-win' zone. Also logically implied by sustainable development is that any future generation should be able to undo our policies. We should try to avoid policies or technologies that would obviously seriously restrict their options or impose very large burdens upon them. These observations can be illustrated by taking the example of Ireland's future energy supply.

Ireland is among the most fossil fuel-dependent states in the EU. The share of oil, coal and gas within the total primary energy demand rose from 84 per cent in 1990 to 93 per cent by 2004.[35] This is clearly unsustainable, but what would be the alternative?

In concrete terms, the choices here would seem to be limited. Does Ireland invest very heavily in less proven renewable energies? Or should Irish utilities simply plug into an emerging European liberalised electricity grid and just buy the extra electricity they need? This might be from nuclear powered grids in nearby UK and France. Given that it is very likely that a large fossil fuel sector will remain for the next few decades, how do we mix and match different energy sources?

How would sustainable development inform these hard choices? First, it would speak against nuclear energy on any reasonable interpretation. Choosing to invest heavily in nuclear energy,[36] as is currently proposed in the UK, obviously offends the sustainable development principle because the nuclear waste generated remains so lethal for so long: 50,000 years. That in itself should be a very strong indication that there is something intrinsically wrong with such solutions.[37]

In the future, new technologies might evolve to manage such wastes, but it is also possible such innovations could take a very long time to emerge.[38] Defenders of the nuclear route often argue that nuclear energy is needed to prevent global warming as it typically has much lower greenhouse gas emissions than fossil fuels.[39] They argue that it would be irresponsible to future generations not to use it. Yet, strictly speaking, nuclear energy is not technically necessary to prevent global warming. A variety of other radical (or draconian) policies could reduce energy wastage and CO_2 emissions without producing toxic waste on the scale the nuclear industry routinely does. More obviously, renewable energies can much reduce CO_2 emissions without any long-term waste problem.

The conclusion to be drawn here is that nuclear energy should be rejected and renewables explored to the fullest extent. Under EU laws, preventing Irish electricity suppliers from hooking up to the British or French part-nuclear powered grids could prove difficult. Technically and legally, it might then be impossible to prevent the transmission of some nuclear-sourced electricity within Ireland. However, it certainly would be possible to put in place domestic renewable energy capacity as a competitive alternative energy supply on the island itself. The Irish state should also be able, through its tax system, to price electricity for consumers according to the environmental properties of the fuel source used by the utility. This could make renewable electricity cheaper for the consumers but more expensive for importers of electricity who have their contracts with nuclear-powered utilities abroad. In short, it is not impossible to adopt a domestic policy of promoting renewables and rejecting nuclear energy.

The fear with renewables has to be that any heavy investment would be speculative and end up leaving a country like Ireland with very expensive energy, low levels of supply, and an exposure to the technological risks of failure. However, such risks are *not* inevitable outcomes. They are merely *possible*. By way of contrast, with any form of nuclear energy it is a *certainty* that it will involve a highly toxic waste product. There is a big difference in risk here. Moreover, wind turbines, tidal barges, biomass and biofuels are all initiatives that can be relatively easily reversed in a generation or two. Current developments of their reliability and cost-effectiveness seem to be very positive. It is true that there has been considerable controversy in Ireland over the location of wind turbines in scenic areas. What would seem badly needed is greater direction through legislation which should specify that local authorities actively zone only the most suitable sites based on scientific evidence. This is what the Danes did in the 1990s.[40] Proximity to ecologically sensitive or designated lands should be avoided, and moving wind farms offshore might reduce some of the volume of objections.

Critics of renewables are on firmer ground when they allege that, even at the most optimistic growth scenarios involving huge public subsidy, such technologies would still leave an energy gap that would have to be filled by fossil fuels. There is a fear that renewables cannot meet the 'baseload'[41] grid requirement. Assuming this hard-headed analysis is correct (although advocates of renewables often reject it outright), what would the sustainable development perspective add here?

First, serious thought ought to be given to improving energy efficiency and energy conservation measures. An extensive degree of technological measures exist to squeeze much greater utility out of each unit of fossil fuels used, especially outside the large industrial sector. However, there is no getting away from a serious examination of the differences *between* various fossil fuels as regards their security of supply, likely cost profile, and environmental characteristics.

Oil appears to have reached a period of systematic peak prices, and supply may well get more unpredictable. Over the last decade, natural gas, which usually has better environmental characteristics, has become the fuel of choice for electricity utilities in advanced economies. Coal has become something of a 'Cinderella'.

Yet in the long term, it is not at all clear that large-scale investment in natural gas is wise. Indeed, natural gas may become much more expensive in future. Its supply is fundamentally scarcer than coal and more open to political risk. This was revealed dramatically when Russian suppliers briefly cut off western European consumers in January 2006. Coal has, by way of contrast, the great merit of enhanced security of supply and diversity of sources, which implies its price should be lower over the longer run.[42]

Coal may be the surer bet, at least in the long-term. Such a conclusion will doubtless leave many environmentalists distraught, being suspicious of coal as a classic dirty fuel.

Yet there is scope to improve the environmental performance of coal-fired electricity generation. A new wave of technologies to do this either exist or are emerging.[43] Doubtless some of these are hyped-up promises by the powerful coal lobbies who seek public subsidies.[44] Yet 'clean coal' technology deserves a more serious consideration, even if it should only be considered with the caveat of technical innovations emerging that can ensure a much reduced environmental impact.[45]

In summary, two interlinked energy policy agendas are needed. The first should be a long-term strategy of exploring renewables to reduce dependence on all fossil fuels. The second would be a more mid-range policy designed to optimize the remaining fossil fuel mix.

Unfortunately, Ireland's policy on renewables has been disappointing, especially when compared with what other EU states have achieved. In 2004, less than 3 per cent of Irish electricity was generated from renewables, and this is predicted to rise to around 8.2 per cent by 2020.[46] Denmark had 10 per cent of her electricity coming from wind energy alone by 2005. Yet the Irish Commission for Electricity Regulation (CER) has taken a bizarrely hostile view of renewables, instituting a ban on such connections in 2004 on technical grounds. The European Commission have had to threaten Ireland with legal action to get this lifted.[47] As of 2005, important elements of a general pricing structure for renewable electricity had not even been put in place for renewable suppliers connecting to the grid.[48] In 2006, the largest renewables utility (Airtricity) simply decided to walk away from trying to sell electricity directly to Irish domestic consumers given all the regulatory hassles they were faced with. This is an appalling indictment of the CER.

Yet both the CER and the state owned former monopoly, ESB, retain a deep technical scepticism towards the reliability of wind energy. They also worry that any subsidies for renewables, which are currently very modest,[49] would detract from the urgency to ensure adequate conventional electricity capacity is renewed first. Yet such views are beyond depressing, given that some studies have indicated tremendous potential for relatively low-cost windpower in Ireland. As much as 7500 MW could be harnessed by 2020. That would be a fifteen-fold increase over the limited capacity of 500 MW as of December 2005.[50]

By way of contrast, Germany, Spain, and Denmark all stand out as EU states that have made major investments in renewables, especially wind power. However, such a turn-around does not come cheaply. The experience of other countries indicates that, without large-scale public investment,[51] the renewables sector cannot easily reach a level for its fledgling industry to take hold.

There is then nothing woolly or vague about sustainable development. Its great merit should be to move debate towards making definitive choices that are well thought out at the strategic level.

Exploring 'ecological modernization': the case of transport

One of the biggest problems with sustainable development approaches is that the conclusions reached can be stark. More bluntly, they are often politically unpalatable. To be really effective as a political strategy, attention has to be paid to winning political support. There is a need for a savvy set of tactics to get its tough insights put into practice. To do this, I advocate that serious consideration be given to ecological modernization (EM) approaches.

That very unattractive term was used to describe how, in Germany, Japan, and other states, a type of environmental debate emerged which has as its key goal the reconciliation of economic growth with necessary environmental adjustments. The message is that environmental concerns can be systematically integrated into business agendas in ways that do not mean a lack of competitiveness, job losses, or industries going bust.

Efficiency is one key goal within the approach. That makes it, in theory, very compatible with currently rather crude debates about the competitiveness of the Irish economy. Such efficiency can be achieved through clever industrial design, but also by applying taxes. Equally important is management of consumption patterns. There is little point having ecologically super efficient production if consumption trends are wildly unsustainable.

One way of making this general discussion tangible is to examine how the ecological modernization approach could be systematically applied to Ireland's problematic transport sector. Obviously, I cannot here discuss all aspects of that sector.[52] It will be recalled from preceding chapters that a number of seriously unsustainable trends were evident: excessive car dependency, poor public transport, and controversial new motorway developments. How could ecological modernization be applied here?

A first goal should be to identify scope for much greater efficiencies. A second objective would be to stress 'softer' social and governmental management approaches to transport problems. Transport policy should not be merely about throwing money at problems and hoping that we can simply 'engineer' them away. A third goal would be ultimately, to steer mobility consumption patterns by state leadership.

With regard to achieving greater efficiencies, one can simply note that public transport is generally the most efficient way of moving large numbers of people in urban centres. This insight is further reinforced by the simple fact that the majority of journeys undertaken are local and routine. People need mobility mostly to get around to work, schools, shops and recreational facilities. Often these will be quite local (less than 10 km). It follows that *local* public transport in cities and towns should be the *first* point of departure of any transport policy rather than an obsession with building grandiose *national* transport infrastructure. The economic case for a high-capacity network of motorways sprawling across a low population density island and all feeding into Dublin is far from obvious.[53] Spending on an ultra modern and low emission local bus fleet should actually be a higher priority.

An EM approach to transport policy has many implications for national competitiveness. Nobody seriously disputes that an open island economy must pay great attention to the quality and cost-base of its export/import infrastructure. But it does not follow that existing investments in Irish transport have necessarily been conducive to that end.

McDonald and Nix, for example, have argued that Rosslare port and the rail connections to it remain heavily under-utilised.[54] Rosslare could be developed to provide a competitor to Dublin port. This would ease some of the Dublin-centric gridlock. At the same time, because of its orientation towards continental Europe, it would afford easier bypassing of the high-cost sterling economy of the UK. Importing from the UK results in Ireland effectively 'importing inflation' through an over-valued sterling price differential. Systematic sourcing within the eurozone should be a competitive priority to escape this geographic capture effect, whereby Ireland must take British prices: an old historic economic problem in a new guise.

The big challenge for public transport is the generally low population densities which make a mass transit system often uneconomic, unless carefully managed. This is a problem which advocates for a metro in Dublin may yet have to face.[55] While some commentators[56] see the proposals for a metro as *the* definitive solution to Dublin's traffic woes, there is rarely one 'silver bullet' solution. Indeed, building a new metro system from the ground up will unquestionably deflect financing and engineering capacity away from refining the existing transport network. By backing yet another much promised quick-fix solution, Dublin risks ending up with no system that really works well.

Successful ecological modernization experiences suggest that environmental goals are usually reached by blending different transport technologies together with sound management practices. The exact transport technology chosen for investment matters less than ensuring changes in the underlying pricing and regulation of mobility.[57] In the end, the issue of political leadership and control is vital. That is not to say that it is an utter irrelevancy whether public investment is either for trams, buses, metros, or trains.[58] Yet sinking money into a 'silver bullet' solution is usually a fantasy.

The obvious point should be that a mix of transport technologies is prudent. However, too many diverse systems are likely to be a recipe for the 'little bit of everything, nothing much of anything' syndrome. This is why adding a metro to Dublin's basic weave of Dublin Area Rapid Transit (DART) rail, other commuter rail, trams, and buses is unlikely to be such a good idea as it first appears.

Beside strictly economic criteria, sociological features are very important in considering transport policy. For example, for guaranteed high-density city routes, investing in tram and train rolling stock is likely to offer better quality, improved frequency and higher capacity. These features help to create their own demand, making the service economic.

One can see this effect with regard to Dublin's light rail system (LUAS). It has been greeted with an enthusiasm by the general public which must deafen the mass of criticism which it suffered. Many 'well-to-do' south Dubliners, who previously would never be seen dead on a bus, now willingly queue to board Dublin's new (and crowded) trams. This 're-conversion' effect of trams (getting the middle classes to re-use public transport) is partly why so many cities in Europe and North America are prepared to shoulder the expense of trams. They are building *quality* into public transport for the long term.

Another serious problem with public mass transport is the issue of financing. The Irish rail sector in particular has a history of stop/go funding arrangements. This has seriously held back the development of viable commuter rail and DART extensions which should have happened in the late 1980s. Dublin Bus has the dubious distinction of being one of the few EU city bus fleets to operate at a very low level of subsidy, meaning its fares are comparatively high.

There is a need to ensure public transport providers have access to long-term funding to finance continual improvements and upgrades. One possible way of doing this would be to create a long-term financial instrument, based on an initially large national government subvention or bond issue. This could be held in trust and actively financially managed by the National Treasury Management Agency (NTMA). Moderate returns could then be delivered on an annual basis for, say, a long cycle of fifteen years. These would provide city- and town-based public transport providers with a source of modest, but steady and reliable, funding for routine upgrades and improvements.

Management of public transport remains another critical variable. It is notable that the Irish government's Transport 21 plan in 2005 featured a promise to create a new 'transport czar' for Dublin. As of 2006, this suggestion has matured into the formation of an *ad hoc* Dublin Transport Authority (DTA) (to be formally established in 2007), which will take over the functions of the Dublin Transportation Office (DTO) and the Railway Procurement Agency (RPA).[59]

Broadly speaking, this is a very welcome move and should provide Dublin with the strategic leadership on transport issues it has deserved for thirty years. However, what is not clear is what will be the exact relationship between the DTA and Dublin's four different local governments, or the state-owned transport companies such as Irish Rail and Dublin Bus. Also of some concern is that this new agency will apparently be given the task of executing the very ambitious Dublin metro project. Will it then be a transport regulatory agency or an executive agency for the delivery of yet more new infrastructure? Given the scale of metro construction and the associated tunnelling, one wonders if they will have any time or energy left for anything else. The risk has to be that an obsession with providing new infrastructure will detract from the less glamorous, but more important, goal of refining and improving the quality of existing networks of buses, trams, and trains. Linking the two bizarrely separated LUAS tram lines and offering trams further north of the Liffey should be more pressing goals.

More generally, there is clearly a need for a much more broadly constituted national sustainable transport agency, which would complement the work of organizations such as SEI in the energy sector. Such an agency could have as part of its mandate an in-built bias towards public transport first and foremost. It could also have genuine regulatory powers to improve the quality of service offered by public transport providers such as Irish Rail or Dublin Bus, and perhaps control the type of financial instruments discussed before.

More profoundly, ecological modernization approaches would stress that there is scope for much greater efficiency by ensuring people live as close as possible to where they work, shop, and access recreational facilities. Because most mobility patterns are largely a reflection of housing patterns, this means decisions on housing have a direct impact on transport. If sprawl is allowed to grow unchecked, then car-based commuting patterns and traffic gridlock will follow. Compact cities and towns must be a vital goal of any spatial development policy.

Unfortunately, the official government mindset is still very much locked into an adolescent conception of transport policy. Their view is that transport means building more roads, railways, and infrastructure; as if Ireland were a giant Lego set. The government's Transport 21 strategy unveiled in November 2005, upon closer examination, was just a series of wish lists of various projects with notional prices attached. There was little mention of the vital link with housing and spatial strategy.

Yet how can compact urban centres become a reality? A debate about high density housing in Ireland is underway. One concern is that there are simply not enough available sites for development within existing city and town limits. In certain cases that may be true. However, it is obvious there are numerous potential sites, such as the giant Guinness brewery zone in Dublin or the nearby Hueston station site. Both could be feasibly developed for a mix of housing, retail, and commercial needs. Similar urban renewal and brownfield sites exist in other cities and towns.[60]

A second and more serious concern is that high density is a codeword for cramped and small apartments of low quality. Historically, Ireland's cities suffered from slum and tenement housing in the city centres. It will take a long time for affluent middle class families to consider investing in anything other than the standard suburban starter home. Currently very few apartment developments are suitable for families, nor under Irish planning law are they necessarily required to be.

Minimum living sizes per housing unit have not been adequately established by law. A confusion of different standards exist.[61] City development plans, notably in Dublin, have tried to increase apartment size. Even these moves are too timid to bring about a culture change where families might desire to invest in urban centres for living. The number of apartments in Dublin which were larger than the three-bed type (80 m^2), was just 11 per cent in 2005.[62] What is needed here are more demanding legislative guidelines. At least 20 per cent of future apartment development should be specified as suitable for family living, meaning three-bed units of at least 90 m^2.

A final area for very significant efficiency gains concerns the private motor vehicle. Environmentalists tend to view cars as *the* problem. However, there is scope for seeing them as part of the solution. A classic EM approach here would be to push very heavily for alternative fuels for ordinary cars, trucks, and vans. Biofuels could have a major part to play here in coming years, and hybrid vehicles (joint petrol or diesel/electric) are emerging. Two EU directives mandate that each country ensure biofuels have a market share of 5.75 per cent by 2010, rising to an ambitious 20 per cent by 2020.[63] Once again it is EU leadership which is setting the pace here. Targeted tax-cuts in successive Irish budgets could encourage the growth of an alternative fuel vehicle market share. Equally effective would be a simple rule that 20 per cent of all state owned vehicles should run on alternative fuels within, say, four years.

Demand management of rising car ownership, but especially car (over)use, would be another key idea here. In practice, demand management means savvy government tax systems are needed to achieve a calming of both the car ownership curve, but especially to control the type of vehicles bought by consumers, and excessive car driving. Unfortunately, the Irish tax regime on motors is anything but savvy. Indeed, from an environmental perspective it is crude beyond belief.

The bulk of existing Irish taxes on motors are levied at the point of sale or are connected to the ownership of the vehicle. Taxes on actual driving are comparatively low: a few road tolls, and moderate duties on fuel. The critical issue from an environmental perspective is to get people to use their cars less, or to use cars in urban areas which are more appropriate. Smaller compact models running on hybrid propulsion would be best, but even just newer compact models rather than diesels or SUVs can help reduce emissions.

A major reform of the entire tax system of motor vehicles would seem needed, but it must be thought out sensibly: not a revenue wheeze. What is required is a re-balancing of the burdens in motor tax. Taxes on hybrids or lower emission compact models should be reduced as far as is practicable. Taxes on heavy, large, inefficient and high emissions vehicles should be increased steeply. From penalizing the very fact of car ownership at point of sale, the tax system should increasingly tax driving itself.

Aside from fuel taxes, the most effective way to price car driving is by a sophisticated road tolling system, together with extensive car parking pricing.[64] However, it is crucial that tolls should be set at a fair level. If they are set too high, that will prove politically unacceptable and lead to a revenue loss.[65] Such revenues earned could be given to local governments and 'ring-fenced' to cross-fund local public transport investment.

To soften this blow and make the system more rational, other car taxes (vehicle registration tax, value added tax, road tax) would have to be phased out as part of a co-ordinated reform. Voters may just accept a phased-in package that is balanced, and if they see a tangible benefit for their taxes whereby revenues generated by tolls would, by law, be ploughed back into expanding public transport alternatives. There is little doubt such fiscal gymnastics would be very complex. Nonetheless, the broad logic of such a direction for reform is sound.

CONCLUSIONS

Reforming Irish environmental policy is more likely to be an art than an exact science. It cannot be a case of simply setting out what needs to be done on paper and then hoping that the force of good ideas alone will win out. Reform is an intensely political question. Powerful interest groups or lobbies will have to be faced down, as would innate civil service caution against any major change. Much might depend on the political complexion of future governments. If the Green Party manages to enter a coalition government, it might just ratchet upwards the political incentives for increased action. That has been the experience in at least some EU countries where Greens have joined cabinets.

Yet do we as voters simply care enough about environmental issues to support an extensive reform agenda? Does the political class have the leadership and sympathy to plunge into a complex series of institutional and other environmental reforms? Based on the past three decades, only a fool would answer optimistically to either of these questions.

Nonetheless, setting down here arguments for reform is a worthwhile exercise. It may contribute to 'starting the ball rolling' in terms of challenging complacency. It is also true that unless people can be convinced as to the possibility and desirability of reform then it will surely never happen.

The central message of this chapter is a positive one: reforms are plausible in terms of benefits they could bring. We are not dealing with intractable social problems where solutions are elusive. The infuriating thing about many environmental problems is that quite straightforward technical and regulatory solutions exist. They just have to be applied and enforced. The problems faced within modern environmental policy are mostly political: willpower, leadership, the mechanics of reform, or distribution of costs.

Another key message of this chapter is that the era of environmental policy being a somewhat boring but worthy area of government activity is at an end. We have entered a new era where the choices are hard and stark. Leadership must be repeatedly shown, and challenges will need to be anticipated and met with ingenuity.

Once again these are, basically, political impediments to be overcome. In that regard, the discussion here has been as much about the strategy of reform as the actual substance. I have not examined reform of policy instruments except by the way, partly to emphasize that reform should be strategic. We should start with tangible institutional problems. Fix those first, if only because institutions matter. By changing the institutional rules one also changes the nature of the political game itself. From a concrete start in overhauling the institutional hardware of the Irish state, momentum can then be gathered for more ambitious goals.

Yet this chapter cannot provide a precise recipe for reform. Indeed, many issues have been left unexplored. In any event, the aim of the chapter has been more to convince the reader about what is possible. We do not have to remain locked into a 'blame game' or stuck in catch-up mode.

There is no reason why Ireland cannot adopt an intelligent, ambitious, and demanding environmental policy. Moreover, such ambition does not mean sacrificing economic progress or a loss in competitiveness. However, it would be wrong to deny that no hard choices would be faced. Yet thinking strategically about an advanced environmental policy can reveal approaches that stress the need for economic efficiency, for intelligent management of resources, and for negotiation over vital questions of public policy.

This chapter, perhaps more than the others, will provoke reflection about where we go from here. Hopefully, it will also stimulate a debate about environmental policy reform among a few policy-makers and even perhaps among some interested citizens. But it should also impart the lesson that there are answers to the problems that emerge in any study of Irish environmental policy. We can, if we really want to, move beyond the 'blame game'.

NOTES

1. Space restrictions preclude this, although mention is made here of legal changes and new tax reforms. It should be evident that following the discussion in Chapters three and four, I advocate Ireland needs to significantly expand her use of eco-taxes, as long as these are not regressive in their income effects. See Flynn, B. (2003) 'Much Talk But Little Action? "New" Environmental Policy Instruments in Ireland', in A. Jordan (et al.) (eds.) Special Issue on New Environmental Policy Instruments, *Environmental Politics*, Vol. 12. No. 1, pp.136–56.

2. Irish Creamery Milk Suppliers Association.
3. See McDonald, F. 'Environmental Advisory Committee appointed by the Minister is unbalanced', *The Irish Times*, 31 March 2006; and McDonald, F. 'EPA nominee sent letter to Roche over illegal dump', *The Irish Times*, 21 March 2006. He points out that Minister Roche changed the provisions of the EPA Act 1992 in relation to the appointment of the advisory committee by statutory instrument (Statutory Instrument (S.I) No. 816 of 2004 Environmental Protection Agency (Advisory Committee) Regulations, 2004). More worryingly, no advisory committee was in place for eighteen months (mid 2004 to January 2006) despite the fact that the EPA Act 1992 specifies that such a committee is mandatory. In 2005, Irish ENGOs had been invited to nominate six members for a new advisory committee, and did so. Yet mysteriously, these nominations were all effectively ditched a year later. See Table 5.1 for a listing of the Directors and Advisory Committee members of the EPA circa 2006.
4. Szarka has pointed out that environmental concerns are a valence issue, meaning ones which are seen as intrinsically a good thing. Survey research tends, then, to overestimate public support for environmental issues. See Szarka, J. *The Shaping of Environmental Policy in France* (New York: Bergham, 2002) and Stokes, D.E. 'Valence politics', in Kavanagh, D. (ed.) *Electoral Politics* (Oxford: Clarendon, 1992), pp.141–64.
5. Alan Dukes, a Fine Gael TD and an ex-leader was one!
6. There has also been for some time a successful Cork Environmental Alliance (CEA) focused on the ongoing pollution problems for Cork Harbour. There is also a Cork harbour Alliance for a Safe Environment (CHASE), focussing on incineration.
7. This is not just my view, see the comments by various environmentalists interviewed by Pocock, I. 'We need to clear the air', *The Irish Times*, 13 November 2004.
8. Allen, R. *No Global: the People of Ireland versus the Multinationals* (London: Pluto Press, 2004), p.221.
9. Moreover, it is surely revealing that such local campaigns were generally at their most effective when they targeted party political candidates during the national and local/European elections of 2002 and 2004 respectively.
10. Services, Industrial, Professional, and Technical Union.
11. These figures come from the EENGOCF's own website, available at: http://www.eengosec.ie/. Pocock quotes a figure of €245,000 being given to environmental organizations from the DEHLG, but notes that only €20,000 of this was to help them make submissions. It is likely she is adding other funding to arrive at this figure. See Pocock, I. 'We need to clear the air', *The Irish Times*, 13 November 2004.
12. See EEB/European Environment Bureau, *Annual Report 2004: Aims, Activities and Achievements*, EEB Publication 2005/005 (Brussels: EEB, 2005), pp.105–6. Available at: http://www.eeb.org
13. Some may object that establishing new local environment and planning inspectors would be very costly for each local council area. Circa seventy-eight new senior posts might be required for every county, city, or borough

council area. A compromise would be to phase in these new statutory offices, and several proximate councils could simply 'share' a particular inspector.

14. Article 21(1) of the EPA Act 1992 says the Director General (DG) 'will be appointed by the government'. It provides for a selection committee to be established to advise the government on who to choose as DG. A shortlist of three candidates should be prepared. This selection committee includes the Chairperson of An Taisce, but state servants predominate. Article 21(7)b notes that the selection committee in considering who to appoint as DG should 'have regard to' their special knowledge and experience and other qualifications, although it does not mandate that this be proven by objective evidence, such as qualifications or work experience. For appointments to the Advisory Committee no expertise on environmental matters need to be taken into account: it is merely the minister's opinion as to their suitability that counts. This is open to partisan political abuse. The power of the government to remove a DG seems excessively vague and discretionary. Under Article 21(16) a Director General can be removed for ill-health, stated misbehaviour, but also 'if his removal appears to the Government to be necessary or desirable for the effective performance by the Agency of its functions'. What does this mean? All a government must do is justify such a removal by providing a written statement before the Oireachtas.

15. See Article 27(5–6), Environmental Protection Act, 1992.

16. Article 15 of the EPA Act 1992 stipulates that the salary of the DG and other directors is agreed by the Minister for Finance and the Minister for the Environment, and the same provisions apply for the directors and even the expenses for the Advisory Committee. This cannot be considered a proper state of affairs. One of the simplest historical interferences with the independence of regulatory officials has been to reduce (or increase) their pay. The DG and directors should be simply guaranteed a level of remuneration equivalent to an appropriate judicial officer (District, Circuit or High Court judge).

17. See Articles 79, 104,105, EPA Act 1992.

18. Currently, all that happens is that the head of the EPA appears before the Oireachtas committee on environmental affairs once a year.

19. In New Zealand an environmental court has been in operation since the early 1990s. The three Australian states which operate some form of an environmental court are Queensland, South Australia, and New South Wales (NSW). The NSW court has been arguably the more interesting model, and was originally founded in 1980. It has pioneered integration of alternative dispute resolution mechanisms and mediation into its court procedures. It has also employed fast-tracking for urgent cases, and more liberal rules on evidence. See Hayward, T. *Constitutional Environmental Rights* (Oxford: OUP, 2005), pp.111–14; Grant, M./DETR/Department of Environment, Transport and the Regions (UK), *Environmental Court Project Final Report* (London: DETR, 2000). Available at: http://www.odpm.gov.uk/; and Macrory, R. and Wood, M. *Modernising Environmental Justice: Regulation and the Role of an Environmental*

Tribunal (London: Centre for Environment and Law, University College London, 2005). Available at: http://www.ucl.ac.uk/laws/environment/ tribunals See: http://www.ucl.ac.uk/laws/environment/ tribunals/

20. See Kehoe, I. 'Commercial Court Service Cuts to the Chase', *The Sunday Business Post*, February 19, (2006).

21. There is a view that the government is perfectly entitled to have its planning policies reflected by the Board in its decisions. After all, Ireland has lacked a cohesive national planning policy for so long, isn't direction badly required? However, should such SPGs or ministerial directives be really addressed to an appellate body deciding particular cases? Arguably the appropriate agency to execute government planning directives are the local governments in their original granting or refusal of planning permission.

22. If this were thought to be too costly, such a minister could focus on the implementation of all EU laws and not just environmental ones.

23. See EPA/Environmental Protection Agency, 'Press Release – A win-win solution for farming, for our Kyoto targets, and for our environment', Wednesday 2 February 2005. Available at http://www.epa.ie/newscentre/ pressrelasearchive; and MacConnell, S. 'EPA urges re-use of farm slurry as fertilisers, energy', *The Irish Times*, 8 February 2005. As of 2005 only four relatively small on-farm systems were operating in the Republic of Ireland, whereas Denmark had over thirty. See 'Great Gas Sorting out Slurry', *The Irish Farmers' Journal*, 8 January 2005 and Nugent, A. 'Putting farm byproducts to work', *The Irish Farmers Journal*, 5 August 2000.

24. See MacEoin, R. 'Residents oppose plan for Wexford waste plant', *The Irish Times*, 16 February 2006 and 'Organic Waste Plant Refused', *The Irish Times*, 1 September 2005.

25. Denmark and Sweden both do, the former since 1990. The Swedish tax is on natural gravel and has been in place since 1996. The Danish tax seems to have been more successful. See Nordic Council of Ministers. *The Use of Economic Instruments in Nordic Environmental Policy, 1999–2001* (Copenhagen: Nordic Council of Ministers, 2002), p.60, 105.

26. See Viney, M. 'Cultivating a new Conservation', *The Irish Times*, 8 February 2003: and Dunford, B. *Farming and the Burren* (Dublin: Teagasc, 2003).

27. DEFRA/Department of Environment, Food and Rural Affairs, 'News Release – Environmental Stewardship payments begin', 8 February 2006a). Available at: http://www.defra.gov.uk/news/2006/060208a.htm

28. See Edmondson, G. and Carlisle, K. 'Italy and the Eco-mafia', *Business Week*, 27 January 2003. Available at: http://www.businessweek.com/ magazine/content/03_04/b3817015.htm

29. Reid, L. 'New move to seize earnings of illegal dumpers', *The Irish Times*, 22 October 2004.

30. The Heritage Council in 2004 operated on a budget of €11.2 million, an increase on 2003 (€8.6 million) and 2002 (€9.3 million). Of this, approximately €6.4 million was awarded in grants – well over half their total income. Administration costs were circa €1.3m or less than 12 per

cent. SEI in 2004 had a total income of €14.1 million. General administration and salaries accounted for circa €3.8 million or roughly 27 per cent of the total budget. Direct grants amounted to roughly €6 million. Sources: Heritage Council. *Annual Report 2004* (Kilkenny: Heritage Council, 2005). Available at: http://www.heritagecouncil.ie/publications/annual2004/HC Annual Report 2004.pdf; and SEI/Sustainable Energy Ireland, *Annual Report 2004* (Dublin: SEI, 2004a). Available at http://www.sei.ie/publications

31. The Heritage Act, 1995, III Schedule 2(2).

32. For an overview of the literature, see Meadowcroft, J. 'Sustainable Development: A New(ish) idea for a New century?', in J.S. Dryzek and D. Schlosberg, (eds.) *Debating the earth: the environmental politics reader,* 2nd edition (Oxford: OUP, 2005/2000), pp.267–84; Carruthers, D. 'From Opposition to Orthodoxy: the Remaking of Sustainable Development', in J.S. Dryzek and D. Schlosberg, (eds.) *Debating the Earth: the environmental politics reader,* 2nd edition (Oxford: OUP, 2005/2001), pp.285–300; and WCED/World Commission on Environment and Development, 'From One Earth to One World: An Overview by the World Commission on Environment and Development', in J.S. Dryzek and D. Schlosberg, (eds.). *Debating the earth: the environmental politics reader,* 2nd edition (Oxford: OUP, 2005/1987), pp.259–84.

33. WCED, 'From One Earth to One World: An Overview by the World Commission on Environment and Development', p.264.

34. Soil, in fact, has been something of a 'Cinderella' in the environmental policies of rich industrial states over the last three decades. Most countries have failed to develop serious policies to protect against soil erosion and contamination. Ireland has experienced soil erosion along the western seaboard upland areas, due to excessive sheep numbers overgrazing. On this view of sustainable development, that problem is really serious.

35. SEI/Sustainable Energy Ireland and Howley, M., O'Leary, F., and Ó Gallachóir, B. *Energy in Ireland, 1990–2004: trends, issues, forecasts and indicators* (Dublin: SEI, 2006), p.10.

36. What is more likely is a scenario whereby Irish-based utilities source a growing share of their energy needs from part-nuclear powered grids in fellow EU states.

37. This is not the only argument against nuclear energy. For a succinct overview of some of these arguments in an Irish context see Fleming, D. 'Why Nuclear Energy cannot provide a major power source', *An Taisce: Biannual magazine of An Taisce/The National Trust for Ireland,* (Summer, 2006), pp.7–8. and Greer, H. 'Nuclear Energy? Ten pointers leading to support for a nuclear presence', *An Taisce: Biannual magazine of An Taisce/The National Trust for Ireland,* (Summer, 2006), p.5–6.

38. See Economist Publications, 'A new way to dispose of radioactive waste', *The Economist,* 16 March 2006.

39. Note there are some greenhouse gas emissions associated with uranium mining and processing.

40. See OPET Network/EPU NTUA, *EU Best Practice in RES: Wind Energy in Denmark* (Commission of the European Communities, DG Energy and Transport, October 2003), p.5. Available at: http://www.opet-chp.net/download/wp6/EUBestPracticeWindinDemark.pdf

41. The baseload is the available power on hand within a grid which is needed to meet minimum customer requirements at various times of the day.

42. Moreover, some studies suggest that when the impact of CO_2 taxes is modelled on prices, coal still performs very cost effectively under a variety of scenarios involving different costs of emissions trading, taxes, and the cost of competitor fuels (mainly natural gas). See IEA/International Energy Agency (2003), *Emissions trading and its possible impacts on investment decisions in the power sector* (IEA: Paris, 2003). Available at http://www.iea.org/dbtw- wpd/textbase/papers/2003/cop9invdec.pdf

43. As of 2005 in the USA, at least one utility was operating a 'clean coal' facility, apparently achieving 90 per cent reductions of SO_2 and 60 per cent reductions of NOx. However, it is not clear if this plant is sequestering CO_2. See OFE/DoE/ Office of Fossil Energy, Department of Energy (USA), 'JEA successfully completes world's largest CFB demonstration', *Clean Coal Today*, 64, (Fall, 2005), pp.4–5. There are also plans to build such facilities in Europe. See Bream, R. 'Powergen's owners backs mix of energy', *The Financial Times*, 06 April 2006, Harvey, F. 'Clean-coal power plant moves step closer', *The Financial Times*, 12 April 2006, and Adams, C. 'New era of 'clean-coal technology', *The Financial Times*, 1 May 2006. There are two large EU-funded research programmes that examine the scope for capturing CO_2 pre-combustion (ENCAP) and post-combustion (CASTOR). For technological details see: IEA/WPFF/International Energy Agency/Working Party on Fossil Fuels (2003), CO_2 *Capture at Power Stations and Other Major Point Sources* (IEA: Paris, 2003).

44. See Flannery, T. *The Weather Makers: the History and Future Impact of Climate Change* (London: Allen Lane), pp.251–75. His main objections to sequesterization are the costs of such plants, and that large volumes of CO_2 might have to be transported long distances for burial. Once buried, the CO_2 would require constant monitoring and prevention of release (not unlike nuclear waste although not as toxic). It may be then that sequesterization should be seen as only a short-term strategy while renewables mature.

45. Some commentators who are in favour of nuclear energy tend to be dismissive of coal. A case in point is Lovelock, J. *The Revenge of Gaia: Why the earth is fighting back – and how we can still save humanity* (London: Allen Lane), pp.72–4 and pp.89–98.

46. SEI (et al.), *Energy in Ireland, 1990–2004: trends, issues, forecasts and indicators*, p.26.

47. See Oliver, E. 'EU to take action on national grid policy', *The Irish Times*, 24 March 2006.

48. Brattle Group and Henwood Energy Resources Inc, *A Study on Renewable Energy in the New Irish Electricity Market. Report prepared for Sustainable Energy Ireland* (Dublin: SEI, 2004), pp.2–3. Available at: http://www.sei.ie/publications.htm

49. According to Staudt, only 47 per cent of the installed wind energy capacity has been based on AER subsidy contracts. Over 50 per cent is from strictly commercial operators, principally from one large company (Airtricity). See: Staudt, L. 'Status and Prospects for Wind Energy in Ireland' (2005). Available at http://www.iwea.com/publications/statuspropsect.pdf. See also Staudt, L. 'Ireland must go down the route of renewable energy', *The Irish Times*, 29 September 2005.

50. See Staudt, L. 'Status and Prospects, etc.' (2005) and SEI/Sustainable Energy Ireland, *Renewable Energy in Ireland. 2005 Update* (Dublin: SEI, 2006), p.2.

51. A subsidy of €5–10 per MW/h would likely be required. See Brattle Group and Henwood Energy Resources Inc, *A Study on Renewable Energy in the New Irish Electricity Market. Report prepared for Sustainable Energy Ireland*, p.3. However, this report estimated that by 2009 the need for subsidy might well decline considerably, to as low as €0.5 per MW/h (ibid.).

52. In particular I cannot make much comment on civil aviation, yet with the rise of low cost carriers there has also come soaring air passenger numbers. The most likely policy option currently on the table at EU level is that the civil aviation sector would be required to enter into the EU emissions trading scheme (ETS).

53. See McDonald, F and Nix, J. *Chaos at the Crossroads* (Kinsale: Gandon Books), pp.288–92. They provide an excellent discussion of the low traffic densities on Irish motorways and the way that the M50 acts as the hub for this traffic. Motorways are designed and specified to cater for 55,000 vehicles per day. Irish motorways are predicted to be handling 3,500 per day.

54. McDonald and Nix, *Chaos at the Crossroads*, pp.308–15.

55. High density property development along the linear path of any metro is an important element in the business plan of those who promote it. In fact, one can argue that it is a giant property play first and foremost, with a metro added as the 'carrot' to entice investors, government support and, ultimately, property buyers.

56. Fitzgerald, G. 'Time to fast track commuter rail services', *The Irish Times*, 2 July 2005.

57. Indeed, it is an oddity of transport policy how old the technological solutions are. Consider that trams, metro trains, cars, buses and cycles all matured as technologies between 1900 and the 1930s! Today most cities are still tinkering around with essentially the same technological solutions, somewhat modernized.

58. See Beuthe, M. Himanen, V., Reggiani, A., Zamparini, L. *Transport Developments and Innovations in an Evolving World: advances in Spatial Science* (Berlin/New York: Springer, 2004), pp.255–74; Wright, R. 'Trams: A streetcar-driven desire to engineer lower floors', *The Financial Times*, 21 September 2004; CER/Community of European Railways, *Railways and the Environment: building of the railways environmental strengths* (Brussels: CEA, 2004). Available at http://www.cer.be/files/CER%20ENV2004–095925A.pdf

59. O'Brien, T. 'Transport Body begins work soon', *The Irish Times*, 12 June 2006.

60. For an interesting exchange of views on the question of how much land is available for development within Dublin City Council precincts, see Quinn, O. 'Let's make full use of the land banks and brown fields', *The Irish Times*, 13 October 2004, and Nolan, K. 'Institutional land required for development', *The Irish Times*, 4 October 2004. Existing Dublin city plans make it clear that 41,000 housing units can be built. The Hueston site would provide a further 3–4,000 and the Docklands site about 7,000.

61. Current DEHLG national guidelines provide that a minimum size for a single bed apartment should be 42m². For two-bed apartments it should be 54m². For three-bed units, it must be not less than 74m². Dublin City Council has specified, as part of its city development plan for 2005–2011, higher minimum sizes for apartments. These are at a level of 65m² for two-bed units and 80m² for three-bed units. See Buckley, D. 'The Apartment Size Debate Heats Up', *Housing Times*, 10, 1 (2006a), pp.12–14.

62. What is also worrying is that a significant number of apartments under 60m² continue to be built. Around half of the apartments built between 1998 and 2005 appear to be around 70m², but another quarter or more were well below this level. The result is that Ireland is developing a city-centre apartment stock that is structurally too small to sustain modern family living in city centre or urban areas. This reinforces the trend whereby families cluster in suburban locations and engage in commuting. See Buckley, 'The Apartment Size Debate Heats Up'.

63. The two directives in question are Directive 2003/30/EC and Directive 2003/96/EC. The latter allows member states scope to alter their tax systems to encourage this market to develop. There has been little response by the Irish government as of 2006.

64. Free car parking in large retail shopping centres on the suburban fringe sprawl is causing problems. Small city and town centre shops lose even more customers, undermining the very viability of a compact sustainable city.

65. It would also seem wise to prefer a system of electronic 'smart' tolling that can avoid physical barriers and queues. Examples of such exist in Oslo, Singapore and Stockholm. This can make allowance for how many passengers are carried and the type of vehicle. Tolls can also be varied for different times of the day: peak rates and off-peak rates.

Postscript

In January 2006, the Minister for Environment and Local Government, Dick Roche, warmly welcomed an international report that gave Ireland a high ranking in terms of its environmental policy record.[1] The Environmental Performance Index, a large-scale study prepared by Columbia and Yale Universities, placed Ireland in tenth best position out of 133 countries.[2] The Minister argued:

> This [was] a tangible measure of the progress this country is making in tackling environmental issues . . . Objective commentators acknowledge that the quality of Ireland's environment is high and that the environmental policies enacted by the Irish Government are advanced and effective . . . [but] there has been a tendency in some quarters, however, to overemphasise the challenges and to ignore the progress we have achieved. I have a very real problem with this. If the people of Ireland who are making a real effort are led to believe that our environmental policies are futile, we are halfway to losing the cooperation which is necessary to make them work. Those who talk down our environmental progress need occasionally to consider the damage that they can do. So it is very helpful to be assured, by objective international experts, that our policies are the right ones and that they are working very effectively.

I beg to differ. It is important to make a few comments here lest this book be accused of being overly negative. The argument has certainly been critical. A systematic culture of complacency within Irish government on environmental questions was alleged. The view held, *sotto voce*, is that environmental problems will be sorted out eventually. Or that we are a pleasant green little island with few genuine problems anyway. The really dangerous thing about uncritical commentary on studies like the Environmental Policy Performance is that they will be used to justify such complacency.

Firstly, to criticize the Irish record on environmental policy is definitely not to say that efforts to date have been futile. The argument here is rather that efforts have not gone far enough in their ambition. The message put out has not been to give up, but to strive harder. The main arguments of this book are very positive.

We need to move away from an adversarial style of environmental policy. Ireland should adopt pragmatic ecological modernization approaches, and take hard decisions informed by sustainable development. A tangible menu of institutional and other reforms was sketched out. These are both feasible and desirable. Such reforms just need to be genuinely explored and engaged with by social and political leaders. If anything, opening up a critical debate about Ireland's environmental record should be welcomed. It forces us to rethink where we should be going as regards environmental policy. The criticisms of this book have been purposeful and not unreasonable.

Secondly, what of the Environmental Performance Index (EPI) itself? Is it really true that Ireland's environmental record is actually very good, and have I got it so wrong? The EPI report is based on secondary data. It does not rely on original scientific measurement. There is nothing wrong with this, but it is only as good as the data it uses. Unfortunately, the authors admit that data problems have reduced the scope for their report to be truly authoritative. In the case of Ireland there would appear to be omissions for indoor air pollution and water consumption.[3]

The EPI is based on sixteen different indicators[4] and tracks performance of these. It only deals with what can be measured. Those environmental problems which are not easily measured (such as soil erosion) are simply not dealt with. Moreover, it is basically an assessment for the year 2006. Some of the data used are single figures for one or two years only, whereas other entries have been taken from longer time-series data sets.[5] The reality is that the EPI does not measure environmental performance over a period of time. It is not very useful to judge each county's *evolving* track record.

Also less than convincing is the absence of a proper assessment of environmental administration or the implementation of laws. In their introduction to the EPI study, the authors make the claim that good environmental policy is correlated with good governance.[6] The problem here is that the EPI (2006) study does not actually measure good governance. Instead, it relies on an earlier study, the Environmental Sustainability Index of 2005.[7] Minister Roche does not mention that this particular assessment ranked Ireland in a much less impressive twenty-first place.

In any event, the variables measured in 2005 under the term 'good governance' were not really useful. Remarkably, they did not include actual measurements of governmental performance on environmental policies – spending on environmental protection or staffing levels – and there is no measure of how many environmental laws are enforced. This means it can only be a snapshot view, based on proxy statistics rather than substantive environmental governance indicators.[8]

Finally, even if one accepts the findings of the EPI report without such criticisms, what is it really saying? For Ireland to come tenth overall is not so impressive. It is notable that a number of the smaller EU states have done better: Finland (third), Czech Republic (forth), Austria (sixth) and Denmark (seventh). Indeed as was argued in Chapter 2, Ireland's environmental record in the EPI is just ahead of Portugal (eleventh) but below Denmark.

Considering that Ireland is now a wealthy state, the real questions posed by the EPI study must be why is Ireland *only* in tenth place, and how soon can it move upwards? If countries like Denmark and Finland can reach the very highest rankings, why can't we achieve the same outcome? The arguments made in this book have never sought to portray Ireland as an environmental disaster zone. Instead the claim has been that our relative performance, compared to other states, should be so much better. But it is not.

Looking back, one strong feature of the arguments made has been a comparative focus. One needs to continually place Ireland's environmental record in perspective with our fellow EU states and a meaningful 'peer' group. Making comparisons with other countries' policies is vital to get a sense of how well or badly we are doing. It should be a critical point in informing future debate.

Yet now that our socio-economic fortunes have changed for the better it will not be appropriate to bracket Ireland with Portugal or Greece as a peer group. Because of our relative wealth, Ireland is probably in the same league as the relatively rich Nordic states. But are we in the same league as them on questions of the environment?

It is fallacy to see these or any other countries as paragons of policy enlightenment. Finland has embarked on building a new nuclear reactor, and Denmark has a penchant for incineration which is not uncontroversial. Most of the Nordic states have high levels of per capita energy consumption as well. The real story is almost always more nuanced and complex.

Yet these countries are pacesetters for some environmental issues, notably eco-taxes. Sweden has even declared, in 2005, a national goal to become the first oil-free economy by 2015. In practice what such rhetoric means is a huge investment boost for Swedish alternative fuels, mass transport, and renewable electricity.[9] Ireland will face major challenges to achieve an environmental 'front-runner' position of this ambition. Nonetheless, Ireland is now wealthy enough, technologically advanced enough, and politically stable enough to play a front-runner role. What is holding us back?

One problem might be a lack of awareness, among ordinary voters and even the policy elite, of what a really proactive environmental policy could look like. This book makes some modest contribution in that regard. Indeed, part of its rationale was to make known the vital concept of 'ecological modernization'. It could better be described as 'eco-innovation' or 'eco-competitiveness'.

Despite its arcane terminology, the idea is simple enough. Pollution, waste, and energy inefficiencies should all be systematically engineered away or managed out of the cycles of production and consumption. This can be achieved by intense industry and government led programmes of ongoing innovation and experimentation. However, that is not only what ecological modernization implies. A focus on government regulation to manage overall societal consumption and demand is clearly implied in the more sophisticated accounts.

There is no question but that it is a challenging vision. Yet it is also a deeply pragmatic and focused strategy. It offers a chance to move beyond a 'blame game' style of adversarial conflict in the courts. If taken seriously, it is not just about searching for technical fixes, nor does it necessarily have to empower a scientific elite. Indeed part of the agenda of ecological modernization is about opening up technological innovation and risks for democratic debate and scrutiny.

Environmentalists could easily become leaders within such a style of environmental policy by negotiating for innovations in mass transport, waste prevention, alternative fuels, and renewable electricity generation. It also offers a straightforward way of making palatable the tough insights revealed by a sustainable development perspective. The idea that these two approaches should be linked is not that commonly made, and yet they are both needed, even if ecological modernization would be in practice the more visible strategy. In fact, critics of ecological modernization have worried that it sells a story to voters and policy-makers that no sacrifices are necessary. By linking the concept to sustainable development, that mistaken view can no longer be tenable. In summary, one of the most distinctive conclusions of this book is a very strong endorsement of the ecological modernization approach.

It is likely that some commentators will find all of this far too neat. The accent here is firmly on reform. For those who self-consciously identify their environmental politics as radical, ecological modernization may seem too technocratic and consensual. Certainly those on the political right who have an ideological aversion to robust state leadership are likely to find the approach anathema to their views. So be it.

Yet those with radical perspectives are likely to be unconvinced by the institutional focus adopted in this book. For those influenced by what could be termed (very loosely) a post-Marxist critique of modern capitalist society, the stress placed here on reform of state institutions would seem naïve. There is a view that capitalist states will always choose to protect profit and property rights over environmental protection. It is only a short inference to argue that their environmental institutions will inexorably be full of bias and contradiction as a result. By this account, national institutional reform in an era of globalized capital can only be at best a token measure.

The problem with such arguments is that they assume a crude and static analysis of modern capitalist states. At their worst they imply a type of vast étatist and capitalist conspiracy. Such claims must also explain why there has been so much inconvenient environmental policy reform since the 1960s, in the same way that historic and even ongoing expansions of welfare entitlements are not obviously placating the interests of capitalism.

The literature on 'varieties of capitalism'[10] has, through careful empirical research, pointed out what such theoretical speculation forgets: modern liberal states and their relationship with capitalist economic forces are simply not uniform. States, their governing elites, and the wider public realm retain an autonomy of politics that rests quite apart from the machinations of structural economic forces. There remains a huge difference between the type of capitalism fostered by the Swedish state, with its recent stress on ecological modernization, compared with say the 'crony capitialism' favoured by the Chinese one-party regime. The latter faces huge environmental problems from wild economic growth. The former is taking solid steps towards a society which has fundamentally lower environmental impacts.

Culture and history cannot be discounted either as to why some states will move faster than others to address environmental problems. But neither can an independent role for the exact institutional structures within states be ignored. Institutions simply matter in influencing policy results. Accordingly, detailed debate about institutional design and reform is justifiable and necessary.

Finally, some critics might be unable to resist accusing this volume of dishing out its own fair share of blame! This rather misses the point. By focusing on institutional reform, and on the strategic approaches to environmental policy, a conscious shift away from recounting 'black/white' narratives has been taken. Few criticisms have been offered of individual political leaders, or of particular parties. The target has been a wider institutional malaise in which they both work. It is true that 'government' has been chastised at several junctures for taking plainly wrong decisions. Yet such objections are backed up and explained as part of a wider analysis. There is no attempt to argue that *all* Irish governments are intrinsically untrustworthy on environmental matters. In fact, the scope for government-led reform has been suggested to be generous.

Some robust comment has also been directed at interest groups and their spin on various environmental issues. They are big enough to take it. I have only done this so that the adversarial nature of the blame game is exposed and revealed for what it is: dysfunctional for everyone.

After three decades of modern Irish environmental policy, it seems that some of its characteristic features remain with us. Environmentalists remain weak and unrespected by the Irish state. Controversy abounds over environmental technology risks: incineration, chemical plants, and nuclear energy all retained a unique mobilizing force as issues from the 1970s right up to the 2000s. Sadly, nobody seems willing to protest *for* renewable energy, *for* trams before motorways, and *for* biofuels to replace petrol or diesel. Ecological modernization approaches have simply not taken hold. The Irish state retains an institutional hardware which, although superficially altered, has not changed so much. Regulatory independence remains problematic and local governance far too weak. When faced with conflict, the Irish state's core impulse is simply to impose its own solution. Implementing environmental laws on paper has probably become worse, if only because there is so much more law now.

How much progress have we really made on environmental issues? Is it not time to leave behind this 'blame game' style of policy for good? Isn't it time we fundamentally rethought Irish environmental policy?

NOTES

1. DEHLG/Department of Environment, Heritage and Local Government, Press Release – 'Ireland's High Standing A Measure Of Progress: Roche', 26 January 2006. Available at http://environ.ie
2. Esty, D.C., Srebotnjak, T., Kim, C., Levy, M.A., de Sherbinin, A., Andersen, B. Dahl, A., Saltelli, A., Saisana, M. (et al.) *Pilot Environmental Policy Index 2006* (New Haven: Yale Centre for Environmental Law and Policy, 2006). Available at http://www.yale.edu/epi. Note that New Zealand came first, followed by Sweden (2), Finland (3), Czech Republic (4), UK (5), Austria (6), Denmark (7). Somewhat surprisingly in view of their advanced environmental policies, the Netherlands was ranked twenty-seventh, Germany twenty-second, and Norway eighteenth.
3. Esty, D.C. (et al.) *Pilot Environmental Policy Index 2006*, p.172.
4. The sixteen indicators used were: (1) child mortality, (2) indoor air pollution, (3) drinking water, (4) adequate sanitation, (5) urban particulates, (6) regional ozone, (7) nitrogen loading, (8) water consumption, (9) wilderness consumption, (10) eco-region protection, (11) timber harvest rate, (12)

agricultural subsidies, (13) over-fishing, (14) energy efficiency, (15) renewable energy, (16). CO_2 per GDP. Esty, D.C. (et al.) *Pilot Environmental Policy Index 2006*.

5. For example, the data on particulate matter PM10 is just for the year 1999. Data for the timber harvest rate is for 2000 and 2004 respectively. The data for wilderness protection is just for circa 2000. Figures for eco-region protection are for 2004 only. The data for CO_2 per unit of GDP PPP is for 2000 only. Esty, D.C. (et al.) *Pilot Environmental Policy Index 2006*.

6. Esty, D.C. (et al.) *Pilot Environmental Policy Index 2006*, p.2.

7. Esty, D.C., Levy, M. Srebotnjak, T., and de Sherbinin, A. (et al.) *2005 Environmental Sustainability Index: Benchmarking National Environmental Stewardship* (New Haven: Yale Center for Environmental Law & Policy, 2005). The 2005 ESI can be found at: http://sedac.ciesin.columbia.edu/es/esi/ESI2005.pdf

8. There are several critics of the ESI reports 2000–5. See Raghbendra, J. and Bhanu Murthy, K.V. 'A Critique of the Environmental Sustainability Index', Australian National University, Economic RSPAS Departmental Working Paper 2003–08 (Canberra, ANU/RSPAS, 2003). Available at: http://ideas.repec.org/p/pas/papers/2003–08.html; and Wackernagel, M. 'Shortcomings of the Environmental Sustainability Index', Redefining Progress, 10 February 2001. Available at: http://www.anti-lomborg.com/ESI%20critique.pdf

9. See: Sahlin, M. 'Sweden first to break dependence on oil! New programme presented', *Dagens Nyheter*, 1 October 2005. Available at: http://www.sweden.gov.se/sb/d/3212/a/51058

10. See, for example: Rhodes, M. 'Varieties of capitalism and the political economy of European welfare states', *New Political Economy*, 10, 3 (2005), pp.363–70; Pop, L., and Vanhuysse, P. 'Varieties of capitalism, varieties of theory? Conceptualizing paths of change and patterns of economic interaction across models of market democracy', *Journal Of European Public Policy*, 11,1 (2004), pp.167–77; and Menz, G. 'Re-regulating the Single Market: national varieties of capitalism and their responses to Europeanization', *Journal Of European Public Policy*, 10, 4, (2003), pp.532–55.

Bibliography

Adams, C. 'New era of "clean-coal; technology"', *The Financial Times*, 1 May 2006.

Ahlstrom, D. 'Investigation set up too late to provide answers', *The Irish Times*, August 10 2001.

Ahlstrom, D. 'Valid questions raised on EPA's methods', *The Irish Times*, 21 November 2002.

Allan, K. *Celtic Tiger – The Myth of Social Partnership in Ireland* (Manchester: Manchester University Press, 2000).

Allen, R. *No Global: the People of Ireland versus the Multinationals* (London: Pluto Press, 2004).

Allen, R. and Jones, T. *Guests of the Nation: People of Ireland versus the Multinationals* (London: Earthscan, 1990).

AM&R/Abfallberatung Müllvermeidung & Recycling. *Reuse of Primary Packaging, Final Report, Part I – Main Report. Study for Commission of the European Communities* (AM&R, 2000). Available at: http://europa.eu.int/comm/environment/waste/studies/packaging/resue.htm.

Amárach Consulting. *Teleworking – the Shortest Route to Work. Report commissioned by Telework Ireland, Telecom Éireann and Dublin Transportation Office* (Dublin: Amárach, 2004). Available at: http://www.amarach.com/study_rep_downloads/telew.htm.

Amárach Consulting/Muldowney, E. *Hooked on Oil: Tomorrow's News – Issue Twenty* (Dublin: Amárach, 2004a). Available at: http://www.amarach.com/news/issue_20htm.

An Taisce. Press Release: 'Hike in Charges a Tax on democracy and Community', 4 April 2003. Available at http://www.antaisce.org.

Bailey, I. *New Environmental Policy Instruments in the European Union: Politics, Economics and the Implementation of the Packaging Waste Directive* (Aldershot (UK): Ashgate, 2003).

Baker, S. 'The Nuclear Power Issue in Ireland; The role of the Irish anti-nuclear movement', *Irish Political Studies*, 3, 1 (1988), pp.14–29.

Barry, J. 'Ecological Modernisation', in J.S. Dryzek and D. Schlosberg (eds.), *Debating the Earth: the environmental politics reader*, 2nd edition (Oxford: OUP, 2005/2003), pp.303–21.

Battersby, E. 'Knocking down Dúchas', *The Irish Times*, 19 April 2003.

Beesley, A. 'Inquiry is ordered as road costs rise 100%', *The Irish Times*, 21 February 2003.

Beesley, A. 'Green Party calls for appointment of new EPA director to be terminated', *The Irish Times*, 28 August 2004.

Beuthe, M., Himanen, V., Reggiani, A., Zamparini, L. *Transport Developments and Innovations in an Evolving World: Advances in Spatial Science* (Berlin/New York: Springer, 2004).

Bergin, A., Fitzgerald, J. and Kearney, I. *The Macro-Economic Effects of Using Fiscal Instruments to Reduce Greenhouse Gas Emissions (2001-EEP/DS8-M1) Final Report: A Report by the Economic and Social Research Institute, prepared for the Environmental Protection Agency* (EPA: Wexford, 2004). Available online at: http://www.esri.ie/

Bergin, A., Fitzgerald, J., Keeney, M., McCarthy, N., O'Malley, E., and Scott, S. *Aspects of Irish Energy Policy.* Policy Research Series No.57, September 2005 (Dublin: ESRI, 2005).

'Bin Charges referred to the Supreme Court', *The Irish Times*, 21 March 2006.

Blackwell, J. and Convery, F. (eds.), *Promise and Performance: Irish Environmental Policies Analysed* (Dublin: Resource and Environmental Policy Centre, University College Dublin, 1983).

Börkey P, and Lévêque, F. 'Voluntary Approaches for Environmental Protection in the European Union – A Survey', *European Environment: The Journal of European Environmental Policy*, 10, 1 (2000), pp.35–54.

Buckley, D. 'A crude way to address a very complex problem', *The Irish Times*, 5 September 2003.

Buckley, D. 'Shedding light on emission debate', *The Irish Times*, 19 March 2004.

Buckley, D. 'Putting Ireland out of business is no answer to climate change', *The Irish Times*, 2 February 2006.

Buckley, D. 'The Apartment Size Debate Heats Up,' *Housing Times*, 10, 1 (2006a), pp.12–14.

Burtraw, D., Evans, D.A., Krupnick, A., Palmer, K. and Toth, R. 'Economics of Pollution Trading for SO_2 and NOx', *Annual Review of Environmental Resources*, Vol.30, (2005), pp.253–89.

Butler, B. 'Industry has risen to challenge of Kyoto', *The Irish Times*, 1 December 2004.

Brattle Group and Henwood Energy Resources Inc.. *A Study on Renewable Energy in the New Irish Electricity Market. Report prepared for Sustainable Energy Ireland* (Dublin: SEI, 2004). Available at: http://www.sei.ie/publications.htm.

Bream, R. 'Powergen's owner backs mix of energy', *The Financial Times*, 6 April 2006.

Brennock, M. 'Greens and Labour voice strong concerns', *The Irish Times*, 14 April 2005.

Cadogan, S. 'EU wants action on pig-rearing, Derrybrien and Nitrates Directive', *The Irish Examiner*, 20 January 2005. Available at http://www.examiner.ie

Callanan, M. and Keogan, J.F. *Local Government in Ireland: Inside Out* (Dublin: IPA/Institute of Public Administration, 2003).

CANE/Climate Action Network Europe. *Qu Quo Vadis, EU ETS? Is the EU's key climate policy tool headed in the right direction? CAN Europe position paper on EU ETS Phase 2 (2008–12)* (Brussels: CANE, 2005). Available at http://www.climnet.org.

Carolan, M. 'Charge for domestic waste is deemed to be lawful', *The Irish Times*, 22 January 2004.

Carruthers, D. 'From Opposition to Orthodoxy: the Remaking of Sustainable Development', in J.S. Dryzek, and D. Schlosberg (eds.), *Debating the Earth: the environmental politics reader*, 2nd edition (Oxford: OUP, 2005/2001), pp.285–300.

Casey, J. *Constitutional Law in Ireland*, 2nd edition (London: Sweet & Maxwell, 1992).

CBC/Carrier Bag Consortium, 'What you have *not* been told about the Irish bag tax', (CBC, 2003). Available at http://www.carrierbagtax.com/notbeentold.htm.

CBC/Carrier Bag Consortium, 'Proposal for Welsh trials of carrier bag alternatives will not help the environment', *Press Information* 03/5888/3, (CBC, 2003a). Available at http://www.carrierbagtax.com/.

CEC/Commission of the European Communities, 'Eleventh annual report on monitoring the application of Community law, 1993', COM/94/500 final, *Official Journal of the European Communities*, C 154, 6/6/94, (1994).

CEC/Commission of the European Communities, 'Twelfth annual report on monitoring the application of Community law, 1994', COM/95/500 final, *Official Journal of the European Communities*, C 254, 29/9/1995, (1995).

CEC/Commission of the European Communities, 'Thirteenth annual report on monitoring the application of Community law, 1995', COM/96/600 final, *Official Journal of the European Communities*, C 303, 14/10/1996, (1996).

CEC/Commission of the European Communities, 'Fourteenth Annual Report on Monitoring the Application of Community Law, 1996', COM/97/299 final, *Official Journal of the European Communities*, C 332, 3/11/1997, (1997).

CEC/Commission of the European Communities, 'Fifteenth Annual Report on Monitoring the Application of Community law, 1997', COM/98/317 final', *Official Journal of the European Communities*, C 250, 10/08/1998, (1998).

CEC/Commission of the European Communities, *Implementation of Council Directive 91/271/EEC of 21 May 1991 Concerning Urban Waste Water Treatment as amended by Commission Directive 98/15/EC of 27 February 1998* (Luxembourg: Office of the Official Publications of the European Communities, 1999).

CEC/Commission of the European Communities, 'Sixteenth Report on Monitoring the Application of Community Law, 1998', COM (1999) 301 final', *Official Journal of the European Communities*, C 354 , 07/12/1999, (1999a).

CEC/Commission of the European Communities, *First Annual Survey on the Implementation of Community Environmental law (1996–1997).* SEC 1999/592. Working Document of the

Commission Services, Directorate-General for the Environment (Luxembourg: Office for Official Publications of the European Communities, 1999b). Available at: http://ec.europa.eu/environment/law/as97.htm.

CEC/Commission of the European Communities, *Second annual survey on the implementation and enforcement of Community environmental law, January 1998 to December 1999*. Working Document of the Commission Services, Directorate-General for the Environment (Luxembourg: Office for Official Publications of the European Communities, 2000a). Available at: http://ec.europa.eu/environment/law/as99.htm.

CEC/Commission of the European Communities, 'Seventeenth Annual Report on Monitoring the Application of Community Law 1999', COM (2000) 92 Final, 23.06.2000. *Official Journal of the European Communities*, C 30, 30.1.2001 (2000b).

CEC/Commission of the European Communities, 'Eighteenth Annual Report on Monitoring the Application of Community Law, 2000', COM (2001) 309 final, 16.7.2001 (Luxembourg: Office for Official Publications of the European Communities, 2001). Available directly from http://www.europa.eu.int/eur-lex.

CEC/Commission of the European Communities, *Implementation of Council Directive 91/676/EEC concerning the protection of waters against pollution caused by nitrates from agricultural sources – synthesis from year 2000 member states reports* (Luxembourg: Office of Official Publication of the European Community, 2002).

CEC/Commission of the European Communities, 'Nineteenth Annual Report on Monitoring the Application of Community Law, 2001', COM (2002) 324 final, 28.6.2002 (Luxembourg: Office for Official Publications of the European Communities, 2002a). Available directly from http://www.europa.eu.int/eur-lex.

CEC/Commission of the European Communities, *Third Annual Survey on the Implementation and Enforcement of Community Environmental Law: January 2000 to December 2001*. SEC 2002/1041. Working Document of the Commission Services, Directorate-General for the Environment (Luxembourg:

Office for Official Publications of the European Communities, 2002b). Available at: http://ec.europa.eu/ environment/law/as01.htm.

CEC/Commission of the European Communities, 'Twentieth Annual Report on Monitoring the Application of Community Law, 2002', COM(2003) 669 final, 21.11.2003 (Luxembourg: Office for Official Publications of the European Communities, 2003). Available directly from http://www.europa.eu.int/eur-lex.

CEC/Commission of the European Communities, *Towards a Thematic Strategy on the Prevention and Recycling of Waste*, COM(2003) 301 final, 27.05. 2003 (Luxembourg: Office of the Official Publications of the European Communities, 2003a).

CEC/Commission of the European Communities, *Fourth Annual Survey on the Implementation and Enforcement of Community Environmental Law 2002. SEC (2003) 804.* Working Document of the Commission Services, Directorate-General for the Environment (Luxembourg: Office for Official Publications of the European Communities, 2003b). Available at: http://ec.europa.eu/environment/law/as02.htm.

CEC/Commission of the European Communities, 'Twenty-first Annual Report from the Commission on Monitoring the Application of Community Law, 2003', COM(2004) 839 final, 30.12.2004 (Luxembourg: Office for Official Publications of the European Communities, 2004). Available directly from http://www.europa.eu.int/eur-lex.

CEC/Commission of the European Communities, *Commission Decision of 7 July 2004 concerning the national allocation plan for the allocation of greenhouse gas emission allowances notified by Denmark in accordance with Directive 2003/87/EC of the European Parliament and of the Council*, C (2004) 2515/6 final, 07.07.2004 (Luxembourg: Office for Official Publications of the European Communities, 2004a).

CEC/Commission of the European Communities (2004), *Commission Decision of 7 July 2004 concerning the national allocation plan for the allocation of greenhouse gas emission allowances notified by Ireland in accordance with Directive 2003/87/EC of the European Parliament and of the Council*, C (2004) 2515/5 final, 07.07.2004 (Luxembourg: Office for Official Publications of the European Communities, 2004b).

CEC/Commission of the European Communities, *Commission Decision of 7 July 2004 concerning the national allocation plan for the allocation of greenhouse gas emission allowances notified by Portugal in accordance with Directive 2003/87/EC of the European Parliament and of the Council*, C (2004) 3982/4 final (Luxembourg: Office for Official Publications of the European Communities, 2004c).

CEC/Commission of the European Communities, *Fifth Annual Survey on the Implementation and Enforcement of Community Environmental law 2003*. SEC (2004)1025. Working Document of the Commission Services, Directorate-General for the Environment (Luxembourg: Office for Official Publications of the European Communities, 2004d). Available at: http://ec.europa.eu/environment/law/as03.htm.

CER/Community of European Railways, *Railways and the Environment: building of the railways' environmental strengths* (Brussels: CEA, 2004). Available at http://www.cer.be/files/CER%20ENV2004-095925A.pdf.

Clancy, L, Goodman, P. Sinclair, H. and Dockery, D.W. 'Effect of air-pollution control on death rates in Dublin, Ireland: an intervention study', *The Lancet*, 360, 19 October 2002, pp.1,210–14.

Clinch, P. and Dunne, L. 'A Theory of Impediments to Environmental Tax Reform', *Environmental Studies Research Series Working Papers*, ESRS 01/14, UCD/ University College Dublin (Dublin: Dept. of Environmental Studies, UCD, 2001). Available at: http://www.ucd.ie/pepweb/publications/workingpapers/

Clinch, P., Convery, F. and Walsh, B. (eds.), *After the Celtic Tiger: Challenges Ahead* (Dublin: The O'Brien Press, 2002).

Coakely, J. and Gallagher, M. *Politics in the Republic of Ireland*. 3rd edition (London: PSAI/Routledge, 1999).

Coffey, M. 'Ireland one of the worst polluters in Europe', *The Irish Times*, 23 January 2002.

Coloe, J./EPA/Environmental Protection Agency. *Indicators for Transport and the Environment in Ireland: A discussion document on key national transport indicators* (Wexford: EPA, 2000).

Commerford, H. *Wildlife Legislation 1976–2000* (Dublin: Roundhall, 2001).

Council of Ministers of the European Communities, 'Council Decision 2002/358/EC of 25th April 2002 concerning the approval on behalf of the European Community, of the Kyoto Protocol to the United Nations Framework Convention on Climate Change and the joint fulfilment of commitment thereunder', *Official Journal of the European Communities*, L 130, 45, 15 May, (2002), pp.1–20.

Cotter, E. and DoT/Department of Transport. *Sustainable Transport Policies* (Dublin: DoT/Department of Transport, Integrated Transport Unit).

CPA/Combat Poverty Agency. *Submission to the Department of Finance on the introduction of a Carbon Energy Tax* (Dublin, CPA, 2003). Available at: http://www.cpa.ie/publications/submissions/2003 Sub CarbonTax.pdf.

CPA/Combat Poverty Agency. *Waste Collection Charges and Low Income Households* (Dublin: CPA, 2003a).

CPA/Combat Poverty Agency and Fitzpatrick Associates. Implementing a waiver system: guidelines for local authorities (Dublin: CPA, 2005). Available at: http://www.cpa.ie/publications/ImplementingAWaiverSystem 2005.pdf.

CSO/Central Statistics Office and ESRI/Economic and Social Research Institute. *Environmental Accounts for Ireland, 1994–2001* (Cork: CSO, 2003). Available at: http://www.cso.ie/publications/enviracc.pdf.

CSO/Central Statistics Office and ESRI/Economic and Social Research Institute. *Environmental Accounts for Ireland, 1995–2002* (Cork: CSO, 2004). Available at: http://www.cso.ie/publications/enviracc.pdf

CSO/Central Statistics Office. *Vehicles Licensed for the First Time*, February 16 (Dublin: CSO, 2006).

Cullen, P. 'Redmond conviction for corruption quashed', *The Irish Times*, 29 July 2004).

D'Alton, M. 'Excessive incineration capacity planned', *The Irish Times*, 12 December 2005.

Daly, M.E. *The Buffer State: The History of the roots of the Department of the Environment* (Dublin: IPA/ Institute of Public Administration, 1997).

Daly, M.E. (ed.). *County and Town: One Hundred Years of Local Government in Ireland* (Dublin: Institute of Public Administration, 2001).

Davies, A. 'Waste wars – public attitudes and the politics of place in waste management strategies', *Irish Geography*, 36, 1, (2003), pp.77–92.

Deegan, G. 'Farmers welcome new report on deaths of animals', *The Irish Times*, 21 November 2002.

Deegan, G. 'ESB can proceed with €200m clean-up of Moneypoint station', *The Irish Times*, 28 February 2004.

Deegan, G. 'Clare County Council to debate stripping An Taisce of status', *The Irish Times*, 17 April 2004a.

Deegan, G. 'An Taisce seeks change on planning', *The Irish Times*, 6 May 2004b.

Deegan, G. 'Clare County Council Moves to dismantle house building restrictions', *The Irish Times*, 21 September 2005.

Deegan, G. 'Investigation urged into health patterns after firm is fined', *The Irish Times*, 16 February 2006.

DEFRA/Department of Environment, Food and Rural Affairs. 'Nitrates – Reducing Water Pollution from Agriculture – Implications' (UK: DEFRA, 2006), available at: http://www.defra.gov.uk/environment/water/quality/nitrate/nitrogen.htm.

DEFRA/Department of Environment, Food and Rural Affairs. News Release – 'Environmental Stewardship payments begin', February 8, (2006a). Available at: http://www.defra.gov.uk/news/2006/060208a.htm.

DEHLG/Department of Environment, Heritage, and Local Government. *Making Ireland's Development Sustainable* (Dublin: Government Stationery Office, 2002).

DEHLG/Department of Environment, Heritage, and Local Government. *Progress Report: Implementation of the National Climate Change Strategy* (DELG, Dublin, 2002a).

DEHLG/Department of Environment, Heritage, and Local Government. *Preventing and Recycling Waste: Delivering Change* (Dublin: Government Stationery Office, 2002b).

DEHLG/Department of Environment, Heritage, and Local Government. *Environmental Bulletin*, No.55 (Dublin: DEHLG, 2002c).

DEHLG/Department of the Environment, Heritage, and Local Government. *Discussion Paper: Strategy to Reduce Emissions of Transboundary Air Pollution by 2010* (Dublin: Government Stationery Office, 2003).

DEHLG/Department of Environment, Heritage, and Local Government. 'Minister Roche Publishes Report on Nitrates

Action Programme', DEHLG Press Release, 14 October 2004. Available at http://www.environ.ie/.

DEHLG/Department of Environment, Heritage, and Local Government, *Planning Statistics 2004* (Dublin, DEHLG, 2004a). Available at: http://www.environ.ie/.

DEHLG/Department of Environment, Heritage, and Local Government, *National Action Programme Under the Nitrates Directive, 28 July 2005* (Dublin: DEHLG, 2005), Section 1.3. Available at http://www.environ.ie/.

DEHLG/Department of Environment, Heritage, and Local Government, Press Release: 'Breakthrough on Chewing Gum. Roche Announces €7 million Industry-Funded Programme', 26 January 2006. Available at http://www.environ.ie/.

DEHLG/Department of Environment, Heritage, and Local Government, Press Release: 'Farm Plastics Recycling: Revised Scheme Will Improve Service To Farmers', 3 May 2006. Available at http://www.environ.ie./

DEHLG/Department of Environment, Heritage, and Local Government. Press Release: 'Ireland's High Standing A Measure Of Progress: Roche', 26 January 2006. Available at http://environ.ie.

Delany, J. and McGettigan, M. *Air Quality Monitoring. Annual Report 2002* (Wexford, EPA, 2004).

DELG/Department of Environment and Local Government, *An Environment Action Programme* (Dublin: DELG, 1990).

DELG/Department of Environment and Local Government, *An Environment Action Programme: 1st Progress Report* (Dublin: DELG, 1991).

DELG/Department of Environment and Local Government, *Ireland: Climate Change/CO$_2$ Abatement Strategy* (Dublin: Government Stationery Office, 1993).

DELG/Department of Environment and Local Government, *Recycling for Ireland* (Dublin: Government Stationery Office, 1994).

DELG/Department of Environment and Local Government, *Moving Towards Sustainability: A Review of Recent Environmental Policy and Developments* (Dublin: DELG, 1995).

DELG/Department of Environment and Local Government, *Local Authorities and Sustainable Development. Guidelines on Local Agenda 21* (Dublin: Government Stationery Office, 1995a).

DELG/Department of Environment and Local Government. *Sustainable Development: A strategy for Ireland* (Dublin: Government Stationery Office, 1997).

DELG/Department of Environment and Local Government. *Changing our Ways* (Dublin: Government Stationery Office, 1998).

DELG/Department of Environment and Local Government. *Planning Statistics 1998* (Dublin, DELG, 1998a). Available at: http://www.environ.ie/.

DELG/Department of the Environment and Local Government. 'Government approves precautionary environmental policy on GMOs', *DELG Press Release*, October 9, (1999). Available at http://www.environ.ie/.

DELG/Department of the Environment and Local Government. *National Climate Change Strategy Ireland* (Dublin: Government Stationery Office, 2000).

DELG/Department of the Environment and Local Government and Drury Research. *Attitudes and Actions: A National Survey on the Environment* (Dublin: Government Stationery Office, 2000a).

DELG/Department of the Environment and Local Government. *Waste Management (Landfill Levy) Regulations 2002, Information Note and Guidance* (Dublin: DELG, 2002)

Demmke, C. 'Implementation and Enforcement in the Member States: internal management of European Environmental Policy', in C. Demmke (ed.), *Managing European Environmental Policy: the role of the member states in the policy process* (Maastrict: EIPA,1997), pp. 41–81.

De Sadeler, N. *Environmental Principles: From Political Slogans to Legal Rules* (Oxford: OUP, 2002).

Dobson, A. *Justice and the Environment: Conceptions of Environmental Sustainability and Theories of Distributive Justice* (Oxford: OUP, 1998).

DoF/Department of Finance. *State Directory* (Dublin: Government Stationery Office, 2000).

DoF/Department of Finance. *Budget 2003 Commentary*. Available at: http://www.budget.gov.ie/2003/esttabsEnviron.asp#Environ.

Dooley, C. 'Resistance in Kilkenny to motorway plan', *The Irish Times*, 21 July 2001.

Doyle, A. 'Environmental Impact and Who Assesses What', *Irish Planning and Environmental Law Journal*, 5, 1, (1998), pp.13–18.

Dunford, B. *Farming and the Burren* (Dublin: Teagasc, 2003).

Dunne, J. 'AA says Dublin is among the least car populated cities in EU', *The Irish Times*, 4 January 1997.

Dunne, T. 'Letters – Farmers and Water Quality', *The Irish Times*, 5 May 2005.

DTEC/ Department of Transport, Energy, and Communications. *Renewable Energy: A Strategy for the Future* (Dublin: DTEC, 1996).

DTO/Dublin Transportation Office. *A Platform for Change: Strategy 2000–2016* (Dublin: DTO, 2001).

DTO/Dublin Transportation Office. *Quality Bus Corridor Monitoring Report* (November, 2004). Available at http://www.dto.ie/.

EA/Environment Australia/Department of Environment and Heritage. *Plastic Shopping Bags – Analysis of Levies and Environmental Impacts Final Report*, December (Canberra: EA, 2002).

Economist Publications. 'A new way to dispose of radioactive waste', *The Economist*, 16 March 2006.

ECOTEC Research and Consulting (et al.). *Study on the Economic and Environmental Implications of the Use of Environmental Taxes and Charges in the European Unions and its Member States*, (Brussels: ECOTEC, April, 2001). Available at: http://ec.europa.eu/environment/enveco/taxation/ch1t4_overview.pdf.

Editor/Irish Times. 'Rethink Required (on forestry budget cuts)', *The Irish Times*, Friday, 22 November 2002.

Editor/Irish Times. 'End of Dúchas', *The Irish Times*, 28 April 2003.

Editor/Irish Times. 'Carbon emissions', *The Irish Times*, 24 February 2004.

Editor/Irish Times. 'Smoke in their eyes', *The Irish Times*, 13 September 2004.

Editor/Irish Times. 'Opinion – Failure on Kyoto', *The Irish Times*, 25 June 2005.

Editor/Irish Times. 'Diluting the Nitrates Directive', *The Irish Times*, 21 February 2006.

Edmondson, G. and Carlisle, K. 'Italy and the Eco-mafia'. *Business Week*, 27 January 2003. Available at: http://www. businessweek.com/magazine/content/03_04/b3817015.htm.

EEA/European Environment Agency. *Environmental taxes – Recent developments in tools for integration. Environmental issue report No 18* (Copenhagen: EEA, 2000). Available at: http://reports.eea.eu.int/Environmental_Issues_No_18/en/tab_content_RLR.

EEA/European Environment Agency. *Hazardous waste generation in EEA member countries: Comparability of classification systems and quantities. Topic Report No.14/2001* (Copenhagen: EEA, 2001). Available at http://reports. eea.eu.int/topic_report_2001_14/en/Hazwaste_web.pdf.

EEA/European Environment Agency. *Indicator Fact Sheet Signals 2001 – Chapter Waste: Biodegradable waste in landfills* (Copenhagen: EEA, 2001a). Available at: http://themes. eea.eu.int/Environment_issues?waste/indicators/landfilling/w4_biodegradable.pdf.

EEA/European Environment Agency. *Europe's Environment: the 3rd Dobris Assessment* (Copenhagen: EEA, 2002).

EEA/European Environment Agency, *Emissions of Atmospheric pollutants in Europe, 1990–99*. Topic Report No. 5 /2002 (EEA: Copenhagen, 2002a). Available at: http://www. reports.eea.eu.int/topic_report_2002_5/en/index_html.

EEA/European Environment Agency. *Analysis and comparison of national and EU-wide projections of greenhouse gas emissions*. Topic report No 1/2002 (EEA: Copenhagen, 2002b). Available at: http://reports.eea.eu.int/topic_report_2002_1/en/tab_content_RLR.

EEA/European Environment Agency. *EEA Signals 2004 – a European Environment Agency update on selected issues* (EEA: Copenhagen, 2004).

EEA/European Environment Agency. *Greenhouse gas emission trends and projections in Europe 2004. EEA Report No. 5/2004*, (EEA: Copenhagen, 2004a). Available at: http://reports.eea.eu.int/eea_report_2004_5/en.

EEA/European Environment Agency. *Indicator Fact Sheet WEU16 Urban Waste Water Treatment* (EEA: Copenhagen, 2004b).

EEA/European Environment Agency. *Sustainable Use and Management of Natural Resources: EEA Report No.9/2005* (EEA: Copenhagen, 2005).

EEA/European Environment Agency. *The European Environment: State and Outlook 2005* (Copenhagen: EEA, 2005a).

EEA/European Environment Agency. *Greenhouse Gas Emissions trends and projections in Europe 2005, EEA Report No.8/2005* (EEA: Copenhagen, 2005b).

EEA/European Environment Agency. *Emissions of primary particles and secondary particulate precursors,* (CSI 003) – May 2005 Assessment (Copenhagen: EEA, 2005c). Available at: http://themes.eea.europa.eu/IMS/IMS/Ispecs/Ispecification 20041001123025/Iassessment1116511151442/view content.

EEA/European Environment Agency. *Transport and Environment: facing a dilemma. TERM2005: Indicators tracking transport and environment in Europe. EEA Report No.3, 2006* (Copenhagen: EEA, 2006).

EEB/European Environment Bureau. *Annual Report 2004: Aims, Activities and Achievements,* EEB Publication 2005/005 (Brussels: EEB, 2005), pp.105–6. Available at: http://www.eeb.org/.

Ellis, G. 'Third party rights of appeal in planning: Reflecting on the experience of the Republic of Ireland', *The Town Planning Review*, 73, 4 (2002), pp.437–47.

ENDS/Environmental Data Services (1999). 'Phosphate detergent phase-out in Ireland', *The ENDS Report*, 299, December, (1999).

ENDS/Environmental News and Data Services. 'OSPAR row over nuclear reprocessing, slow progress on chemicals', *The ENDS Report*, 306, July, (2000).

EORG/European Opinion Research Group/DG Environment/ Eurobarometer. *Eurobarometer 58.0: The attitudes of Europeans towards the environment* (Luxembourg: Office for Official Publications of the European Communities, 2002). Available at: http://www.europa.eu.int/comm/ environment/barometer/barometer 2003 en.pdf.

EPA/Environmental Protection Agency. *Proposed national hazardous waste management plan* (Wexford: EPA, 1999).

EPA/Environmental Protection Agency. *National Waste Database Report 1998* (Wexford: EPA, 2000).

EPA/Environmental Protection Agency. *Ireland's Environment: a millennium report* (Wexford: EPA, 2000a).

EPA/Environmental Protection Agency. *Annual Report and Accounts 2001* (Wexford: EPA, 2001).

EPA/Environmental Protection Agency and Lehane, M., Le Bolloch, O., and Crawley, P. (eds.), *Environment in Focus 2002: key environmental indicators for Ireland* (Wexford: EPA, 2002a).

EPA/Environmental Protection Agency/Office of Environmental Enforcement/OEE. *The Quality of Drinking Water in Ireland. A Report for the Year 2002 with a review of the period 2000–2002* (Wexford: EPA, 2002b).

EPA/Environmental Protection Agency. *Annual Report and Accounts 2002* (Wexford: EPA, 2002c).

EPA/Environmental Protection Agency/Smith, D. (et al.). *Urban Waste Water Discharges in Ireland with population equivalents greater than 500 persons: a Report for the years 2000 and 2001* (Wexford: EPA, 2003).

EPA/Environmental Protection Agency. *Annual Report and Accounts 2003* (Wexford: EPA, 2003a).

EPA/Environmental Protection Agency. *Ireland's Environment 2004* (Wexford: EPA, 2004).

EPA/Environmental Protection Agency. *The Quality of Drinking Water in Ireland: A Report for the Year 2003 with a Review of the Period 2001–2003* (Wexford: EPA, 2004a).

EPA/Environmental Protection Agency. *National Waste Database 2003. Interim Report* (Wexford: EPA, 2004b).

EPA/Environmental Protection Agency. *National Allocation Methodology* (Wexford: EPA, 2004c). Available at: http://www.epa.ie/Licensing/EmissionsTrading/NationalAlloc ationPlan/finalmethodology/.

EPA/Environmental Protection Agency/OEE/Office of Environmental Enforcement/Smith, D. (et al.). *Urban Waste Water Discharges in Ireland with population equivalents greater than 500 persons: a Report for the years 2002 and 2003* (Wexford: EPA, 2004d).

EPA/Environmental Protection Agency. *National Waste Prevention Programme. Outline Work Plan 2004–2008* (Wexford: EPA, 2004e).

EPA/Environmental Protection Agency. *Annual Highlights, 2004* (Wexford: EPA, 2004f).

EPA/Environmental Protection Agency/Toner, P. (et al.). *Water Quality in Ireland 2001–2003* (Wexford: EPA, 2005).

EPA/Environmental Protection Agency. *The Quality of Drinking Water in Ireland: A Report for the Year 2004* (Wexford: EPA, 2005a).

EPA/Environmental Protection Agency. *Report on Objections and Oral Hearing. Indaver (Ringaskiddy) Waste Licence Register 186–01. Volume 1. Main Report and Recommendations* (Wexford: EPA, 2005b), pp.91–123.

EPA/Environmental Protection Agency. Press Release: 'The Nature and Extent of Unauthorised Waste Activity in Ireland', Thursday, 15 September (Wexford: EPA, 2005c).

EPA/Environmental Protection Agency. Press Release: 'EPA Prosecutes Offaly County Council', Thursday, 29 September (Wexford: EPA, 2005d).

EPA/Environmental Protection Agency. Press Release: 'EPA Prosecutes Roscommon County Council', Tuesday, 2 August (Wexford: EPA, 2005e).

EPA/Environmental Protection Agency. Press Release: 'Judge Refuses Jurisdiction in EPA Court Cases Against Waterford County Council and Waterford City Council', Friday, June 10 (Wexford: EPA, 2005f).

EPA/Environmental Protection Agency. Press Release: 'EPA Prosecutes Cavan County Council', Friday, December 9 (Wexford, EPA, 2005g).

EPA/Environmental Protection Agency and Collins, C, Le Bolloch, O., and Meaney, B. *National Waste Report 2004* (Wexford: EPA, 2005h).

EPA/Environmental Protection Agency. Press Release: 'EPA invites local authorities to participate in a waste prevention demonstration grant-in-aid programme', Wednesday November 30, (2005i). Available at: http://www.epa.ie/NewsCentre/PressReleaseArchive/2005/MainBody,8214,en.html.

EPA/Environmental Protection Agency. Press Release: 'A win-win solution for farming, for our Kyoto targets, and for our environment', Wednesday, February 2 (2005j). Available at http://www.epa.ie/newscentre/pressrelasearchive.

EPA/Environmental Protection Agency. *Annual Highlights, 2005* (Wexford: EPA, 2005j).

EPA/Environmental Protection Agency. Press Release: 'Ireland's greenhouse gas emissions increased slightly in 2004 – final figures released', Wednesday, March 29 (Wexford: EPA, 2006). Available at: http://www.epa.ie/NewsCentre/PressReleases/MainBody,9033,en.html.

EPA/Environmental Protection Agency. Press Release: 'Technological solutions to environmental issues – EPA initiative provides €2 million in funding', Thursday, March 2 (EPA: Wexford, 2006a). Available at: http://www.epa.ie/NewsCentre/PressReleases/MainBody,8890,en.html.

EPA/Environmental Protection Agency. 'Improvements in the Enforcement of the Packaging waste Regulations', *EPA Newsletter*, April (Wexford: EPA, 2006b). Available at: http://www.epa.ie/NewsCentre/Newsletter/epaNewsApril200 6/FileUpload,9451,en.pdf

EPA/Environmental Protection Agency. 'EPA Holds First EU Auction for Emissions Trading', *EPA Newsletter*, April (2006c).

'EU imposes €21,600 fine in peat extraction row', *Irish Independent*, Friday, 30 September 2005.

Eurobarometer/Commission of the European Communities. *Special Eurobarometer 217: the attitudes of European citizens towards the environment* (Luxembourg: Eurobarometer, 2005).

Eurostat. *Energy Efficiency Indicators: Data 1990–1999* (Luxembourg: Office for Official Publications of the European Communities, 2002). Available at: http://epp.eurostat.cec.eu.int/portal/.

Eurostat. *Source book of environmentally relevant data on industry: Data 1990–1999* (Luxembourg: Office for Official Publications of the European Communities, 2002a).

Eurostat. *Energy, Transport and Environment indicators pocketbook. Data 1990–2000* (Luxembourg: Office for Official Publications of the European Communities, 2003).

Eurostat. *Population Statistics – 2004 edition* (Luxembourg: Office for Official Publications of the European Communities, 2004). Available at: http://epp.eurostat.cec.eu.int/portal/.

Eurostat. *A selection of environmental pressure indicators for the EU and Candidate Countries* (Luxembourg: Office for Official Publications of the European Communities, 2004a). Available at: http://epp.eurostat.cec.eu.int/portal/.

Eurostat. *Energy, transport, and environment indicators –
pocketbook – Data 1991–2001* (Luxembourg: Office for
Official Publications of the European Communities, 2004b).
Available at: http://epp.eurostat.cec.eu.int/portal/.

Eurostat. *Energy, Environment and Transport Indicators: Data
1992–2002* (Luxembourg: Office for Official Publications of
the European Communities, 2005).

Esty, D.C., Levy, M., Srebotnjak, T., and de Sherbinin, A. (et al.),
*2005 Environmental Sustainability Index: Benchmarking
National Environmental Stewardship* (New Haven: Yale
Center for Environmental Law & Policy, 2005).

Esty, D.C., Srebotnjak, T., Kim, C., Levy, M.A., de Sherbinin, A.,
Andersen, B. Dahl, A., Saltelli, A, and Saisana, M. (et al.),
Pilot Environmental Policy Index 2006 (New Haven: Yale
Centre for Environmental Law and Policy, 2006). Available
at http://www.yale.edu/epi.

Faughnan, C. 'Luas light rail system should not be about trying
to curb transport by car in the capital', *The Irish Times*, 21
August 1997.

Faughnan, C. 'New Tax would not cut traffic jams', *The Irish
Times*, 15 July 2003.

Faughnan, P. and McCabe, B. *Irish Citizens and the
Environment: A cross-national study of environmental
attitudes, perceptions and behaviours. Report for the
EPA/Commission of the European Communities* (Dublin:
UCD, Social Science Research Centre, 1998).

Farrell, A.E. and Lave, L.B. 'Emission Trading And Public Health',
Annual Review of Public Health, 25 (2004), pp.119–38.

FJ/Farmers' Journal. 'Water Pollution', 20 January 2001. Available
at: http://www.farmersjournal.ie/2001/0120/environment/.

Fenlon, R.M. 'The Water Pollution Control Act: An evaluation',
in J. Blackwell, J. and F. Convery (eds.), *Promise and
Performance: Irish Environmental Policies Analysed* (Dublin:
Resource and Environmental Policy Centre, University
College Dublin, 1983), pp.5–12.

FIE/Friends of the Irish Environment. *Forestry Network
Newsletter/FNN 138: Parliamentary Replies*, 12 May 2004.
Available at: http://www.friendsoftheirishenvironment.net/fnn/.

FIE/Friends of the Irish Environment. *Forestry Network
Newsletter/FNN 136: The Hunt for the Missing Broadleaves*,

31 March 2004. Available at: http://www.friendsoftheirish environment.net/fnn/.

Fields, S./An Taisce. *Monitoring and Evaluation of the Rural Environmental Protection Scheme* (Dublin: An Taisce, 2002).

Finnegan, P./GRIAN. *2003 Budget Submission, December 1, 2003* (Dublin: GRIAN, 2002). Available at http://www.grian.net or http://www.grian.ie/Policy/CarbonTax.htm.

Finnegan, P./GRIAN. *Recommendations On Ireland's Draft National Allocation Plan 2005–7, March 10 2004* (Dublin, GRIAN, 2004). Available at http://www.grian.net or http://www.grian.ie/Policy/CarbonTax.htm.

FIOSRÚ/Centre for Public Inquiry/Connolly, F. and Lynch, R. *The Great Corrib Gas Controversy* (Dublin: CPI, 2005).

Fischer, F. and M. Black (eds.). *Greening environmental policy: the politics of a sustainable future* (New York: St. Martin's Press, 1995).

Fitzgerald, G. 'Time to fast track commuter rail services', *The Irish Times*, 2 July 2005.

Fitzgerald, J. 'Council may have to refund €12.8m in refund levies', *The Irish Times*, 20 May 2005.

FitzGerald, J. and McCoy, D. (eds.). *The Economic Effects of Carbon Taxes*. ESRI Policy Research Series No.14 (Dublin: ESRI, 1992).

FitzGerald, J., McCarthy, C. Morgenroth, C.E. and O'Connell, P. (eds.). *The Mid-Term Evaluation of the National Development Plan and Community Support Framework for Ireland, 2000–2006. Report to the Department of Finance by the ESRI in association with DKM Economic Consultants, ESB International and Gesellschaft für Finanz und Regionalanalysen.* Economic and Social Research Institute, Policy Research Series, No. 50 (Dublin: ESRI, 2003).

Flannery, T. *The Weather Makers: the History and Future Impact of Climate Change* (London: Allen Lane, 2005).

Fleming, D. 'Why Nuclear Energy cannot provide a major power source', *An Taisce: Bi-annual magazine of An Taisce/The National Trust for Ireland*, Summer, (2006), pp.7–8.

Flynn B. 'Is supranational participation possible? The EU's attempt to enhance participation in Dublin's Transport Initiative', in F.H.J.M Coenen, D. Huitema, and L.J. O'Toole (eds.), *Participation and the quality of environmental decision-making* (Dordrecht, Kluwer, 1998), pp. 203–22.

Flynn, B. 'Voluntary environmental policy instruments: Two Irish success stories', *European Environment: The Journal of European Environmental Policy*, 12, 1 (2002), pp.1–12.

Flynn, B. 'Much Talk But Little Action? New Environmental Policy Instruments in Ireland', in Jordan, A. et al. (eds.), Special Issue on New Environmental Policy Instruments, *Environmental Politics*, 12, 1 (2003), pp.136–56.

Flynn B. and Kröger, L. 'Can Policy Learning Really Improve Implementation? Evidence From Irish Responses to the Water Framework Directive', *European Environment*, 13, 3, (2003a), pp.150–63.

Flynn, T. *The Planning and Development (Strategic Infrastructure) Bill, 2006 – A Critical Analysis of its Implications For Environmental Law*. Paper given at the Fourth Law and the Environment Conference, Faculty Of Law, University College, Cork, Thursday 27 April 2006. Available at: http://www.ucc.ie/en/lawsite/eventsandnews/previousevents/e nvironapr2006/.

Forfás (2005). *Annual Competitiveness Report 2005*, October (Dublin: Forfás). Available at: http://www.forfas.ie/ncc/ reports/ncc annual 05/ch03 03.html. Forfás/Hirsch, R.L. *A Baseline Assessment of Ireland's Oil Dependence. Key Policy Considerations*. April 2006 (Dublin: Forfás, 2006).

Galligan, E. 'Case Notes', *Irish Planning and Environmental Law Journal*, 3, 4 (1996), pp.180–8.

Galway Corporation, Galway County Council, M.C. O'Sullivan Ltd, and COWI. *Draft Connaught Waste Management Plan* (Galway: Galway Corporation/Galway County Council, 1999).

Greenfacts.org, 'Particulate Matter', available at: http://www. greenfacts.org/glossary/pqrs/PM10-PM2.5-PM0.1.htm.

GOI/Government of Ireland. *Ireland National Development Plan 2000–2006: Economic and Social Infrastructure Operational Programme* (Dublin: Government Stationery Office, 2000).

GOI/Government of Ireland. *The National Spatial Strategy for Ireland, 2002–2020: People, Places and Potential* (Dublin: Government Stationery Office, 2001).

GOI/Government of Ireland and CSO/Central Statistics Office. *Census 2002* (Dublin, CSO, 2004a).

Goulder, L. *Environmental Policy Making in Economies with Prior Tax Distortions* (Cheltenham: Edward Elgar, 2002).

Grant, M./DETR/Department of Environment. Transport and the Regions (UK), *Environmental Court Project Final Report* (London: DETR, 2000). Available at: http://www. odpm.gov.uk/.

'Great Gas Sorting out Slurry', *The Irish Farmers' Journal*, 8 January 2005.

Green 2000 Advisory Group. *Green 2000 Advisory Group Report* (Dublin: Stationery Office, 1993).

Greer, H. 'Nuclear Energy? Ten pointers leading to support for a nuclear presence', *An Taisce: Bi-annual magazine of An Taisce/The National Trust for Ireland*, (Summer, 2006), pp.5–6.

Grist, B. 'Wildlife legislation – The Rocky Road to special areas of conservation surveyed', *Irish Planning and Environmental Law Journal*, 4, 2 (1997), pp.87–95.

Hanlon, K. 'Councillors and officials in row over free bin scheme', *The Irish Times*, 30 November 2004.

Hanlon, K. 'Council discusses bin service row', *The Irish Times*, 17 August 2005.

Hartley, N. and Wood, C. 'Public participation in environmental impact assessment: implementing the Åarhus Convention', *Environmental Impact Assessment Review*, 25, 4 (2005), pp.319–41.

Harvey, F. 'Clean-coal power plant moves step closer', *The Financial Times*, 12 April 2006.

Hatch, M (ed.), *Environmental Policy-making: Assessing the use of alternative policy-making instruments* (New York: State University of New York Press, 2005).

Hawke, N. *Environmental Policy: Implementation and Enforcement* (Aldershot: Ashgate, 2002).

Hayward, T. *Constitutional Environmental Rights* (Oxford: OUP, 2005).

Healy, A. 'Geologist questions Askeaton report', *The Irish Times*, 19 January 2004.

Hederman, W. 'Battlefield Ireland', *Village Magazine*, May 20–26, (2005), pp.24–5.

Helm, D (ed.), *Environmental Policy: Objectives, Instruments and Implementation* (Oxford: OUP, 2000).

Hempel, L. C. 'Climate Policy on the Installment Plan', in. Vig, N.J and Kraft, M.E. *Environmental Policy: New Directions for the Twenty-First Century*. Sixth edition (Washington: CQ press, 2006), pp.294–5.

Hennessy, M. 'Fast-track planning body may face legal challenges', *The Irish Times*, 7 April 2004.

Hennessy, M. 'Changes can be made to carbon plan, says EPA', *The Irish Times*, 11 June 2004.

Hennessy, M. 'No emission cut for big industry', *The Irish Times*, 6 February 2004.

Hennessy, M. 'Incineration firm executive joins EPA', *The Irish Times*, 17 July 2004.

Heritage Council. *Forestry and the National Heritage* (Kilkenny: The Heritage Council, 1999).

Heritage Council. *The Heritage Council Annual Report 2003* (Kilkenny: Heritage Council, 2003).

Heritage Council. *Impact of Agricultural Schemes and Payments on aspects of Ireland's heritage* (Kilkenny: Heritage Council, 2004). Available at http://www.heritage.ie/.

Heritage Council. *Annual Report 2004* (Kilkenny: Heritage Council, 2005). Available at: http://www.heritagecouncil.ie/publications/annual2004/HC_Annual_Report_2004.pdf.

Hogan, T. 'Time for Ireland to quench thirst for oil', *The Irish Independent*, 5 April 2006, p.17.

Howley, M. and Ó Gallachóir, B./SEI/Sustainable Energy Ireland. *Energy in Ireland, 1990–2003: Trends, issues and indicators* (Cork: Energy Policy Statistical Support Unit, 2005).

HRB/Health Research Board. *Environmental Effects of Landfilling and Incineration of Waste – A Literature Review* (Dublin: HRB, 2003). Available at: http://www.hrb.ie/publications/

Humphreys, J. 'IBEC gives cautious welcome', *The Irish Times*, 6 February 2004.

Humphreys, J. 'File on Waterford council official for DPP', *The Irish Times*, 30 November 2005.

IBEC/Irish Business and Employers Confederation. *IBEC Environmental Policy* (Dublin: IBEC, 1997).

IBEC/Irish Business and Employers Confederation. 'Waste Management Amendment Act 2001 is enacted', IBEC Press Release, 24 March 2001. Available at: http://www.ibec.ie/ibec/Press/Publicationsdoclib3.nsf.

IBEC/Irish Business and Employers Confederation. 'Dempsey proposes levy on land-filled waste', IBEC Press Release, 5

November 2001. Available at: http://www.ibec.ie/ibec/Press/
Publicationdoclib3.nsf.

IBEC/Irish Business and Employers Confederation. 'Cool heads
needed to move forward on Climate Change', IBEC Press
Release, 11 April 2001. Available at: http://www.ibec.ie/ibec/
buspolicies/buspolciesdoclib3.nsf/.

IEA/International Energy Agency (2003). *Emissions trading and
its possible impacts on investment decisions in the power
sector* (IEA: Paris, 2003). Available at http://www.iea.org/
dbtw-wpd/textbase/papers/2003/cop9invdec.pdf.

IEA/WPFF/International Energy Agency/Working Party on Fossil
Fuels. CO_2 *Capture at Power Stations and Other Major
Point Sources* (IEA: Paris, 2003).

Imhoff, D. *Paper or Plastic: Searching for Solutions to an Over-
packaged World*, (San Francisco: Sierra Club Books, 2005).

JOCELG/Joint Oireachtas Committee on Environment and Local
Government. *Parliamentary Debates*, 42, (2005a), February
9. Available at http://www.oireachtas.ie

JOCELG/Joint Oireachtas Committee on Environment and Local
Government. *Parliamentary Debates*, 64, (2005b), December
6. Available at http://www.oireachtas.ie

Jordan A. 'The implementation of EU environmental policy: a
policy problem without a political solution?', *Environment And
Planning C – Government And Policy*, 17, 1 (1999), pp. 69–90.

Jordan, A., Wurzul, R.K.W., and Zito, A.R. (eds.), *'New'
Instruments of Environmental Governance? National
Experiences and Prospects* (London: Frank Cass, 2003).

'Judgement reserved in waste disposal challenge', *The Irish
Times*, 27 February 2003.

Kay, J. 'Key to Carbon trading is to keep it simple', *The Financial
Times*, 8 May 2006.

Keatinge, P., Laffan, B., and O'Donnell, R. 'Overview', in P.
Keatinge, (ed.), *Ireland and EC membership evaluated*
(London: Pinter, 1991), pp.279–91.

Kehoe, I. 'Commercial Court Service cuts to the Chase', *The
Sunday Business Post*, 19 February 2006.

Kelly, M. *Attitudes to the environment in Ireland. How much
have we changed between 1993 and 2002?* Paper presented
to the Environmental Protection Agency Conference:
Pathways to a Sustainable Future, Dublin, 15–16 May 2003.

Kelly, M. 'Baseline Health Data', Letter to Michael Kelly, Secretary General Department of Health and Children, 25 March 2003, available at: http://www.epa.ie/Licensing/WasteLicensing/OralHearings/186–1IndaverOralHearingReport/.

Kelly, M. 'EU should be wary of backing Kyoto', *The Irish Times*, 11 April 2001.

Kelly, O. 'Output of "greenhouse gas" is double Kyoto target', *The Irish Times*, 8 August 2004.

Kelly, O. 'Manager to proceed with plan for waste incinerator', *The Irish Times*, 16 September 2004.

Kelly, O. 'Dublin Council may fall unless city manager changes waste charges', *The Irish Times*, 29 November 2004.

Kelly, O. 'Roche critical over lack of consultation', *The Irish Times*, 12 April 2005.

Kennedy, J. 'Survey finds low level of nitrates in Irish waters', *Irish Farmers Journal*, 16 October 2004. Available at: http://www.farmersjournal.ie/2004/1016/farmmanagement/environment/feature.shtml.

Kennedy, J. 'Revised Nitrates Action plan sent to Brussels', *The Irish Farmers Journal*, 27 May 2006.

Keogh, E. 'Anger at rezoning of area near site of battle', *The Irish Times*, 24 May 2004.

Keogh, E. 'Ability of EPA to handle incinerator hearing queried', *The Irish Times*, 3 March 2005.

King, T. 'EU chides Ireland over wild birds', *The Irish Times*, 30 January 2004.

King, T. 'Belgians to ship back 1,000 tonnes of illegal waste to Ireland', *The Irish Times*, 28 February 2004.

Knox, C. and Haslem, R. 'Local government', in N. Collins (ed.), *Political Issues in Ireland Today* (Manchester: MUP, 1999), pp.55–69.

Krämer, L. *Casebook on EU environmental Law* (Oxford: Hart, 2002).

Krarup, S. 'Danish Municipalities' Monitoring Efforts', *AKF Working Paper*, February 1, (Denmark, 2006), pp.17–19. Available at: http://www.akf.dk/udgivelser/workingpaper/2006/pdf/01 monitoring effort.pdf/.

Laffan, B. 'National Co-ordination in Brussels: The Role of Ireland's Permanent Representation', in H. Kassim, A.

Menon, B.G. Peters, and V. Wright (eds.), *The National Co-ordination of EU policy* (Oxford: OUP, 2001), pp.277–96.

Laffan, B. and O'Mahony, J. 'Mis-fit, politicisation and Europeanisation: the implementation of the Habitats Directive in Ireland', *OEUE Occasional Paper*, 1.3, September, (2004). Available at: www.oeue.net/papers/ ireland-implementationofthehab.pdf.

Laffan, B and Tannam, E. 'Ireland: the rewards of pragmatism', in K. Hanf and B. Soetendorp (eds), *Adapting to European Integration: small states and the European Union* (Harlow: Longman,1998), pp.69–83.

Lampinen R., and Uusikyla, P. 'Implementation deficit – Why member states do not comply with EU directives', *Scandinavian Political Studies*, 21, 3(1998), pp. 231–51.

Langendoen, R. 'Irish Tax Cuts Plastic Use Dramatically', (2003). Available at http://www.futurenet.org/29globalhope/ indicatorlangendoenplastic.htm

Landman, T. *Issues and Methods in Comparative Politics* (London: Sage, 2000).

Larson, E.T. 'Why Environmental Liability Regimes in the United States, the European Community, and Japan have grown Synonymous with the Polluter Pays Principle', *Vanderbilt Journal of Transnational Law*, 38, 2 (2005), pp.541–677.

LGMSB/Local Government Management Services Board, *Service Indicators in Local Authorities 2004. Report to the Minister for Environment, Heritage and Local Government, June 2005* (Dublin: LGMSB, 2005), p.12.

Lopez-Claros, A. (ed.), Porter, M., and Schwab, K./WEF/World Economic Forum, *The Global Competitiveness Report 2005-2006: Policies underpinning Rising Prosperity* (London: Palgrave, 2005).

Lovelock, J. *The Revenge of Gaia: Why the earth is fighting back – and how we can still save humanity* (London: Allen Lane, 2005).

Lucey, A. 'Alert issued over contaminated water', *The Irish Times*, 26 November 2004.

Lucey, A. 'Planning Chief Denies Hidden Agenda Claims', *The Irish Times*, 15 December 2004.

Lucey, A. 'Councillors de-list Valentia house to allow development', *The Irish Times*, September 22, (2004b).

Lucey, A. 'An Taisce criticises one-off holiday homes', *The Irish Times*, 14 January 2005.

Lucey, A. 'Killarney councillors vote for rezoning', *The Irish Times*, 8 March 2006.

Lucey, A. 'Killarney manager not to act on rezoning motion', *The Irish Times*, 5 April 2006.

MacConnell, S. 'Farmers buy less fertilizer but use more', *The Irish Times*, 2 July 2002.

MacConnell, S. 'EPA urges re-use of farm slurry as fertilisers, energy', *The Irish Times*, 8 February 2005.

MacCormaic, R. 'The tidiest town with the dirtiest water', *The Irish Times*, 22 October 2005.

MacEoin, R. 'Residents oppose plan for Wexford waste plant', *The Irish Times*, 16 February 2006.

Mackie, T. and Marsh, D. 'The comparative method', in D. Marsh, and G. Stoker (eds.), *Theory and Methods in Political Science* (Basingstoke: Macmillian/Palgrave, 1995), pp.173–88.

Macrory, R. and Wood, M. *Modernising Environmental Justice: Regulation and the Role of an environmental Tribunal* (London: Centre for Environment and Law, University College London, 2005). Available at: http://www.ucl.ac.uk/laws/environment/tribunals

Magner, D. 'Annual plantings at 20 year low', *The Irish Farmers Journal*, 27 May 2006, p.26.

Maguire, B., O'Reilly, M., and Roche, M.S. *Irish Environmental Legislation* (Dublin: Round Hall Sweet and Maxwell, 1999).

Mansergh, M. 'What ordinary people want still counts for something', *The Irish Times*, 13 March 2004.

Markusen, J.R. 'Costly pollution abatement, competitiveness and plant location decisions', *Resource and Energy Economics*, 19, 4 (1997), pp.299–320.

Mattila, M. *Fiscal Redistribution in the EU and the Enlargement* (Helsinki: Department of Political Science, Helsinki University, 2005). Working paper available at: http://www.valt.helsinki.fi/staff/mmattila/euredist/redist.pdf.

Mawhinney, K. 'Environmental Conservation: Concern and Action, 1920–1970', in M.J. Bannon, J. Hendry, and K. Mawhinney, *Planning: The Irish Experience 1920–1988* (Dublin: Wolfhound, 1997), pp.86–104.

McAleer, M. 'SUV sales up 34 per cent last year', *The Irish Times*, 26 January 2005.

McDonald, F. *The Destruction of Dublin* (Dublin: Gill and MacMillan, 1985).

McDonald, F. 'CO_2 emissions not an issue in hearing', *The Irish Times*, 7 July 1998.

McDonald, F. 'At the heart of our towns', *The Irish Times*, 11 November 2000.

McDonald, F. '30 per cent of group water schemes found to be contaminated', *The Irish Times*, 10 January 2003.

McDonald, F. 'An Taisce questioned over housing', *The Irish Times*, 24 August 2003a.

McDonald, F. 'Number of Bord Pleanála appeals queried', *The Irish Times*, 13 June 2003b.

McDonald, F. 'Bin charges are just part of 'polluter pays' policy, *The Irish Times*, 22 September 2003c.

McDonald, F. 'Break–up of Dúchas may be unlawful', *The Irish Times*, 23 April 2003d.

McDonald, F. 'Running up a big bill for our rotten track record', *The Irish Times*, 17 July 2004.

McDonald, F. 'Planners Despair as Profit drives new housing policy', *The Irish Times*, 16 March 2004a.

McDonald, F. 'Bill to fast track incinerators and motorways is withdrawn', *The Irish Times*, 12 December 2004b.

McDonald, F. 'Policing the waste land', *The Irish Times*, 3 September 2005.

McDonald, F. 'Order for bird protection area made without authority', *The Irish Times*, 27 May 2005a.

McDonald, F. 'Irish Cement gets right to emit more CO_2', *The Irish Times*, 23 February 2005b.

McDonald, F. 'Roche tones down populist rhetoric', *The Irish Times*, 14 April 2005c.

McDonald, F. 'Roche defends housing policy', *The Irish Times*, 14 April 2005d.

McDonald, F. 'EPA nominee sent letter to Roche over illegal dump', *The Irish Times*, 21 March 2006.

McDonald, F. 'Environmental Advisory Committee appointed by the Minister is unbalanced', *The Irish Times*, 31 March 2006.

McDonald, F. and Nix, J. *Chaos at the Crossroads* (Kinsale: Gandon, 2005).

McKenna, P. and Clerkin, S. *Ireland's Compliance with EU environmental law.* A report Commissioned for Patricia McKenna MEP (1999-2004), June (2004). Available at http://www.greenparty.ie/en/content/download/946/6403/filec ompliance_report_pmckenna-sml.pdf

McWilliams, D. 'Time to discuss our nuclear option, without a meltdown', *The Irish Independent*, 5 April 2006, p.23.

Meadowcroft, J. 'Planning for sustainable development; Insights from the literatures of political sciences', *European Journal of Political Research*, 31, 4 (1997), pp.427–54.

Meadowcroft, J. 'Sustainable Development: A New(ish) idea for a New century?', in J.S. Dryzek, and D. Schlosberg (eds.), *Debating the earth: the environmental politics reader,* 2nd edition (Oxford: OUP,2005/2000), pp.267–84.

Menz, G. 'Re-regulating the Single Market: national varieties of capitalism and their responses to Europeanization', *Journal Of European Public Policy*, 10, 4, (2003), pp.532–55.

Mol, A.P.J. 'Ecological modernization and the environmental transition of Europe: between national variations and common denominators', *Journal of Environmental Policy and Planning*, 1, 2 (1999), pp.167–81.

Mol, A.P.J., Liefferink, D. and Lauber, V. *The Voluntary Approach to Environmental Policy: Joint Environmental Policy-Making in Europe* (Oxford: OUP, 2000).

Morrison, K. 'Emissions trade prices drop again', *The Financial Times*, 27 April 2006.

Morgera, E. 'An Update on the Åarhus Convention and its Continued Global Relevance', *Review of European Community and International Environmental Law*, 14, 2 (2005), pp.138–47.

Mullally, P. 'A policy for the Environment: What happened to it?', in J. Blackwell and F. Convery (eds.), *Promise and Performance: Irish Environmental Policies Analysed* (Dublin: Resource and Environmental Policy Centre, University College Dublin, 1983), pp.407–10.

Murphy, J. 'Editorial – Ecological Modernisation', *Geoform*, 31,1 (2000), pp.1–8.

Murphy, J. (2001) *Ecological Modernisation: The Environment and the Transformation of Society.* March, OCEES Research Paper No. 20 (Oxford: OCEES, 2001).

Murphy, J. and Cohen, G. (eds.), *Exploring Sustainable Consumption: Environmental Policy and the Social Sciences* (Oxford: Pergamon, 2001).

Murphy, J. and Gouldson, G. 'Environmental policy and industrial innovation: integrating environment and economy through ecological modernisation', *Geoforum*, 31,1 (2000), pp.33–45.

Murtagh, P. 'EU may be about to judge us wanting on the environment – yet again', *The Irish Times*, 30 May 2005.

Naughton, D. 'Dáil question 37780/05 with reply by Minister Roche', *Parliamentary Debates*, 611, 4, (2005), p.43 (available at http://www.oireachtas.ie).

Neale, A. 'Organising Environmental Self-regulation: Liberal governmentality and the Pursuit of Ecological Modernisation in Europe', *Environmental Politics*, 6,4 (1997), pp.1–24.

Neill, M. 'Nitrate concentrations in river waters in the south-east of Ireland and their relationships with agricultural practice', *Water Research*, 23, (1989), pp.1,339–55.

Network of Heads of European Environment Protection Agencies. *The Contribution of Good Environmental Regulation to Competitiveness*, November 2005. Available at: http://www.umweltbundesamt.de/ius/downloads/prague statement-en.pdf.

Newman, C. 'Heritage group is critical of economic goals in national plan', *The Irish Times*, 27 April 2000.

Newman, C. 'Checkpoints in Dublin to stop illegal dumping', *The Irish Times*, 31 January 2004.

Nix, J. 'When it comes to developing a truly national motorway plan, less is more', *The Irish Times*, 27 December 2002.

Nix, J. 'Sick of jams? Take the bus', *The Irish Times*, 2 February 2004.

Nolan, K. 'Institutional land required for development', *The Irish Times*, 4 October 2004.

Nordic Council of Ministers. *The Use of Economic Instruments in Nordic Environmental Policy, 1999–2001* (Copenhagen: Nordic Council of Ministers. 2001).

Nugent, A. 'Putting farm byproducts to work', *The Irish Farmers Journal*, 5 August 2000.

O'Brien, T. 'Big firms that fail to recycle face prosecution', *The Irish Times*, 1 July 1999.

O'Brien, T. 'State agency warned of castle danger', *The Irish Times*, 18 August 2002.

O'Brien, T. 'Brennan to accelerate motorway plans', *The Irish Times*, 13 August 2003.

O'Brien, T. 'Almost 76,000 one-off houses constructed', *The Irish Times*, 7 November 2003a.

O'Brien, T. 'McCreevy accelerates roads programme', *The Irish Times*, 2 January 2004.

O'Brien, T. 'NRA aims to raise €2bn from new toll charges', *The Irish Times*, 15 April 2004a.

O'Brien, T. 'An Taisce to sue State over dumping', *The Irish Times*, 14 December 2004b.

O'Brien, T. 'EU criticism on waste rejected as outdated', *The Irish Times*, 24 September 2004c.

O'Brien, T. 'Roche angry over action by EC on environment', *The Irish Times*, 14 January 2005.

O'Brien, T. 'M50 plaintiffs sue Cullen over court remarks', *The Irish Times*, 11 August 2005a.

O'Brien, T. 'Warning of a high price to be paid for services to houses', *The Irish Times*, 14 April 2005b.

O'Brien, T. 'Council rezones flood plain for housing', *The Irish Times*, 26 July 2005c.

O'Brien, T. 'Licences given for waste plants in Cork, Meath', *The Irish Times*, 26 November 2005d.

O'Brien, T. 'Recycling price rise on electrical goods', *The Irish Times*, 13 August 2005e.

O'Brien, T. 'Danish firm to invest €1bn in Poolbeg Incinerator', *The Irish Times*, 20 August 2005f.

O'Brien, T. 'Anti-pollution drive not sufficient', *The Irish Times*, 4 March 2006.

O'Brien. T. 'Ireland exceeds quota for harmful emissions', *The Irish Times*, 16 May 2006a.

O'Brien, T. 'Ireland now recycling 66 per cent of used packaging', *The Irish Times*, 22 May 2006b.

O'Brien, T. 'Transport Body begins work soon', *The Irish Times*, June 12, 2006c.

O'Donnell, R. 'Environmental Policy', in P. Keatinge, (ed.), *Ireland and EC membership evaluated* (London: Pinter, 1991), pp.119–25.

O'Dowd, F. 'EPA's Askeaton report slated', *The Sunday Business Post*, 2 December 2001.

OECD/Organisation for Economic Co-operation and Development. *Environmental Performance Reviews–Denmark* (Paris: OECD, 1999).

OECD/Organisation for Economic Co-operation and Development. *Environmental Performance Reviews–Ireland* (Paris: OECD, 2000).

OECD/Organisation for Economic Co-operation and Development. *Voluntary Approaches for Environmental Policy: An assessment* (Paris: OECD, 2000a).

OECD/Organisation for Economic Co-operation and Development. *Environmental Performance Reviews–Greece* (Paris: OECD, 2000b).

OECD/Organisation for Economic Co-operation and Development. *Environmental Performance Reviews–Portugal* (Paris: OECD, 2001).

OECD/Organisation for Economic Co-operation and Development. *Indicators to measure decoupling of environmental pressure from economic growth* (Paris: OECD, 2002). Summary available at http://www.oecd.org/dataoecd/0/52/1933638.pdf.

OECD/Organisation for Economic Co-operation and Development. *Energy Policies of IEA Countries–Ireland–2003 Review* (Paris: OECD, 2003).

OECD/Organisation for Economic Co-operation and Development. *Energy to 2050 – Scenarios for a Sustainable Future* (Paris: OECD, 2003a).

OECD/Organisation for Economic Co-operation and Development. Environment Directorate General, *Pollution, Abatement and Control expenditures in OECD countries* (Paris: OECD, 2003b).

OECD/Organisation for Economic Co-operation and Development. *Environmental Data Compendium 2004* (Paris: OECD, 2005).

OFE/DoE/Office of Fossil Energy, Department of Energy (USA). 'JEA successfully completes world's largest CFB demonstration', *Clean Coal Today*, 64 (Fall 2005), pp.4–5.

Oliver, E. 'B of I to facilitate emissions trading', *The Irish Times*, 23 May 2005.

Oliver, E. 'EU to take action on national grid policy', *The Irish Times*, 24 March 2006.

OPET Network/EPU NTUA. *EU Best Practice in RES: Wind Energy in Denmark* (Commission of the European Communities, DG Energy and Transport, October 2003). Available at: http://www.opet-chp.net/download/wp6/EUBest PracticeWindinDemark.pdf.

O'Reilly, A. 'REPAK says legal loopholes hindering recycling', *The Irish Times*, 5 October 2001.

'Organic Waste Plant Refused', *The Irish Times*, 1 September 2005.

O'Riordan, A. 'The Rise and Rise of Recycling', *Local Authority News*, 25, 6 (2006), p.31.

O'Toole, F. 'Trim plan a monument to stupidity', *The Irish Times*, September 27, (2005).

Oydssee/CEC – Commission of the European Communities/ Ademe/Enerdata S.A./Fraunhofer Institute. Systems and Innovation Research, *Energy efficiency in the European Union, 1990–2000. SAVE-ODYSSEE Project on Energy Efficiency Indicators. Report prepared by ENERDATA S.A. in collaboration with FhG/ISI*, (2001). Available at: http://www.odyssee-indicators.org/Publication/PDF/ RapFra.pdf.

Pearce, D. 'Book Review: The Porter Hypothesis and the economic consequences of environmental regulation: a neo-Schumpeterian approach, by Thomas Roediger-Schluga', 2004, *European Environment: the Journal of European Environmental Policy*, 15, 6, (2005) p.391.

Pearce, F. 'Climate Change: Menace or myth?', *New Scientist*, 185, 2486 (2005), pp.38–43.

PIFA/ Packaging and Industrial Films Association. 'Three essential reasons why a tax on plastic carrier bags will not help the environment', Press Release 02/5007/5, (2002). Available at http://www.carrierbagtax.com/.

Pocock, I. 'State loses water pollution case', *The Irish Times*, 13 March 2004.

Pocock, I. 'Slurry hits the fan', *The Irish Times*, 22 May 2004.

Pocock, I. 'Director of EPA is excluded from vote', *The Irish Times*, 27 August 2004.

Pocock, I. 'We need to clear the air', *The Irish Times*, 13 November 2004.

Pop, L, and Vanhuysse, P. 'Varieties of capitalism, varieties of theory? Conceptualizing paths of change and patterns of economic interaction across models of market democracy', *Journal Of European Public Policy*, 11, 1 (2004), pp.167–77.

Porter, M.E. and van der Linde, C. 'Toward a New Conception of the Environment-Competitiveness Relationship', *The Journal of Economic Perspectives: a journal of the American Economic Association*, 9, 4 (1995), pp.97–112.

Porter, M.E. *The Comparative Advantage of Nations*. 2nd edition (Basingstoke: Palgrave, 1998).

Pressman, J.L. and Wildavsky, A. *Implementation*, 3rd edition (Berkeley: University of California Press,1984).

Quinn, O. 'Let's make full use of the land banks and brown fields', *The Irish Times*, 13 October 2004.

Raferty, M. 'Comparing apples and oranges', *The Irish Times*, 15 July 2004.

Raftery, M. 'Not a record to boast of', *The Irish Times*, 1 July 2004a.

Raftery, M. 'We will pay for Carbon emissions', *The Irish Times*, 16 September 2004b.

Raftery, M. 'Farm profit put before our health', *The Irish Times*, 28 April 2005.

Raftery, M. 'Motoring down the road to perdition', *The Irish Times*, September 22, 2005a.

Raftery, M. 'Nitrates and vested interests', *The Irish Times*, 23 February 2006.

Raghbendra, J. and Bhanu Murthy, K.V. 'A Critique of the Environmental Sustainability Index', Australian National University, Economic RSPAS Departmental Working Paper 2003–08 (Canberra, ANU/RSPAS, 2003). Available at: http://ideas.repec.org/p/pas/papers/2003-08.html.

Reid, L. 'Ombudsman criticises lack of enforcement of planning laws', *The Irish Times*, 28 April 2004.

Reid, L. 'Illegal NI dumps had waste from South', *The Irish Times*, 3 February 2004a.

Reid, L. 'Council staff playing cat and mouse game with illegal operators', *The Irish Times*, 29 March 2004b.

Reid, L. 'EU Ruling due on Ireland's illegal dumping', *The Irish Times*, 17 September 2004c.

Reid, L. 'Putting a price on the main cause of global warming', *The Irish Times*, 31 December 2004d.

Reid, L. '106 companies in emissions trading scheme', *The Irish Times*, 31 December 2004e.

Reid, L. 'EPA chief disappointed at shelving of carbon tax', *The Irish Times*, 12 November 2004f.

Reid, L. 'Kyoto shortfall to cost Government EUR185m', *The Irish Times*, 31 December 2004g.

Reid, L. 'Government 'underestimated' effect of abandoned carbon tax', *The Irish Times*, 11 November 2004h.

Reid, L. 'The Garden of Ireland', *The Irish Times*, 9 September 2004i.

Reid. L. 'Illegal dumping controls are still rubbish', *The Irish Times*, 9 September 2004j.

Reid, L 'Dumping ground: Part 2. Satellite technology to identify illegal dumps', *The Irish Times*, 29 March 2004k.

Reid, L. 'Dublin taskforce to tackle illegal waste activity', *The Irish Times*, 10 June 2004l.

Reid, L. 'New move to seize earnings of illegal dumpers', *The Irish Times*, 22 October 2004m.

Reid, L. 'IBEC alarmed at planning delay', *The Irish Times*, 12 January 2005.

Reid, L. 'Agency warns of drought threat in the south-east and need to control emissions', *The Irish Times*, 16 February 2005a.

Reid, L. 'State faces €400m bill for failing to meet Kyoto target', *The Irish Times*, 22 September 2005b.

Reid, L. 'Planning rules for waste projects to be eased', *The Irish Times*, 4 May 2005c.

Reid, L. 'Taxpayers will pay high price for broken promises on Kyoto', *The Irish Times*, 3 March 2006.

Reid, L. 'SUVs blamed for increasing greenhouse gas emissions', *The Irish Times*, 3 April 2006a.

Reid, L. 'Ireland to delay farm anti-pollution measures', *The Irish Times*, 19 May 2006b.

Reid, L. 'Greens call for reform of EPA', *The Irish Times*, 16 March 2006c.

Reuters. 'Irish tax on shopping bags nets US$3.45 million', 21 August 2002. Available at http://www.enn.com/news/wire-stories/2002/08/08212002/reu_48207.

Revell, A. 'Ecological Modernization in the UK: Rhetoric or Reality?', *European Environment: the Journal of European Environmental Policy*, 15, 6 (2005), pp.344–61.

Richardson, J., Gustafsson, G. and Jordan, G. 'The concept of policy style', in J. Richardson, (ed.), *Policy Styles in Western Europe* (London: Allen and Unwin,1982), pp.1–16.

Roche, B. 'Council rejects incinerator for Cork', *The Irish Times*, 11 November 2005.

Roche, B. 'Medical evidence cited by objectors', *The Irish Times*, 2 March 2005a.

Roche, B. 'Appeals process flawed, says EPA', *The Irish Times*, 6 August 2005b.

Roche, B. 'Opponents may take legal action to block incinerator', *The Irish Times*, 26 November 2005c.

Roche, D. 'Irish Compliance with EU law', *The Irish Times*, 13 July 2004.

Rhodes, M. 'Varieties of capitalism and the political economy of European welfare states', *New Political Economy*, 10, 3 (2005), pp.363–70.

Ronayne, D. 'Letters – Electrical Waste Directive and the costs of recycling', *The Irish Times*, 23 August 2005.

Ryall Á. 'The EIA Directive and the Irish Planning Participation Fee', *Journal of Environmental Law*, 14, 3 (2002), pp.317–29.

Ryan, E. 'Action on climate change makes sense', *The Irish Times*, 18 February 2005.

Sahlin, M. 'Sweden first to break dependence on oil! New programme presented', *Dagens Nyheter*, 1 October 2005. Available at: http://www.sweden.gov.se/sb/d/3212/a/51058.

Scannell, Y. *The Law and Practice relating to Pollution Control in Ireland* (London: Graham and Trotman, 1982).

Scannell, Y. *Environmental and planning law in Ireland* (Dublin: Round Hall Press, 1995).

Schall, J. 'Does the Solid Waste Management Hierarchy Make Sense? A Technical, Economic & Environmental Justification for the Priority of Source Reduction and Recycling', October, 1992, *Working Papers of the Yale School of Forestry and Environmental Studies*. Available at: http://www.yale.edu/pswp/#schall.

Scott, S. *Fertiliser Taxes – Implementation Issues (2001-EEP-DS9-M2). Final Report. A Report prepared for the Environmental Protection Agency by the Economic and Social Research Institute* (Dublin: ESRI, 2005). Available at http://www.esri.ie/.

Scott, S. and Eakins, J. *Carbon Taxes: Which Households Gain or Lose? (2001-EEP/DS7-M1). Final Report. A Report prepared for the Environmental Protection Agency by the Economic and Social Research Institute* (Dublin: ESRI, 2004). Available at: http://www.esri.ie/.

Segerson K, and Miceli, T.J. 'Voluntary environmental regulation: good or bad news for environmental protection?', *Journal of Environmental Economics and Management*, 36, 2 (1998), pp.109–30.

SEI/Sustainable Energy Ireland. *The Route to Sustainable Commuting: an employer's guide to Mobility Management Plans* (Dublin: SEI, 2001).

SEI/ Sustainable Energy Ireland. *Energy and CO_2 Efficiency in Transport: Analysis of New Car Registrations in Year 2000* (Dublin: SEI, 2003). Available at: http://www.sei.ie/ publications.

SEI/Sustainable Energy Ireland. *Combined Heat and Power in Ireland – Trends and issues 1991–2002* (Dublin: SEI, 2004). Available at http://www.sei.ie/publications.

SEI/Sustainable Energy Ireland. *Annual Report 2004* (Dublin: SEI, 2004a). Available at http://www.sei.ie/publications.

SEI/Sustainable Energy Ireland and O'Leary, F. *Energy Efficiency in Ireland 1990–2002: An analysis based on the ODYSSEE database of energy efficiency indicators* (Dublin: SEI, 2004b). Available at http://www.sei.ie/publications.

SEI/Sustainable Energy Ireland and Howley, M., O'Leary, F., and Ó Gallachóir, B. *Energy in Ireland 1990–2004: Trends, issues, forecasts and indicators* (Dublin: SEI, 2006).

SEI/Sustainable Energy Ireland. *Renewable Energy in Ireland: Update 2005* (Dublin: SEI, 2006a).

Shanahan, E. 'Waste Disposal Law is ignored – Repak', *The Irish Times*, 6 October 2001.

SF/Sinn Féin. 'Sinn Fein call for Nitrates reassessment', Press Release, 2 June 2004. Available at: http://sinnfein.ie/news/detail/4997.

Shipan, C.R. *Independence and the Irish Environmental Protection Agency: a comparative assessment.* Working Paper of the Policy Institute, Trinity College Dublin, December 16 (Dublin: The Policy Institute, TCD, 2005), p.25. Available at: http://www.policyinstitute.tcd.ie/working_papers/PIWP08%20-%20Shipan.pdf

Siggins, L. 'Motorways and housing developments add to strain on inland waterway system', *The Irish Times*, 23 July 2001.

Siggins, L. 'Pollutants found in Galway city water', *The Irish Times*, 30 June 2001.

Siggins, L. 'Public water supply at centre of row in east Galway town', *The Irish Times*, 14 February 2002.

Siggins, L. 'Council rejects plan for Galway city incinerator', *The Irish Times*, 12 October 2004.

Siggins, L. 'Housing row is more than a one-off', *The Irish Times*, 16 April 2005.

Siggins, L. 'Several key Shell Corrib work not authorised, board finds', *The Irish Times*, 2 June 2006.

Smyth, J. 'Tax rate among EU's lowest', *The Irish Times*, 18 May 2006.

Smyth, J. 'State accused of impeding participation in planning', *The Irish Times*, 26 April 2006.

Staudt, L. 'Status and Prospects for Wind Energy in Ireland' (2005). Available at http://www.iwea.com/publications/statuspropsect.pdf

Staudt, L. 'Ireland must go down the route of renewable energy', *The Irish Times*, 29 September 2005.

Staunton, D. 'State in breach of EU environmental law', *The Irish Times*, 14 July 2004.

Staunton, D. 'Brussels approves carbon dioxide emissions plan', *The Irish Times*, 8 July 2004.

Staunton, D. 'Ireland accused of breaching EU rules on Health environment', *The Irish Times*, 12 April 2005.

Staunton, D. 'EU censures Ireland over illegal dumping', *The Irish Times*, 27 April 2005.

Statistics Denmark. *Transport 2005* (Copenhagen: Statistics Denmark, 2005). Available at: www.dst.dk/transport2005

Stokes, D.E. 'Valence politics', in D. Kavanagh (ed.) *Electoral Politics* (Oxford: Clarendon, 1992), pp.141–64.

Sullivan, K. 'US Study raises new fears over Dioxins', *The Irish Times*, 18 May 2000.

Swanson, I. 'Plastic tax did not leave Irish down in the dumps', *Evening News*, 2 November 2005. Available at http://news.scotsman.com/.

Szarka, J. *The Shaping of Environmental Policy in France* (New York: Bergham, 2002).

Taylor, C. 'Cabinet abandons plan to introduce carbon tax', *The Irish Times*, 10 September 2004.

Taylor, C. 'Proposed carbon tax could benefit poorer house-holds', *The Irish Times,* 22 July 2004a.

Taylor, C. 'Carbon tax could lead to job losses – industries', *The Irish Times,* 18 February 2004b.

Taylor, C. 'Enterprise Ireland chief calls for flexibility on carbon taxation', *The Irish Times,* 27 January 2004c.

Taylor, G. 'Conserving the Emerald Tiger: the politics of Environmental Regulation in Ireland', *Environmental Politics,* 7, 4 (1998), pp.55–74.

Taylor, G. 'Environmental Democracy, Oral Hearings and Public Registers in Ireland: Methinks thou do'st protest too much', *Irish Planning and Environmental Law Journal,* 5, 4 (1998a), pp.143–51.

Taylor, G. *Conserving the Emerald Tiger: The Politics of Environmental Regulation in Ireland* (Galway: Arlen House, 2001).

Taylor, G. and Horan, A. 'From cats, dogs, parks and play-grounds to IPC licensing: policy learning and the evolution of environmental policy in Ireland', *British Journal of Politics & International Relations,* 3, 3 (2001), pp.369–92.

Teagasc, 'Teagasc Rejects Dillon Statement on Nitrates Directive' – Press Release, 26 May 2004. Available at: http://www.teagasc.ie/news/2004/200405-26.htm.

Timmins, E. 'Recycling revisited', *The Irish Times,* 7 May 2000.

Toke, D. 'Ecological Modernisation: A Reformist Review', *New Political Economy,* 6, 2, (2001), pp.279–91.

UNDP/ United National Development Programme and Fukuda-Parr, S. (et al.), *Human Development Report 2002: Deepening Democracy in a fragmented world.* (New York: Oxford University Press, 2002). Available at http://hdr.undp.org/reports/

UNDP/United National Development Programme and Watkins, K. (et al.), *Human Development Report 2005: International cooperation at a crossroads: Aid, trade and security in an unequal world.* (New York: UNDP, 2005). Available at http://hdr.undp.org/reports/.

UNFCC/United Nations Framework Convention on Climate Change. 'Compliance under the Kyoto Protocol', (UNFCC, 2006). Available at http://www.unfccc.int/kyoto_mechanisms/compliance/items/3024.php.

van Calster, G. 'Waste', in T.F.M. Etty et al. *The Yearbook of European Environmental Law*, Volume 5 (Oxford: OUP, 2005), pp.408–28.

van Waarden, F. 'Persistence of national policy styles: a study of their institutional foundations', in B. Unger and F. van Waarden (eds), *Convergence or Diversity: Internationalisation and Economic Policy Response* (Aldershot: Avebury, 1995), pp.333–72.

Vehmas, J. (et al.), 'Environmental Taxes on fuels and electricity – some experiences from Nordic countries', *Energy Policy*, 27, 6, (1999), pp.343–55.

Viney, M. *A living Island: Ireland's responsibility to nature. A Comhar Pamphlet* (Dublin: Comhar/The National Sustainable Development Partnership, and Ashfield Press, 2003).

Viney, M. 'Brooding on the politics of conservation', *The Irish Times*, 10 May 2003a.

Viney, M. 'Cultivating a new Conservation', *The Irish Times*, 8 February 2003b.

Vogel, D. *Trading Up: Consumer and environmental regulation in a global economy* (Cambridge, Mass: Harvard University Press, 1999).

VOICE/VOICE of Irish Concern for the Environment. *Response to Seminar reviewing EU Drinking Water Directive (98/83/EC). Submitted by VOICE of Irish Concern for the Environment*', October 27–8 (Dublin: VICE, 2003). Available at: http://www.npwa.freeserve.co.uk/voice.html.

VROM/Dutch Ministry of Housing, Spatial Planning, and the Environment. *Waste Prevention* (VROM: The Hague, 2001). Available at http://www2.vrom.nl/Docs/internationaal/03waste%20prevention.pdf.

Wackernagel, M. 'Shortcoming of the Environmental Sustainability Index', Redefining Progress, 10 February 2001. Available at: http://www.anti-lomborg.com/ESI%20critique.pdf.

Wagner, M. and Schaltegger, S. 'The Effect of Corporate Environmental Strategy Choice and Environmental Performance on Competitiveness and Economic Performance', *European Management Journal*, 22, 5 (2004), pp.557–73.

Wall, M. 'Ireland's poor record cited on implementing environmental laws', *The Irish Times*, 20 August 2004.

Wallace D. *Environmental Policy and Industrial Innovation: Strategies in Europe, the US and Japan* (London: RIIA/ Earthscan, 1995).

WCED/World Commission on Environment and Development. 'From One Earth to One World: An Overview by the World Commission on Environment and Development', in J.S. Dryzek and D. Schlosberg (eds). *Debating the earth: the environmental politics reader.* 2nd edition (Oxford: OUP, 2005/1987), pp.259–84.

Weale, A. *The New Politics of Pollution* (Manchester: MUP, 1992).

Weale, A., Pridham, G. Cini, M., Konstadakopulos, D., Porter, M. and Flynn, B. *Environmental Governance in Europe* (Oxford: OUP, 2000).

WHO/CEC/ World Health Organisation/Commission of the European Communities. *Eutrophication and Health* (Luxembourg: Office for Official Publications of the European Communities, 2002).

Wickham, J. *Contextualising Car Dependency, Paper prepared for the ECMT/OECD workshop on managing car use for sustainable urban travel.* Dublin, 1–2 December 1999 (Dublin: Employment Research Centre, Dept. Sociology, TCD, 1999). Available at www.cemt.org/UrbTrav/ Workshops/Carscities/Dubldoc.htm

Wickham, J. and Lohan, M. *The Transport Rich and the Transport Poor: car dependency and social class in four European Cities.* Paper for conference, 'Urbanism and Suburbanism at the End of the Century', Friday, November 26th and Saturday, November 27th, 1999, National University of Ireland, Maynooth (Dublin: Employment Research Centre, Dept. Sociology, Trinity College Dublin, 1999). Available at: www.tcd.ie/ERC/pastprojectcars.php/

World Resources Institute. *Earth Trends: the Environmental Information Portal* (2004). Available at: http://earthtrends. wri.org/text/climate-atmosphere/country-profiles.html

Wright, R. 'Trams: A streetcar-driven desire to engineer lower floors', *The Financial Times*, 21 September 2004.

Xepapadeas, A. and de Zeeuw, A. 'Environmental Policy and Competitiveness: The Porter Hypothesis and the Composition of Capital', *Journal of Environmental Economics and Management*, 37, 2, (1999), pp.165–83.

Zito, A.R. 'Integrating the Environment into the European Union: the History of the Controversial Carbon Tax', in A. Jordan (ed.), *Environmental Policy in the European Union: Actors, Institutions and Process* (London: Earthscan, 2002), pp. 241–55.

Index

Note: Page numbers in italics denote tables or charts.

The letter 'n' indicates an endnote, for example, 213n25 indicates endnote 25 on page 213 and 35(nn 21, 22) notes 21 and 22 on page 35.

improper implementation of Directives, 3, 68, 82(nn 87, 89), 98–100, 138–40, *141*, 167(nn 54, 55); planning laws, 17, 36n42, 37n44, 107, 114
European Economic Community *see* European Union
European Environment Agency *see* EEA
European Environmental Bureau (EEB), 184
European Union, 10, 16, 19, 47, 87–8, 201; CAP, 101, 102, 114, 180; funding from, 101, 104, 115, 120n37, 121n40; importance of, 25–6, 27, 85, 88, 114–16, 160–1; leadership role, 27, 112, 127, 207; precautionary principle, 70, 75, 166n47; waste prevention, 77n28, *see also* European Court of Justice
European Union Directives, 146; access to information and participation, 33n6; biofuels, 207, 217n63; bird protection, nature and habitats, 102, 146–8, 169n69; EIA, 98–100, *99*, 138; implementation record, 3, 11, 68, 82(nn 87, 89), 98–100, *99*, 138–49, *141*, *142*, *143*, 167(nn 54, 55), 168(nn 57, 61, 63); IPPC licences, 118n16; large combustion plants, 92; nitrates, 3–4, 68, 70, 82(nn 87, 88), 83n98; packaging waste, 54–5, 95–6; urban waste water, 120n37; waste electrical/electronic

equipment, 155–6, 174(nn 110, 112); water framework, 96, 146
eutrophication, 34n20, 69

farmers/landowners, 68, 90, 102, 109, 136, 179; designated sensitive habitats, 102, 146–8, 149, 192, 193–4, *see also* IFA
'fast-tracking' infrastructure projects, 17, 23, 37n44, 109–10, 114, 189, 190
Faughnan, Conor, 5, 56–7
FEASTA/Foundation for the Economics of Sustainability, *181*
fertilizers, 13, 71–3, *72*, 74, 193
filtration systems, 193
Finance, Department of, 188
fines, 68, 82n89, 86, 138, 148–9, 167n55, 194
Finland, 23, 168n61, 220, 221
Flood Tribunal, 106
Foras Forbartha, An, 88, 90, 106, 116, 117n3, 118n9
forests, 8, 35n23, 105
Forfás, 59, 66, 67, 80n62
fossil fuels, 14, 41, 63, 198, 200–1; coal, 7, 65, 92–3, 118n12, 177, 200–1, 215(nn 42–5); natural gas, 63, 65, 109, 200; oil, 59–60, 63, 65, 66, 67, 200
France, 139, 140, 144, 168(nn 57, 63), 198–9
Friends of the Earth, Ireland, *181*, 183
Friends of the Irish Environment (FIE), 35n23, *181*

Galway, 105
Galway City, 101, 128, 162n12, 164n25